Eyewitness Accounts of the American Revolution

The Diary
of
Frederick Mackenzie

The New York Times & Arno Press

Reprinted with the permission of
Harvard University Press

*

The maps included in this edition are reprinted from
A British Fusilier in Boston, edited by Allen French,
published by Harvard University Press, 1926.

*

Library of Congress Catalog Card No. 67-29038

*

Manufactured in the U.S.A.

DIARY OF
FREDERICK MACKENZIE

LIEUTENANT FREDERICK MACKENZIE

From a picture in oils in the possession of his descendants

DIARY OF
FREDERICK MACKENZIE

GIVING A DAILY NARRATIVE OF HIS MILITARY
SERVICE AS AN OFFICER OF THE REGIMENT
OF ROYAL WELCH FUSILIERS DURING THE
YEARS 1775–1781 IN MASSACHUSETTS
RHODE ISLAND AND NEW YORK

VOLUME I

HARVARD UNIVERSITY PRESS
Cambridge, Massachusetts
MCMXXX

PRINTED AT THE HARVARD UNIVERSITY PRESS

CAMBRIDGE, MASS., U. S. A.

PUBLISHERS' PREFACE

Lieutenant Frederick Mackenzie was the only son of Mr. William Mackenzie, sometime merchant of Dublin, by his wife Mary Ann (born Boursiquot), who was of French descent, and who belonged to one of the numerous Huguenot families which escaped to Ireland at the time of the revocation of the Edict of Nantes. The son is believed to have received his first commission in the 23rd Regiment (Royal Welch Fusiliers) in the year 1745. He was promoted to a captaincy in Boston in the fall of 1775 and obtained his majority in August, 1780. During a part of the British occupation of New York he acted as deputy adjutant-general. In 1787 he transferred from his old regiment to become lieutenant-colonel of the 37th Foot. He appears to have gone on half-pay for a time and to have lived in or near Exeter, for in 1794, at the time of the fear of a Napoleonic invasion, he raised and commanded the First Exeter Volunteers. He afterwards became "Assistant Barrack-Master General" at Headquarters, and was for some time Secretary of the Royal Military College. He died in the early part of 1824 at Teignmouth, Devon, but the exact date cannot be determined.

Throughout the period of his service in America he regularly kept a diary. For many years the only part of it available to historians was a fragment dealing with Lord Percy's expedition to Lexington on the 19th of April, 1775. That fragment was communicated by Mrs. Frances Rose-Troup, an American woman married in England, to the Massachusetts Historical Society and printed in its *Proceedings* for March, 1890. The rest of the diary was thought to have been lost. In 1925 Mr. Allen French, well known as an untiring and scholarly investigator into our early local history, was led to question whether in fact more of the diary were not still in existence. As a result of his enterprise and persistence he discovered that much of it was still preserved in England — the property of Lieutenant-Colonel Frederick Mackenzie, a direct descendant of the diarist. Colonel Mackenzie kindly placed it at the disposal first of Mr. French and then of the Harvard University Press.

As originally written, the diary, copied in a fair hand by the diarist after he had retired from service, is reported to have covered the period from 1748 to 1791. But all of the volumes have been lost that dealt with the years before 1775, and, most unfortunately for American history, also the volume in which were described the battle of Bunker Hill and the siege of Boston. Of the eight volumes that remain, the first covers the events in Boston from January 5, 1775, to the April 30 following. Then, after the gap already noted, come four volumes detailing what happened in and around Rhode Island in the years 1776 to 1778; and finally, three volumes, dated New York, that cover the twelve months from January to December, 1781, and that not only describe events in the city but also report the news received at headquarters of the doings of the fleet and of the campaign farther south that culminated in the surrender of Lord Cornwallis. In the Boston division occurs the fullest and most satisfactory account of the Boston Massacre Oration delivered by Warren in the Old South Church. His narrative of the embarkation of the Concord expedition is the only one that comes from an eye-witness. The story of Percy's march to and from Lexington is unique and of great historical value. Subsequent volumes are also important. There is, for example, a detailed description of a part of the Rhode Island campaign on which there is little elsewhere in the way of personal narrative written from the British point of view. This section of the diary fills a real gap in history. The description of the capture of General Prescott in 1777 with its accompanying diagram explains the event with an accuracy not hitherto equalled. The account of the burning of New York has considerable vividness, and the allusion to the behavior of Colonel Francis Smith on the occasion confirms the impression of that officer's stupidity which students first derived from his mismanagement at Lexington and Concord. The illustrations reproduce certain especially significant pages of the diary and drawings inserted in it, some of which at least are by Mackenzie himself.

As a diarist, Mackenzie is strictly professional. His record of facts has a soldierly precision. Day after day passes with no entry except the date and a notation of the weather, but when he does write he gives in the clearest and most direct style information that is of real value. He shows no rancor toward the Americans. He gives the facts as he saw them in a notably impersonal way. His cool-headedness, his judiciousness, his competence as a soldier, his keenness as an observer, and his dry exactness of style inspire the reader with the greatest confidence and make his one of the best British diaries of the Revolutionary period that we have.

The part of the diary describing the Concord and Lexington fight was edited by Mr. French and published in 1926 by the Harvard University Press under the title "A British Fusilier in Revolutionary Boston." It is the standard British version of that dramatic event. The book now published contains not only that part of the diary but all the rest of it that is still preserved and forms a whole that historians must consult if they are to form a true estimate of the events with which it deals. It is printed without editing as an historical document of distinct value.

CONTENTS

VOLUME I

I
BOSTON

I

BOSTON

5th Jan^y [1775]

Orders given that when working parties are ordered, the Quarter Master of the day is to parade them, and see them march off.

6th Jany. Two men p^r Regiment have been employed daily for some time past in making Musquet Cartridges for the use of the Army.

7th Jan^y.

8th. It has been signified to the Army, that if any Officers of the different Regiments are capable of taking Sketches of a Country, they are to send their names to the Deputy Adjutant General.

I am afraid not many Officers in this Army will be found qualified for this Service. It is a branch of Military education too little attended to, or sought after by our Officers, and yet is not only extremely necefsary and useful in time of War, but very entertaining and instructive. We have only one profefsed Engineer here, and altho it is natural to suppose that he has taken every opportunity of making himself thoroughly acquainted with, not only the ground within a certain distance of this town, (in case by any change of circumstances there should be a necefsity for a minute knowledge of it) but that of the surrounding Country, I am apprehensive he has at this moment a very imperfect knowledge of either the one or the other.

Some of the Officers who have been appointed Afsistant Engineers, hardly know the names of the different parts of a Fortification. They should have been called overseers of the works, or rather Workmen, and then they would not have been laughed at for their ignorance, as they now are.

9th Jan^y

10th

11th Jan^y

12th

13th Jan^y

14th. The Troops ordered to receive four days salt, and three days fresh, provisions p^r week, 'till further orders. To begin receiving at 9 in the Morning, and an hour allowed for each Corps.

The Marines and Hospitals to continue to receive fresh provisions 'till further notice.

15th Jany. The Regiments are frequently practiced at firing with ball at marks. Six rounds p^r man at each time is usually allotted for this practice. As our Regiment is quartered on a Wharf which projects into part of the harbour, and there is a very considerable range without any obstruction, we have fixed figures of men as large as life, made of thin boards, on small stages, which are anchored at a proper distance from the end of the Wharf, at which the men fire. Objects afloat, which move up and down with the tide, are frequently pointed out for them to fire at, and Premiums are sometimes given for the best Shots, by which means some of our men have become excellent marksmen.

16th Jan^y

17th

18th Jany. This being the Anniversary of The Queen's birthday, 21 Guns were fired by The Royal Artillery; and the Picquets of the Line, drawn up below the Town house, fired three Vollies, at 12 oClock. The Ships of War fired at One oClock.

There was a numerous meeting of the Members of the Blue and Orange Society, who dined together at the British Coffee house.

19th

20th Jany. 2^{ed} Lieu^t John Boadil Forlow of the 23rd Regiment, who died a few days ago, was buried this day with the usual Military honors.

21st. As there was some disturbance last night, and a quarrel between some Officers and the town Watch, the General has ordered a Court of Enquirey, composed of five Field Officers, to examine into the cause and circumstances of it, and report thereon to him.

22^{ed} Jan^y

$\quad\quad\quad\quad\quad\quad\quad\quad\quad\quad$ C S S C D P

23rd. A Detachment consisting of $-1-3-4-4-2-100$, embarked this afternoon on board The Armed Schooner Diana, and the Sloop Britannia, with 7 days provisions, thier Barrack bedding, a few necefsaries, and baggage sufficient for ten or 14 days. This Detachment is under the Command of Captain Balfour of the 4th Regiment, and is going to some town on the Coast not far distant.

24th Jany The General being much displeased with the conduct of the Officers concerned in the late disturbance, and anxious to prevent just cause of complaint on the part of the Townspeople, has, in a private order, directed the Commanding Officers of Corps to afsemble their Officers, and shew them the impropriety of the conduct of some of them, which has afforded the King's enemies the very advantage they seek, and given room for reflections which dishonor the Service. To point out to them the ills that must arise from their afsembling to game and drink, which lays the foundation for Quarrels and Riots, and that the attacking the Watch of any Town in all parts of the World, must be attended with bad consequences: for as they are appointed by Law, the Law will protect them. They will also shew them that no person who quarrels with them will obtain satisfaction for the injuries he may receive, but on the contrary will be condemned. They are desired to inform their Officers that the Commander in Chief is determined to make the strictest enquirey into the conduct of all Officers concerned in quarrels or Riots with the Towns people, and try them if in fault. They will remind the Officers of the orders already given out in that respect, and of the directions given to the Guards to prevent them.

25th Jany. The Detachment which sailed on the 23rd Inst^t has landed at Marshfield.

26th

27th Jan^y

28th

29th Jany. Fourteen days Salt provisions have been ordered to be sent to Marshfield, for the Detachment stationed there under the Command of Captain Balfour.

30th. There has been no material alteration of late in the Detail of the public duties; but the duty is done with the utmost strictnefs, as the ferment among the people has by no means subsided.

We have a free intercourse with the Country, but the people are evidently making every preparation for resistance. They are taking every means to provide themselves with Arms; and are particularly desirous of procuring the Locks of firelocks, which are easily conveyed out of town without being discovered by the Guards.

31st January.

1st February. A Garrison Court Martial afsembled this day for the trial of some Soldiers for selling firelocks, and locks to the Country people.

2^{ed} Feby. Notwithstanding the pains which have been taken to prevent Spirituous liquors from being sold to the Soldiers, Soldiers wives and others find means to dispose of the New England Rum to them in such quantities, and at so cheap a rate, that numbers of them are intoxicated daily. Some of them have sold Spirits of so pernicious a quality, that two men died in one night, affected by it in an extraordinary manner. The towns people encourage this excefsive drinking, as when the Soldiers are in a State of intoxication they are frequently induced to desert.

3rd Feb. It has been customary of late, and approved of by The General, for some of the Regiments to go out of town, with their Arms, Accoutrements, and knapsacks, when the weather permits and they are off duty, and march three four or five miles into the Country. This practice is conducive to the health of the troops; and may enable the General to send Regiments or Detachments to particular parts of the Country without occasioning so much alarm as would otherwise take place.

Our Regiment marched out this day towards Cambridge. The people appear apprehensive that something particular is concealed under these movements; and there are always some persons appointed to Watch the motions and direction of the Troops.

Boston, 4th Feb. 1775. A Soldier of the 4th Reg^t who was tried a few days ago for disposing of Arms to the towns people, has been found guilty and sentenced to receive 500 lashes.

A Serjeant and two Soldiers of the 38th Reg^t tried for the same crime, have been acquitted.

5th. The Detachment under the Command of Captain Balfour of the 4th Regiment, remains at Marshfield.

6th Feb.

7th

8th Feb. The 23rd Regiment marched into the Country this day towards Watertown. The Country people seem extremely jealous of these movements (which are more frequent than they were), as they apprehend they are intended to cover some design the General has formed.

9th

10th Feb. The Soldiers wives and other persons, ſtill find means of selling Spirituous liquors to the Troops, which occasions much drunkenneſs and many irregularities.

11th. Fourteen days pay and provisions at a time is regularly sent to the Detachment at Marshfield.

12th Feb.

13th

14th Feb.

15th

16th Feb. The General having ordered a reinforcement of 9 men to the Magazine guard this Evening; and direĉted the several patroles in going their rounds to be watchful, and to report if they observe numerous parties of people aſsembled in bye lanes or otherwise; gives reason to suppose that he has received information of some intended tumultuous aſsemblage of the Seditious party.

17th. A Guard of a Serjeant, Corporal and 12 Privates, ordered to mount at the Artillery work Shop on the Common.

18th Feb.

19th

20th Feb.

21st

22^{ed} Feb. Very soft, mild day. Thermometer 52°.

23rd. Cold, raw weather. Wind E. Therm^r 40°.

24th Feb. Cold day. Rain; which froze as it fell.

25th

26th Feb.

27th

28th Feb.

1st March. This being S^t. David's Day, the Officers of The 23rd Regiment, or Royal Welch Fusiliers, dined together according to Custom. All the General & Staff Officers, The Admiral, and several other persons were invited to dine with the Regiment.

Officers of the Regiment. Present, 1st March 1775.	Persons invited were.
Lieu^t. Col^o. Bernard	General Gage
Major Blunt	Maj^r Genl. Haldimand
Captain Grove	
" Blakeney	Brig^r Genl Earl Percy
" I. Ferguson	" Pigot.
" D. Ferguson	" Jones.
" Donkin	Admiral Graves.
" Horsfall	Major Kemble — Dep. Adj^t Genl
" Evans	Major Shirreff — Dep-Q Mr Genl
1st Lieu^t Mackenzie	Major Hutcheson. Maj^r of Brigade
" Douglas	
" Gibbings	Mr Kemble. Sec^y to Com^r in Chief
" Welsh	Mr Gefferina. Sec^y to The Admiral.
" Cochran	
" Beckwith	Capt Rooke ⎫ Aides de Camp
" Ridley	Capt Brehm ⎭
2^{ed} Lieu^t Bernard	Capt Pawlett ⎫ Formerly in the Reg^t.
" Fitzgerald	L^t. Carmichael ⎭
" Julian	
" Blucke	Capt Ferrier ⎫ Welchmen
" Apthorp	Lieu^t Lewis ⎭
Surgeon Robertson	Revd Bush — Chaplain
	All came but Genl Pigot, who was unwell

2^{ed} March

3rd

4th March. Robt Vaughan, a Soldier of the 52^{ed} Regiment was apprehended laſt night at Charleſtown Ferry, attempting to Desert; and this day a General Court Martial was ordered to aſsemble to try him for the same.

5th This being Sunday, the Annual Oration, delivered in consequence of what is called by the Rebellious party, the Massacre of the 5th March 1770, on which day some rioters were killed & wounded by the Military; was poſtponed until to-Morrow.

6th March. Warm day. Therm^r 54°.

This day having been appointed by the Seleċtmen of Boſton for the delivery, according to Annual cuſtom, of an Oration in commemoration of the 5th March 1770, on which day some Inhabitants of this town were killed and wounded, in a Riot, by the Military: at 10 o'Clock the Old South Meeting was opened for the purpose, and an immense concourse of people aſsembled therein. As this aſsemblage was undoubtedly intended to inflame the minds of the people, and The Troops conceived it was a great insult, under the present circumſtances, to deliver an Oration on the Occasion, a great number of Officers aſsembled in the Church and seemed determined to take notice of, and resent any expreſsions made use of by The Orator, reflecting on the Military. About 11 o'Clock, Doċtor Joseph Warren, an Apothecary of Boſton came in, and ascended the Pulpit; which was hung with Black Cloth. He was attended by all the moſt violent fellows in town, particularly Hancock, the Adams's, Church, Cooper, and the reſt of the Seleċt Men. Every person was silent, and every countenance seemed to denote that some event of consequence might be expeċted. The Oration, which, tho severe on the conduċt of the Military, and evidently calculated to excite the resentment of the populace againſt them, contained nothing so violent as was expeċted, was delivered without any other interruption than a few hiſses from some of the Officers.

As this meeting was called an Adjournment of a former Town meeting, as soon as the Oration was ended, Mr Saml Adams came forward from a Pew in which he and the other

Select men sat, very near the Pulpit, and moved, "that the "thanks of the Town should be presented to Doctor Warren for "his Elegant and Spirited Oration, and that another Oration "should be delivered on the 5th of March next, to commemorate "*the Bloody Massacre* of the 5th of March 1770." On this several Officers began to hiss; others cried out, "*Oh! fie! Oh! fie!*" and a great bustle ensued. As everyone was now in motion, intending to go out, there was a good deal of noise, and the exclamation was mistaken for the cry of *Fire! Fire!* Numbers immediately called out *Fire! Fire!* which created a Scene of the greatest confusion imaginable. As there were numbers of Women in the Meeting, their cries encreased the confusion, which was further encreased by the Drums & fifes of the 43rd Regiment which happened to be passing by from Exercise. Some persons leaped out of the lower windows, and in a short time the Meeting was nearly cleared. As soon as the mistake was discovered, and things grew quiet, The Select men proceeded to the Choice of some public Officers, which being finished, the people dispersed. Some of the Select men were extremely alarmed when they heard the Drums of the 43rd Regiment, as it is supposed they expected to be apprehended.

The towns people certainly expected a Riot, as almost every man had a short stick, or bludgeon, in his hand; and it was confidently asserted that many of them were privately armed. — They no doubt supposed that some violent expressions in the Oration would have induced the Officers to act improperly, and strike, or lay hands on some of the party, which would have been the signal for Battle. It is certain both sides were ripe for it, and a single blow would have occasioned the commencement of hostilities. Fortunately nothing of the kind happened, nor was any person hurt in the confusion. General Gage also was apprehensive of a Riot, and had ordered the Regiments to be in readiness to get under arms in case of an alarm.

7th March. It was thought by most people, that last night would have been productive of some riot, or disturbance, but contrary to expectation, all was quiet.

8th A Country fellow was detected this day in buying arms from a Soldier of the 47th Regt. The men of that Regiment immediately secured him, and having provided the proper materials, they stripped, and then Tarred & feathered him, and setting him upon a Truck, in that manner paraded him, in the afternoon, through most parts of the town, to The Neck. This matter was done with the knowledge of the Officers of the Regiment, altho they did not appear in it, and it gave great Offence to the people of the town, and was much disapproved of by General Gage. Arms of all kinds are so much sought after by the Country people, that they use every means of procuring them; and have been succefsful amongst the Soldiers, several of whom have been induced to dispose of Arms, or such parts of Arms, as they could come at. Perhaps this transaction may deter the Country fellows from the like practices in future.

The practice of Tarring & Feathering as a punishment is very ancient. When Richard the 1st of England resolved to go to The Holy Land, with Philip King of France, several very severe Regulations were made by him at Chinon in France in the year 1189, for keeping the Soldiers and Sailors in awe whom he embarked for that Country. Among others, "Thieves were to "have their heads shaved, to have boiling Pitch dropped upon "their Crowns; and after having Cushion-Feathers stuck upon "the Pitch, they were to be set on shore, in that figure, at the "first place they came to." Rymer's Faedera. Vol. 1st Page 65.

9th March. Robt Vaughan, the Soldier of the 52ed Regt who was apprehended the night of the 3rd Inst, attempting to desert, by way of Charlestown ferry, was tried on the 6th and 7th, and being found guilty, was ordered to be shot for the same, as this morning; but about 9 oClock last night it was notified to the Troops, that his Execution was respited till further orders.

☞This man was afterwards pardoned, but deserted to the Rebels in a short time.

10th. The Guards ordered to mount with fixed Bayonets for the future.

11th March. The Advanced Guards at the Lines have of late been ordered to send out patroles towards Roxbury. A patrole going out last night, fell in with a party of the Roxbury people, with Arms, patroling towards our Lines, but as soon as the latter perceived our people they took to their heels towards Roxbury.

12th. [No entry, but on a following page is the memorandum:] Strength of the Rank & file of the 1st brigade. 12th March.

4th	 315	
23rd	 314	} 1261
47th	 296	
Marines	 336	

13th March 1775. Rob[t] Vaughan of the 52[ed] Regiment, whose execution was respited on the 8th Ins[t] has since been pardoned.

14th. The lenity shown to Rob[t] Vaughan has not had the effect the General expected, as some Soldiers have deserted since that event; — He has therefore notified to the Army, that as he finds his Clemency has had so little effect in bringing the Soldiers to a sense of their duty to their King and Country, and to reflect seriously on the Sin they commit in deserting the Service of both, this is the laſt man he will pardon who shall be condemned for desertion.

15th March.

16th Rain from 12 o'Clock.

The Provincial Congreſs having recommended a General Faſt on this day throughout the Province, the same was ſtrictly observed by the Inhabitants of this town. All the Shops were shut up, and all busineſs suspended.

17th March. The former part of this month has been extremely mild and pleasant, and without Froſt. But there was Snow from 8 laſt night 'till 9 this morning. Very Cold day.

There was a very full meeting this day of The Friendly Brothers of S[t] Patrick, who went in procefsion to Church. There was no general meeting of the Irish.

18th. The January Mail arrived this day from England by way of New York.

A Country man was Stopped at the Lines, going out of town with 19,000 ball Cartridges, which were taken from him. When liberated, he had the insolence to go to Head quarters to demand the redelivery of them. When asked who they were for, he said they were for his own use; and on being refused them, he said he could not help it, but they were the laſt parcel of a large quantity which he had carried out at different times. Great numbers of Arms have been carried out of town during the Winter; and if more ſtrict search had been made at the Lines, many of them, and much Ammunition might have been seized.

19th March.

20th. Orders given for those Regiments that were encamped last Summer, and delivered their tents to the Quarter Mr General, to send for them, and repair them immediately.

21st March. The working parties ordered for work at the Lines are discontinued; but as some work there is necessary, 20 men have been added to the numbers for duty there, and the Officer Commanding is directed to order 20 men of the Guard to be employed to work under the direction of the Engineer, & to be releived every hour or two hours, as may be thought proper.

22ed

23rd March. The Artillery not being able to make up Cartridges sufficient to supply the Troops, orders are given to supply each Corps with a proportion of the several materials, which they are to make up into Cartridges for their own use.

24th

25th March.

26th. The Asia of 64 Guns, Capt Vandeput, went down the harbour, and anchored in King road. She is going to New York.

27th March. There was a dispute lately on the Evening parade of the 5th Regiment, between Lieut Colo Walcott, and Ensign Patrick of that Corps, at the close of which the former struck the latter, and drew his Sword upon him, which occasioned a Challenge; but the Officers having interfered, and the matter having been reported to Genl Gage, he ordered them both to be put under arrest, and tried by a General Court Martial, which assembled this day for that purpose. Ensign Patrick is related to the Lieut Colonel.

28th March. Whenever the weather is fine, some of the Regiments off duty continue the practice of marching into the Country to the distance of from 4 to 8 Miles, with Arms, Knapsacks, &c, and return before dinner.

The people of the Country are extremely jealous of these movements, and some of them constantly attend, apparently to observe if there is any particular object in view, and to convey intelligence if necessary.

29th. The Guard at the Lines ordered to be reduced to its former Number of 120 men. And a working party of an Officer and 20 men ordered to be sent there.

The Detachment under Capt Balfour of the 4th continues at Marshfield. — Pay and Provisions are sent to them once a fortnight.

30th March. Orders were given last night about 8 o'Clock, for the 1st Brigade to be under arms on the Grand parade at 6 oClock this Morning with their knapsacks on. The 4 Companies of Light Infantry, and 4 Companies of Grenadiers on the right of the whole.

1st Brigade — 4th 23rd 47th Regiments, & Marines.

31st March. Slight frost at night.

1st April. Frost at night. Mild day.

2^{ed} April. A vessel arrived at Salem which sailed from Falmouth in England the 14th February. It appears by the letters and papers brought by her, that a large reinforcement of Ships and Troops may be soon expected to arrive in this Country.

Orders given for the Troops to repair their Camp-kettles and other Utensils, in case they should be suddenly wanted before others arrive.

3rd Slight frost last night.

4th April. Frost last night. Mild day.

5th Snow from 4 'till 8 last night, then rain for some hours; after which it Snowed 'till 12 this day. All the surrounding Country is covered with it.

9th April. Cold weather.

7th. The following order was given out this day.

"As Regiments are often ordered to take Marches, and con-
"tinue out too long to get their dinners dressed at proper hours;
"and may hereafter more frequently be ordered, either by
"Regiments or Brigades; every Corps will have one day's
"pork ready cooked, which the men may carry out with them
"in their knapsacks or Havresacks, with bread in proportion."
From this order, and several other circumstances, it is supposed the General has some object in view, and means to familiarize

the people of the Country with the appearance of Troops among them for a longer time than usual, without creating an alarm.

8th April. Frost last night.

9th. The weather begins now to grow mild and pleasant.

Weekly Return of the 23rd Regt or R. W. Fusiliers. *Apl. 1775*								
	S	C	D	P	S	C	D	P
Effectives........................	..	..	..	..	20	30	12	296
Sick in quarters					..	..	..	..
Sick in hospital					..	..	..	..
Absent with leave					..	..	..	..
On Furlow					..	..	..	..
Recruiting					..	..	..	..
Music not doing duty					..	..	..	..
Public Employ					..	..	..	..
With the Artillery					..	..	..	..
Armourers					..	..	..	..
Prisoners					..	..	..	..
Hospital Guard, and orderly men	..	..	..	..				
Barrack Guard	..	..	..	..				
Rear Guard	..	..	..	..				
Quarter Guard	..	..	..	..				
Ordinary Guards	..	..	..	..				
Off Duty	..	..	..	..				
Total .	..	..	..	..	20	30	12	296

Given in at 2 o'Clock every Monday

Fredck Mackenzie Lt & Adjt
R. W. Fusiliers.

10th April. The 38th and 52ed Regiments marched out this Morning as far as Watertown, and did not return to Boston 'till 5 oClock in the Afternoon. As Watertown is farther than the Regiments have usually gone, and they remained out longer, the Country was a good deal alarmed on the Occasion.

11th. Fine weather.

As the Tents belonging to our Regiment have all been repaired, we pitched them on Fort Hill this day, by way of airing them, and seeing that every thing was in proper order.

12th April. Rain mixed with hail from 12 laſt night, and during the whole of this day. The Rain was very heavy about 6 in the Evening, with a Strong wind at Eaſt.

Orders given for the Officers to provide themselves with Baggage Saddles, at the rate of 3 p^r Company; vizt One for the Captain, One for the Companies tents, and one for the two Subalterns. As Pack Saddles cannot be had in this Country, Sunks and Sods (a kind of Baggage Saddle used by the troops during the German war) are recommended as the beſt ſubſtitutes.

Materials for Sunks or Sods — a
kind of baggage Saddle.

	s d		s
2 Yards of Sail Cloth at 1.6			3.0
4 yards of Osnabrucks 1			4.0
Leather			1.6
Twine			6
			——
Besides labor			9.0

13th April.

14th. Arrived The Nautilus Sloop of War of —— Guns, Captain ——, in 30 days from England. Letters dated the 12th March have been received by her.

The Contractors having declined giving fresh meat to the Troops, orders have been given for their being supplied with Salt provisions 'till further orders.

15th April. The Grenadier and Light Infantry Companies were this day Ordered to be off all duty 'till further orders, as they will be ordered out to learn the Grenadier Exercise, and some New Evolutions for the Light Infantry.

The Sentence of the General Court Martial which sat for the trial of Lieu^t Col^o Walcott and Ensign Patrick of the 5th Regiment, was this day published in Orders, in the following words.

The General Court Martial of which Brigadier Pigot is President, for the trial of Lieu^t Col^o Walcott, and Ensign Patrick of the 5th Reg^t of Foot, for quarreling, and the consequences that ensued, which were reported to be blows given, and a Challenge to fight; is of Opinion that the said Lieu^t Col^o Walcott is Guilty, firſt, of quarreling with Ensign Patrick; Secondly of making use of reproachful, menacing and abusive language; thirdly, of giving a blow, to and drawing his Sword upon the said Ensign Patrick, on the public parade in presence

of the Officers of the Regiment, when addreſsing the former as
Commanding Officer; which conduct the Court considers as
highly prejudicial to good order and Military discipline, as well
as ungentlemanlike; which the Court find to be a breach of the
1st Article of the 7th Section, & of the 3rd article of the 20th Section, of The Articles of War; therefore sentence the said Lieut
Colo Walcott to ask Ensign Patrick's pardon at the head of the
5th Regiment (The 2ed brigade under arms) for the insult given
him, and then and there to be reprimanded for unmilitary,
and ungentlemanlike behavior; and also to be suspended for the
space of three months.

The Court acquits Lieut Colo Walcott of giving Ensign
Patrick a Challenge to fight.

It is further the opinion of the Court Martial that Ensign
Robert Patrick is not guilty, either of quarreling with Lieut
Colo Walcott on the Evening of the 23rd March, or of giving a
blow: and it appearing also to the Court, that the evidence produced does not prove Ensign Patrick guilty of giving Lieut Colo
Walcott a Challenge to fight, the said Ensign Robert Patrick is
acquitted of every part of the charge exhibited againſt him.

The Commander in Chief approves of the above Sentences.

The above General Court Martial is diſsolved.

The 2ed Brigade to be under arms on Monday Morning the
17th Inſtant, at 11 oClock, on the Common, when The Brigadier Commanding the 2ed brigade will reprimand Lieut Colo
Walcott, agreeable to the Sentence of the General Court Martial.

16th April. The Majors and Adjutants of Regiments, ordered
to inſtruct the Grenadiers of their own Corps in the Grenadier
Exercise. — It was also notified in Orders that the Light Companies would be inſtructed in the New Manoeuvres by Lieut
Mackenzie, Adjutant of the 23rd Regiment, who would fix with
respective Captains the time of aſsembling.

17th

18th April 1775. An order was received this afternoon before
6 o'Clock, signifying the Commander in Chief's pleasure that
the suspension ordered Lt Colo Walcott of the 5th Regt shall be
taken off, from this day inclusive. — It also ſtated, that it has
appeared throughout the course of the trial of Lt Colo Walcott,
and Ensign Patrick, that the said Ensign Patrick did behave

disrespectfully to his Commanding Officer, but it not being inserted in his Crime, the Court did not proceed upon it, and Lt Col^o Walcott now excuses it, and will not bring it to a trial; but the Com^r in Chief thinks proper to warn Ensign Patrick, that he behaves with more respect for the future to his Commanding Officer.

At 8 this night the Commanding Officers of Regiments were sent for to Headquarters, and ordered to have their respective Grenadier and Light Infantry Companies on the beach near the Magazine Guard exactly at 10 oClock this night, with one day's provisions in their Havresacks, and without knapsacks. — They were directed to order their Companies to parade quietly at their respective Barracks, and to march to the place of Rendezvous in small parties, and if Challenged to answer "*Patrole.*" — The Companies of our Regiment (the 23rd) marched accordingly, and were the first, complete, at the place of parade; Here we found a number of the Men of War's and Transports boats in waiting. — As there was no public Officer attending to superintend the Embarkation, which it was evident would take up a good deal of time, our two Companies, with the approbation of the Officers of the Navy, embarked in the nearest boats, and pushed off a little way from the shore. As the other Companies arrived soon after, as many men embarked as the boats would contain. By this time Lieu^t Col^o Smith of the 10th, who was to have the Command, arrived, and with him Major Pitcairn of the Marines. The boats then put off, and rowed towards Phipps's farm, where having landed the troops they returned for the remainder and landed them at the same place. This was not completed untill 12 o'Clock.

The Companies embarked are,

Grenadiers — 4th, 5th, 10th, 18th, 23rd, 38th, 43rd, 47th, 59th Reg^{ts}. 1st & 2^{ed} Marines.

Light Infantry — 4th, 5th, 10th, 23rd, 38th, 43rd, 47th, 59th, & 1st & 2^{ed} Marines.

Lt Col^o Smith, & Major Pitcairn are the two Field Officers first for duty, and the Senior of each rank.

The town was a good deal agitated and alarmed at this Movement, as it was pretty generally known, by means of the Seamen who came on shore from the Ships, about 2 o'Clock, that the boats were ordered to be in readiness.

19th April. At 7 o'Clock this morning a Brigade order was received by our Regiment, dated at 6 o'Clock, for the 1st Brigade to afsemble at ½ paſt 7 on the Grand parade. We accordingly afsembled the Regiment with the utmoſt expedition, and with the 4th, and 47th were on the parade at the hour appointed, with one days provisions. By some miſtake the Marines did not receive the order until the other Regiments of the Brigade were afsembled, by which means it was half paſt 8 o'Clock before the brigade was ready to march. Here we underſtood that we were to march out of town to support the troops that went out laſt night. A quarter before 9, we marched in the following order, Advanced Guard, of a Captain and 50 men; 2 Six pounders, 4th Reg^t, 47th Regiment, 1st Battⁿ of Marines, 23^{ed} Reg^t, or Royal Welch Fusiliers, Rear Guard, of a Captain & 50 men. The whole under the Command of Brigadier General Earl Percy. We went out of Boston by the Neck, and marched thro' Roxbury, Cambridge and Menotomy, towards Lexington. In all the places we marched through, and in the houses on the road, few or no people were to be seen; and the houses were in general shut up. When we arrived near Lexington, some persons who came from Concord, informed that the Grenadiers & Light Infantry were at that place, and that some persons had been killed and wounded by them early in the morning at Lexington. As we pursued our march, about 2 o'Clock we heard some ſtraggling shots fired about a mile in our front: — As we advanced we heard the firing plainer and more frequent, and at half after 2, being near the Church at Lexington, and the fire encreasing, we were ordered to form the Line, which was immediately done by extending on each side of the road, but by reason of the Stone walls and other obſtruċtions, it was not formed in so regular a manner as it should have been. The Grenadiers & Light Infantry were at this time retiring towards Lexington, fired upon by the Rebels, who took every advantage the face of the Country afforded them. As soon as The Grenadiers & Light Infantry perceived the 1st Brigade drawn up for their support, they shouted repeatedly, and the firing ceased for a short time.

The ground we firſt formed upon was something elevated, and commanded a view of that before us for about a mile, where it was terminated by some pretty high grounds covered with wood. The Village of Lexington lay between both parties. We could observe a Considerable number of the Rebels, but they were much scattered, and not above 50 of them to be seen in a body in any place. Many lay concealed behind the Stone walls and fences. They appeared moſt numerous in the road near the Church, and in a wood in the front, and on the left flank of the line where our Regiment was poſted. A few Cannon Shot were fired at those on, and near the road, which dispersed them. The flank Companies now retired and formed behind the brigade, which was soon fired upon by the Rebels moſt advanced. A brisk fire was returned, but without much effeƈt. As there was a piece of open Morafsy ground in front of the left of our Regiment, it would have been difficult to have pafsed it under the fire of the Rebels from behind the trees and walls on the other side. Indeed no part of the brigade was ordered to advance; we therefore drew up near the Morafs, in expeƈtation of orders how to aƈt, sending an Officer for one of the 6 pounders. During this time the Rebels endeavored to gain our flanks, and crept into the covered ground on either side, and as close as they could in front, firing now and then in perfeƈt security. We also advanced a few of our beſt marksmen who fired at those who shewed themselves. About ¼ paſt 3, Earl Percy having come to a resolution of returning to Boſton, and having made his disposition for that purpose, our Regiment received orders to form the Rear Guard. We immediately lined the Walls and other Cover in our front with some Marksmen, and retired from the right of Companies by files to the high ground a Small diſtance in our rear, where we again formed in line, and remained in that position for near half an hour, during which time the flank Companies, and the other Regiments of the Brigade, began their march in one Column on the road towards Cambridge. As the Country for many miles round Boſton and in the Neighbourhood of Lexington & Concord, had by this time had notice of what was doing, as well by the firing, as from exprefses which had been from Boſton and the adjacent places in all direƈtions, numbers of armed men on foot and on horseback, were continually coming from all parts guided by the fire, and before the Column had advanced a mile on the road, we were fired at from all quarters, but particularly from the houses on the roadside, and the Adjacent Stone walls. Several of the Troops were killed and wounded in this way, and the Soldiers were so enraged at suffering from an unseen Enemy, that they forced open many of the houses from which the fire proceeded, and put to

death all those found in them. Those houses would certainly
have been burnt had any fire been found in them, or had there
been time to kindle any; but only three or four near where we
first formed suffered in this way. As the Troops drew nearer to
Cambridge the number and fire of the Rebels encreased, and
altho they did not shew themselves openly in a body in any part,
except on the road in our rear, our men threw away their fire
very inconsiderately, and without being certain of its effect: this
emboldened them, and induced them to draw nearer, but whenever a Cannon shot was fired at any considerable number, they
instantly dispersed. Our Regiment having formed the Rear
Guard for near 7 miles, and expended a great part of its ammunition, was then relieved by the Marines which was the next
Battalion in the Column.

Lord Percy, judging that the returning to Boston by way of
Cambridge, (where there was a bridge over Charles river, which
might either be broken down, or required to be forced) and Roxbury, might be attended with some difficulties and many inconveniences, took the resolution of returning by way of Charlestown, which was the shortest road, and which could be defended
against any number of the Rebels. Accordingly where the roads
separate, the Column took that to the left, and passing over
Charlestown Neck, drew up on the heights just above, and
which Command it. This was about 7 oClock in the Evening.
During the March, the Marines had been relieved in the duty of
forming the rear guard by the 47th Regiment, and that Corps by
the 4th. The Grenadiers and Light Infantry being exceedingly
fatigued by their long march, kept at the head of the Column,
where indeed, latterly, the fire was nearly as severe as in the
rear. During the whole of the march from Lexington the Rebels
kept an incessant irregular fire from all points at the Column,
which was the more galling as our flanking parties, which at
first were placed at sufficient distances to cover the march of it,
were at last, from the different obstructions they occasionally
met with, obliged to keep almost close to it. Our men had very
few opportunities of getting good shots at the Rebels, as they
hardly ever fired but under cover of a Stone wall, from behind a
tree, or out of a house; and the moment they had fired they lay
down out of sight until they had loaded again, or the Column
had passed. In the road indeed in our rear, they were most
numerous, and came on pretty close, frequently calling out,

"*King Hancock forever.*" Many of them were killed in the
houses on the road side from whence they fired; in some of them
7 or 8 men were deſtroyed. Some houses were forced open in
which no person could be discovered, but when the Column had
paſſed, numbers sallied out from some place in which they had
lain concealed, fired at the rear Guard, and augmented the numbers which followed us. If we had had time to set fire to those
houses many Rebels muſt have perished in them, but as night
drew on Lord Percy thought it beſt to continue the march.
Many houses were plundered by the Soldiers, notwithſtanding
the efforts of the Officers to prevent it. I have no doubt this in-
flamed the Rebels, and made many of them follow us farther
than they would otherwise have done. By all accounts some
Soldiers who ſtaid too long in the houses, were killed in the very
aćt of plundering by those who lay concealed in them. We
brought in about ten prisoners, some of whom were taken in
arms. One or two more were killed on the march while prisoners
by the fire of thier own people.

Few or no Women or Children were to be seen throughout the
day. As the Country had undoubted intelligence that some
troops were to march out, and the Rebels were probably determined to attack them, it is generally supposed they had previously removed their families from the Neighbourhood.

As soon as the troops had paſſed Charleſtown Neck the
Rebels ceased firing. A Negro (the only one who was observed
to fire at the Kings troops) was wounded near the houses close
to the Neck, out of which the Rebels fired to the laſt.

When the troops had drawn up on the heights above Charlestown neck, and had remained there about half an hour, Lord
Percy ordered the Grenadiers and Light Infantry to march
down into Charleſtown, they were followed by the brigade,
which marched off by the right, the 4th Regiment leading, and
the 23rd being in the rear. Boats being ready to receive them,
the wounded men were firſt embarked, then the flank Companies, the 4th & 47th. The boats returned with the Picquets of
the 2ed, & 3rd brigades, the 10th Regiment, and 200 of the 64th
who had been brought up from Caſtle William. Those troops
were under the Command of Brigadier General Pigot, and were
ordered to take poſſeſsion of Charleſtown, and the heights
Commanding the Neck. As these movements took up a considerable time, the 23rd, and Marines were ordered into the

Town house. Here we remained for two hours, when the boats being ready, we marched out and embarked; but it was paſt 12 at night before the whole of our Regiment was landed at the North end, Boſton, from whence we marched to our Barracks.

Lieu^t Rooke of the 4th Regiment, Aide-de-Camp to Genl Gage, marched out in the Morning with the firſt Brigade, and juſt as the firing began he was sent back by Lord Percy to inform the General of the situation of affairs; but as he was obliged to crofs the Country and keep out of the road, in order to avoid the numerous parties of Rebels who were coming from all parts to join those who attacked us, he did not arrive in Boſton, by way of Charleſtown, 'till paſt 4 o'Clock.

Lord Percy behaved with great spirit throughout this affair, and at the same time with great coolnefs. His determination to return by way of Charleſtown prevented the lofs of many men.

Return of the Killed, Wounded, & Mifsing in the Action of the 19th April 1775.

Corps.	Killed. W^d. Mifsing	Reg^t	Names of Officers Wounded.
4th	7 – 25 – 8	4th	Lieu^t Knight.........Died 20th Ap^l
5th	5 – 15 – 1	–	Lieu^t Gould...........In the Foot
10th	1 – 13 – 1	5th	Lieu^t Tho: Baker.........Hand
18th	1 – 4 – 1	–	Lt Hawkshaw............Cheek
23rd	4 – 26 – 6	–	Lt Cox.................Arm
38th	4 – 12 – .	10th	Lt Col^o Smith...........Leg
43rd	4 – 5 – 2	–	Capt Parsons....Arm. — Contusion
47th	5 – 22 – .	–	Lt Kelly................Arm
52^{ed}	3 – 2 – 1	–	Ens. Lister.............Arm
59th	3 – 3 – .	23rd	Lieu^t Col^o Bernard.......Thigh
Marines	31 – 38 – 2	38th	Lieu^t Sutherland ..Breast. Slight
Artillery	. – 2 – .	43rd	Lieu^t Hull { Body / & 2 other places } Died 2^d May
Total...	68 –167 –22	47th	L^t McLeod.............Breast
		–	Lt Baldwin.............Throat
Officers Not Included.		Marines.	Capt Souter.........Leg
		–	L^t McDonald ....Slight
		–	Lt Potter ....Slight

Return of the Rank & file of the Royal Welch Fusiliers under arms in the Action at Lexington. 19th Ap^l. 1775.

	Rank & file.
Grenadier Company	29
Light Infantry Company	35
Eight Battalion Companies	218
Total	282

The lofs of The King's Troops is ſtated on the opposite page. It is almoſt impoſsible to ascertain the lofs of the Rebels, but in the opinion of moſt persons, they muſt have loſt above 300 men, moſt of whom were killed. It is extremely difficult to say what number of men they had opposed to us, as their numbers were continually encreasing; but I imagine there was not lefs than 4000 actually afsembled towards the latter part of the day.

The whole of The Kings troops did not exceed 1500 men.

The following is another Account of the Action of the 19ᵗʰ of April, by an Officer of one of the Flank Companies.

The Grenadier & Light Companies of the Regiments in Boston were ordered to afsemble on the Beach near the Magazine at 10 o'Clock laſt night. The whole was not afsembled 'till near 11; and as there were not boats enough to embark them at once, as many as they could contain were embarked, and landed at Phipps's farm. The boats then returned for the remainder, and it was near One oClock in the Morning before the whole were landed on the opposite shore. Two days provisions which had been drefsed on board the Transports, were diſtributed to the troops, at Phipps's farm, which detained them near an hour; so that it was 2 oClock before they marched off. Their march acrofs the marshes into the high road, was haſty and fatiguing, and they were obliged to wade, halfway up their thighs, through two Inlets, the tide being by that time, up. This should have been avoided if pofsible, as the troops had a long march to perform. In order to make up for the time they had loſt, the Commanding Officer marched at a great rate, 'till they reached Lexington, where, about daybreak, they found a body of Rebels, amounting to about 100 men, drawn up, under arms. They were haſtily called to, to disperse. Shots were immediately fired; but from which side could not be ascertained, each party imputing it to the other. Our troops immediately rushed forward, and the Rebels were dispersed, 8 of them killed, and several wounded. One Soldier was wounded, and Major Pitcairn's horse was wounded.

Colᵒ Smith was not then in front, owing to the troops marching so fast, and his being a heavy man.

When the firing had ceased, and the troops were put in order, several of the Officers advised Colᵒ Smith to give up the idea of prosecuting his march, and to return to Boſton, as from what they had seen, and the certainty of the Country being alarmed and afsembling, they imagined it would be impracticable to advance to Concord and execute their orders. But Col° Smith determined to obey the orders he had received, and accordingly pursued his march, and arrived at Concord without further interruption. Soon after leaving Lexington, he was met by Major Mitchel of the 5th Regt, and some other Officers, who had been sent out from Boston on Horseback the Evening before towards Concord, with directions to stop all persons going that way in the night with intelligence. These Officers had been informed that Col° Smith would meet them within a few miles of Concord at day break. From the place where Major Mitchel met the troops, an Officer was dispatched to inform Genl Gage of the situation of affairs. It was 10 o'Clock before the troops arrived at Concord. Col° Smith was here informed that at some distance from the town there were two bridges, which it was necessary to secure, in order to prevent the Rebels from interrupting the troops while they were destroying those Military Stores at Concord, which it was the object of the Expedition to effect; Accordingly three Companies of Light Infantry were detached to the bridge on the right, which proved to be 3 miles distant; and 3 Companies to that on the left. The houses at Concord were now searched, and some pieces of Cannon, Carriage-wheels, Ammunition, & flour, found. The Trunnions of the Guns were knocked off, the wheels broken, & the ammunition destroyed. During this time the Rebels were afsembling in considerable numbers opposite the bridges, and at other places, but did not attempt to fire on the detached Companies, altho they drew up within shot of them. As soon as the Stores were destroyed, orders were sent to the detached Companies to return; at one of the bridges they retired in a confused manner, and some shots were exchanged by which two of the Light Infantry were wounded. The whole being re-afsembled at Concord about 12 oClock, they began their march back towards Lexington. The Rebels now appeared in considerable numbers, drawn up in a regular manner, keeping principally on the high grounds, firing occasionally on the troops, but never attempting to make any regular or serious attack. As soon as they found the troops had got into a Column of march, they grew bolder, extended themselves on the flanks and rear of the Column, and fired briskly from behind any thing which afforded them shelter. The Troops returned their fire, but with too much eagerneſs, so that at firſt moſt of it was thrown away for want of that coolneſs and Steadineſs which diſtinguishes troops who have been inured to service. The contempt in which they held the Rebels, and perhaps their opinion that they would be sufficiently intimidated by a brisk fire, occasioned this improper conduct; which the Officers did not prevent as they should have done. A good deal of this unſteady conduct may be attributed to the sudden and unexpected commencement of hoſtilities, and the too great eagerneſs of the Soldiers in the firſt Action of a War. Moſt of them were young Soldiers who had never been in Action, and had been taught that every thing was to be effected by a quick firing. This ineffectual fire gave the Rebels more confidence, as they soon found that notwithſtanding there was so much, they suffered but little from it. During the march to Lexington the numbers of the Rebels encreased, and the fire became more serious; several men were killed, and some Officers, and many men wounded. Colo Smith was wounded in the leg, but walked on to Lexington. The arrival of Lord Percy, with the 1st brigade and 2 6-pounders, who joined Colo Smith's detachment about ½ paſt 2 oClock at Lexington, checked the Rebels, who remained on the eminences near, and were a good deal alarmed at some Cannonshot which were fired at them.

The troops now drew up on the high grounds on the Boſton side of Lexington; and the Grenadiers and Light Infantry assembled in the rear of the brigade and were put in order. Soon after which, Lord Percy gave orders for the whole to begin their march towards Boſton. Colo Smith's detachment marched in front, as they were a good deal fatigued, and had expended moſt of their ammunition. Flanking parties were sent out, and the Welch Fusiliers ordered to form the rear Guard. As soon as the rear Guard began to move, the Rebels commenced their fire, having previously crept round under cover, and gained the walls and hedges on both flanks. The firing continued without intermiſsion, from Lexington, until the troops paſsed over Charlestown Neck. Those Rebels who came in from the flanks during the march, always poſted themselves in the houses and behind the walls by the roadside, and there waited the approach of the Column, when they fired at it. Numbers of them were mounted, and when they had faſtened their horses at some little diſtance from the road, they crept down near enough to have a Shot; as soon as the Column had pafsed, they mounted again, and rode round until they got ahead of the Column, and found some convenient place from whence they might fire again. These fellows were generally good marksmen, and many of them used long guns made for Duck-Shooting.

The troops drew up on Charleftown heights about dusk; soon after which some of the Corps began to embark and pafsed over to Bofton. The laft Regiment did not get to their Barracks 'till paft 12 at night. The 10ᵗʰ Regiment, and the Picquets of the 2ᵉᵈ & 3ʳᵈ brigades, with a Detachment of the 64ᵗʰ Regiment, came over to Charleftown, took poft on the heights, and placed their advanced pofts at Charleftown Neck.

We brought off moft of our Wounded men.

20ᵗʰ April. During the absence of the troops yefterday, orders were given for all those in Bofton to remain in their Barracks, ready to turn out with arms, ammunition, and provisions, the moment they are ordered. General Gage was not without some apprehensions that the Rebels might make some attempt upon the town while so considerable a part of the troops were in the Country.

As soon as the troops from Bofton took poft on Charleftown heights laft night, they began to throw up a redoubt to command the Neck; it was in a good ftate of forwardnefs this morning, when Genˡ Gage, having determined to abandon Charlestown, gave orders for its being demolished, and the Troops to be withdrawn into Bofton; which was done by 4 oClock in the afternoon.

Great numbers of the Rebels are in arms at Roxbury, and there has been no free communication with the Country this day.

It is conceived by many, that the expedition to Concord for the deftruction of the Military Stores, which it was said were deposited there in considerable quantities, might have been conducted with greater secrecy, and been effected without the lofs which ensued and, the consequences which muft now inevitably follow. It had been usual for some of the troops, whenever the weather was favorable, to march several miles into the Country, and return in the Afternoon. The 38ᵗʰ & 52ᵉᵈ Regiments marched once to Watertown, which indeed occasioned some alarm, and Cannon were fired, bells rung, and exprefses sent off, to give the alarm; but as they returned again the same

Evening after refreshing their men, the people were eased of their fears, and there was no afsemblage of any consequence. This mode might have been continued, ſtill encreasing the number of troops, and going different roads, until the time intended for putting the design in execution; when the troops deſtined for that service, might have marched as far as Watertown, which is near 11 Miles on one of the roads to Concord, whence, after remaining 'till towards Evening to reſt the men, inſtead of returning to Boſton, they might have pursued their march to Concord, where they would have arrived & effected their purpose before the Country could pofsibly have been sufficiently alarmed to have afsembled in any numbers, either to prevent them, or moleſt them in their return to Boſton. For greater security a brigade might have marched by different roads from Boſton at daybreak, which would have prevented the Rebels afsembling in one point, and have secured the return of the troops without any material lofs. But as it was, it was known early in the day, the 18th, that provisions were drefsing on board the transports for a body of troops, that the boats were ordered to be on the beach near the Common at night, and that several Officers had gone out towards Concord in the afternoon. As the people in Boſton were conſtantly on the watch, these indications of some enterprize, were sufficient; accordingly exprefses were sent out early in the Evening, and the whole Country was soon alarmed. It was not until 10 at night that orders were sent to The Lines to prevent any person from going out there. There is no doubt but the Country had information of the movement of the troops, as a Company was found under arms at Lexington at daybreak.

There was a general Muſter of all the Neighbouring Militia only the day before, (whether by accident, or in consequence of information of the General's intention is not certain; but moſt probable the latter) so that every man was in a ſtate of preparation and equipment. This should have been known, because, if their meeting was not on purpose to oppose the troops, there was hardly time for them to disperse and return to their several homes. I believe the fact is, that General Gage was not only much deceived with respect to the quantity of the Military Stores said to be collected at Concord, but had no conception the Rebels would have opposed The King's troops in the manner they did. But the temper of the people, the preparations they had been making all the winter to oppose the troops should they move out of Boston with hostile intentions, and above all their declared resolution to do so, made it evident to most persons, that opposition would be made, on any attempt to destroy Stores and Ammunition which they had avowedly collected for the defence of the Province.

An Officer of more activity than Col° Smith, should have been selected for the Command of the troops destined for this service.

Orders were given this day for the Officers to lay in their men's barracks 'till further orders.

From the want of proper accomodations for Officers in most of the Barracks, they have been under the necefsity of hiring lodgings as near as they could to them. It is conceived that in case of an alarm, or sudden insurrection, the Officers might be prevented from repairing to their posts. Every Regiment is now ordered, in case of alarm, to afsemble at their respective Barracks, and not march to the Alarm posts which had been afsigned them.

The troops ordered to lay drefsed in their Barracks this night.

21ˢᵗ Apˡ 1775. The town is now surrounded by armed Rebels, who have intercepted all communication with the Country.

The Guards ordered to mount at 4 o'Clock in the afternoon 'till further orders.

The Orderly hour fixed at 5 in the Afternoon.

Lieuᵗ Knight of the 4ᵗʰ Regiment, who died yesterday of a wound received in the action of the 19ᵗʰ, was buried this afternoon with the usual Military honors. He was an Excellent Officer, and a good man, and is universally regretted.

22ᵉᵈ April The troops ordered to be completed to 60 rounds pʳ man.

A working party consisting of 1 Captᵗ 3 Subˢ 4 Serjᵗˢ 4 Corpˡˢ 2 Drummers and 100 Privates, with their arms and ammunition, marched this afternoon to the Block house near the Neck, where a Battery is immediately to be constructed.

Five Serjeants, 5 Corpˡˢ and 100 Privates, with their Arms and Ammunition, were sent this day to do duty with the Royal Artillery.

The following order was given out this day.

As by the report from Lord Percy and the Officers in general, the men in the late affair, tho they behaved with much courage and spirit, shewed great inattention and neglect to the Commands of their Officers, which if they had observed, fewer of them would have been hurt, the General expects on any future occasion, that they will behave with more discipline and in a more Soldierlike manner: and it is his most positive orders that no man quit his rank to plunder or pillage, or to enter a house unlefs ordered so to do, under pain of death; and each Officer will be made answerable for the Platoon under his Command.

23rd April The Working party at the Block house consisted this day of 2 Cap^{ts} 6 Sub^s 6 Serj^{ts} 6 Corp^{ls} 3 Drum^{rs} and 150 Privates.

A Reinforcement consisting of 1 Field Officer, 5 Captains, 10 Sub^s 10 Serj^{ts} 10 Corp^s 5 Drum^{rs} and 250 men, from the brigade on duty, marched this afternoon at half after 6 o'Clock to The Lines; leaving a Capt and 30 men at the Neck. A Surgeon is ordered to attend this party.

From all the measures which have been taken since the 19th Inst, it appears that the General is apprehensive the Rebels will make some desperate attempt on the town. The numbers which are afsembled round it, and their violent and determined spirit, make it prudent to guard against what they may do.

24th April. Orders given for part of the Troops to Encamp to Morrow: and that no person whatever shall be permitted to go beyond the lines, unlefs on duty, or by permifsion from the General.

The working party at the Blockhouse reduced to 1 Capt 4 Sub^s & 100 men.

All working parties ordered to parade with arms for the future.

The Officers have continued to lie in the Barracks with the men every night since the 19th Instant.

The Brigadier of the Day, with his Major of Brigade, and a Surgeon, has remained all night at the Lines since the above mentioned day.

The Duty at this time is very severe upon the Troops.

25th April Our Regiment Encamped this morning on Fort Hill; The 4th Regiment on Mount Whoredom, and the Marines on the Common.

The Barrack bedding and furniture has been given up to the Barrack Master, and the troops have been supplied with a

Blanket p^r man and three paillaſses p^r tent, by the Q^r Maſter General.

The Officers and men are ordered to lie dreſsed in their tents, and ready to turn out on the ſhorteſt notice. The men take their arms into their tents.

26th April The 47th Regiment encamped this Morning on the Common.

The Commander in Chief has ordered 100 days Bat and Forage money to be iſsued to the troops.

27th April. The General has allowed the troops encamped, to take some of the boards used in the bottoms of their births in the Barracks, to put under their paillaſses in the tents. This arrangement will preserve the health of the Soldiers, as the ground is ſtill damp.

Orders given for all the Regiments to deliver in whatever number of ball Cartridges they may have above 60 rounds p^r man; and to employ their men in making more, which are to be delivered twice a week into the Ordnance Stores.

28th April. The Commander in Chief has ordered another hundred days Bat and forage money to be iſsued to the troops.

The Commander in Chief has allowed two gills of Rum to be given daily, for the future, to those men employed on the works. One Gill is to be given to them in the morning, and the other in the Evening. For this purpose a hogshead of Rum is to be iſsued to each Corps, and the Quarter Maſter is to diſtribute it to the working parties, and account to the Q^r Maſter General for it when expended.

A work is conſtruĉting on Beacon hill.

29th April. Numbers of the Inhabitants having applied to the General for permiſsion to leave the Town, an Officer was ordered to attend at Charleſtown ferry this Morning at 8 o'Clock, to examine and receive the paſses signed by The Town Major for those who have received the General's permiſsion to go out.

Some of the troops having begun to deſtroy fences and other property, the General has given ſtriĉt orders that no property whatever shall be touched or damaged without orders for so doing.

Detail of the Duty in Boston — 29ᵗʰ April 1775

Guards &c—	F.O	C	S	S	C	D	P
Main Guard.......................	.	1	2	3	3	2	50
Advanced works.................	1	2	4	4	4	2	120
Block houfe.....................	.	.	1	1	1	1	30
Neck...........................	.	.	1	1	2	1	30
Artillery.......................	.	1	2	4	4	2	60
Artillery work house..............	.	.	.	1	1	.	12
Wood yard.....................	.	.	.	1	1	.	9
Brigadiers Guards...............	.	.	.	.	1	.	12
Reinforcement to the Lines.........	1	5	10	10	10	5	200
4 Quarter Guards................	.	.	4	4	8	4	120
4 Rear Guards..................	.	.	.	4	4	.	36
Barrack Guards of 11 Corps.........	.	.	5	11	11	5	160
Hospital .. Dᵒ	.	.	.	.	11	.	40
4 Picquets of Regiments encamped	.	4	8	8	8	8	160
Orderlies.......................	.	.	.	11	1	.	50
Total.................	2	13	37	63	70	30	1089

Working parties, not included.

30ᵗʰ April.   Warm weather Thermʳ 64°.

Arrived The Faulcon, and Otter, Sloops of war from England.

We hear by some persons who came in within a day or two, that there are a good many British deserters in arms with the Rebels. They have also a few of The Stockbridge Indians with them, who Shew themselves at the ferry at Charlestown.

Lᵗ Hull of the 43ʳᵈ Regiment who was dangerously wounded on the 19ᵗʰ Inſtant, was left in a house in the Village of Menotomy. 'Tis said the Rebels placed three deserters from the 43ʳᵈ Regᵗ over him while he lay on a bed unable to move, and that one of those Villains threatened to shoot him for having formerly brought him to a Court Martial.

At Boſton in the Spring of 1775 two General Courts Martial were sitting at one time, for the trial of Officers, an inſtance hardly known before in the British Service, in one Garrison.

In Ireland about the year 1770, or 1771, a General Court Martial was afsembled to try a Captain Garſtang of the Dragoons. A Captain who had, some time before, given in his resignation, and signified his desire to sell out, was one of the Members, and the Court proceeded so far as to give their Sentence, by which the Officer who was tried, was censured; but before the Sentence was made public, a Commiſsion, dated before the date of the Warrant for holding the Court Martial, came over from England, appointing another person in the room of the above Captain: the opinion of the Lawyers was taken, who declared, that as, during the whole proceedings of the Court Martial, a person who was not then an Officer, sat as a Member, the Sentence was illegal. On which the whole affair was dropped, as the prisoner could not be tried twice for the same offence.

N. B. Told me by Lᵗ Dutton 38ᵗʰ Regᵗ. April 1775.

If during the sitting of a General Court Martial a Member dies, the whole of the Evidences muſt be examined over again in the presence of the new Member: but, if after Sentence has been paſsed, and before its being approved, or made public, a Member dies, or sells out, the Sentence will stand good.

II

LONG ISLAND

II

LONG ISLAND

4th Sep^t 1776

The Rebels fired a good deal at the Rose, yesterday and this day, but as she lies under Blackwell's Island, in such a manner that her Hull is not seen by their batteries, they can do her no great damage with Cannon Shot. This day they threw several Shells over the Island at her, but without effect. She lies however in a dangerous situation.

Great numbers of Waggons came to Headquarters from the Eastern part of the Island, to be employed in the service of the Army. One hundred Waggons brought from Staten Island, were dismifsed yesterday.

40 Fascines were ordered to be made by each Regiment this morning. In the Evening they were carried down to Genl Clinton's quarters near Hellgate, where a Battery is to be raised to destroy the Enemy's works on the opposite side.

Most of the Ships of War and Transports came up yesterday from Gravesend Bay and Staten Island, and anchored between Red-hook and Governor's Island.

The Niger and Brune Frigates, and the Halifax armed Brig, are in the Sound, between Flushing and Whitestone.

A Detachment of 200 Hefsians have taken post on Governor's-Island, and two Companies of Light Infantry are posted on Blackwell's Island.

When the Army was on Staten Island, we were made to expect that as soon as we should land on this Island, many thousands of the Inhabitants would show their loyalty and join the Army. But we have seen very little to induce us to believe that the Inhabitants of this Island are more loyal than others. The only circumstance that had the appearance of it, was on the Morning of the 27th August. While the first Column was lying on their arms near Howard's house, before we pafsed the hills to Bedford, a small body of men appeared on our right flank, with arms, carrying before them on a long pole, a white Shirt, by

way of a flag of truce. A small party under an Officer being sent
to examine who they were, they proved to be 49 men from the
Neighborhood of Oyster Bay, who having heard that the Army
had landed, afsembled, and set out to join us. During their
march they very narrowly escaped falling into the hands of the
Rebels.

Major Cuyler, aide de Camp to the Commander in chief,
went on board the Packet, with his dispatches for England.

5th Sept

The Rose moved lower down this morning near to Newtown
Creek, where she is in a safer situation. One of the shells which
the Rebels threw at her yesterday fell within 8 feet of her side.
Some splinters from others fell on her decks. The ship has
suffered a good deal of damage from their shot since she first
came up.

The Detachment on Blackwell's Island was withdrawn this
day, soon after which the Rebels sent over a detachment and
took pofsefsion of it.

We began last night to erect a Battery against the work,
which the Rebels have near Mr. Walton's house at Hellgate. It
is to consist of 3 24 prs and 3 12 prs. Ten small Mortars have
also been sent down there. The distance is said to be 850 yards.

By the information received, the Rebels are removing everything they can from New York, and mean to strengthen themselves as much as pofsible at the pafs at Kingsbridge.

It is probable that the next object of our army is to pafs over
to New York Island somewhere about Hellgate, and endeavor,
while the Shipping secure the Rivers, to prevent the retreat of
those who may remain near New York. Perhaps a part of the
Army may at the same time pafs over to the Continent above
Kingsbridge, in order to intercept the Supplies for those posted
there. Should this be the plan, and it succeeds, the whole of
the Rebels posted on New York Island must fall into our hands.
The ground immediately beyond Kingsbridge, entirely commands the North end of York Island.

It appears by the most authentic accounts that the Rebel
Army is much dispirited by their late defeat, and the abandon-
ment of their lines at Brooklyn which had cost them so much
time and pains. It is said numbers of them desert daily, notwithstanding every precaution taken to prevent it, and return

to their own homes declaring they have been betrayed and sold by their leaders.

Many Inhabitants of this Island who were in the Rebel Army on the 27th August, and escaped into the woods, have returned to, and are now at their own homes. Little or no notice has as yet been taken of them, altho they are well known.

General Sullivan, who was taken prisoner the 27th Augt went to New York a few days ago on parole, and returned. He is now gone to Philadelphia, to The Congrefs, supposed on the subject of an exchange of prisoners. Sullivan was bred to the law, and is said to be one of their beft officers. He is a short-set, rough, ill-looking fellow.

An exchange of prisoners is talked of. The measure may be right and politic; but it appears rather extraordinary that under the present circumftances we should treat with them as if on an equality; and for the sake of releasing a few of our officers and Soldiers, give up some of the principal actors in the Rebellion. Rebels taken in arms forfeit their lives by the laws of all Countries. The keeping all the Rebel prisoners taken in arms, without any immediate hope of release, and in a ftate of uncertainty with respect to their fate, would certainly ftrike great terror into their army; whereas now, captivity has nothing dreadful in it; and it rather encourages them to continue their opposition to the utmoft extremity, when they find, contrary to every expectation that capital punishment has not been inflicted on any of those who have fallen into our hands. Not one Rebel has suffered death yet, except in Action. We act thus either from an apprehension that they might retaliate upon our prisoners in their hands, or from a desire to bring them back to a sense of their duty by an extraordinary degree of lenity.

6th Sep^t — Fine pleasant weather for some days paft.

The Rose moved her Station again laft night, and went lower down the River. The Rebels fired some shot at her again laft Evening.

Considerable numbers of Cattle and Sheep, and large quantities of forage, are daily bringing in, and collecting for the use of the Army.

The pofts now occupied by the Army extend from Flushing, round by Jamaica and Newtown, to Flatbush and Gravesend. The 17th Dragoons and 71st Regiment are at Flushing and

Jamaica, four Brigades at Newtown, the Guards, 1ˢᵗ brigade, Grenadiers, Light Infantry, and 33ʳᵈ Regiment at Hellgate and on the Communication from thence to Newtown. The Hefsian Grenadiers and Jagers at Bushwick. General De Heiſter, with the principal part of the Hefsian troops at Brooklyn. The 42ⁿᵈ Regiment at Flatbush, with Detachments at Gravesend and New-Utrecht. The 4ᵗʰ brigade at Bedford. Staten Island is also occupied with Two brigades of Hefsians under Major Genˡ Stirn, and the Corps under the Command of Colᵒ Dalrymple, composed of Detachments of the 6ᵗʰ, 14ᵗʰ, and 16ᵗʰ Regiments.

The Rebels are committing great outrages on the loyaliſts in Weſt Cheſter County, and are selling their effects by public auction. Many of the loyal Inhabitants of this Province whom the Rebels carried away lately into New England, have been removed again from the places of their confinement, to others of which their friends are ignorant.

7ᵗʰ Sepᵗ — Thick weather, inclining to rain

The Battery at Hellgate is nearly completed, and it is said will be opened tomorrow. It consiſts of 3 24 prˢ 3 12 pdrˢ and 8 or 10 Small Mortars.

A few of the Rebels landed about 20 miles to the Eaſtward laſt night, and after committing some outrages upon the loyal-iſts, went off again, taking with them some Cattle, and other matters.

The troops having committed great irregularities of late, the Commander in Chief has authorized the Provoſt Marshal to execute upon the spot any Soldier he finds guilty of Marauding, and to take up all Soldiers he shall find one mile from their poſts.

The Army is ordered to be supplied with two days fresh pro-visions in the week till further orders.

Number of horses belonging to Officers of the 5ᵗʰ Brigade

22ⁿᵈ Regiment	4
43ʳᵈ	12
54ᵗʰ	11
63ʳᵈ	6
	33
Brigadier Genˡ Smith	4
Brigade Maʲ Mackenzie	1
Total	38

8th Sep^t — The Army continues in the same position

The Battery at Hellgate opened this morning at daybreak, upon the Rebel Redoubt on the opposite side.

The Rebels had 3 or 4 12 pr^s in their work from whence they fired now and then. We kept a very brisk fire upon them with Cannon and Mortars, and as the Artillery officers said dismounted their Guns more than once. If so, they mounted them again and fired occasionally. About 12 o'Clock their work was a good deal damaged, and the Merlon between two of the Embrazures almost destroyed. The firing continued till Evening. The distance is too great to batter in breach, as tis full 800 yards from work to work, and theirs upon ground something higher than ours. We had one man wounded.

9th Sep^t

The Rebels having repaired their work last night, remounted or replaced their Guns, and brought some Mortars into it, plied our battery briskly this morning with Shot and Shells. They killed one man, and dismounted one of the 12p^{rs}. One of our 24 p^{rs} ran yesterday, with the continual firing.

A large quantity of fascines were carried down to Hellgate this Evening, as it is intended to erect another battery there against the Enemy's works. The Guns are to be brought from Red-hook, where some heavy ones have been landed from the Ships.

The 71st Regiment marched from Flushing and Jamaica towards Hellgate, leaving some detachments in that Neighbourhood.

Two Ships of War are expected up the East River, as soon as the Wind and tide serves for their passing the town. Many of the flat boats have come up the River during the late nights, and are assembled in Hallet's Cove near Hellgate. More are expected up this night, and the whole will be collected there.

Everything indicates that we shall soon attempt something decisive against the Rebels, but considering the nature of the Shore at Hellgate, and rapidity of the tides and variety of Eddies there, I do not suppose the landing will be made in that place. It appears probable that the erecting batteries against the Enemy's works at Hellgate, and making so much demonstration there, is intended to draw their attention from some other point, for owing to the situation and construction of their principal work, it is extremely difficult to destroy it effectually. The Rebels appeared at first to intend confining the defence of New York Island to that part of it near Kingsbridge, but as by so doing we should have had no chance of destroying or Capturing any considerable number of them, it was perhaps thought proper to give them some confidence, and induce them to remain and defend New York, and by so doing, give us an opportunity of cutting off a considerable part of their army, which their situation, on a long narrow Island, without the means of crossing either of the Rivers makes them liable to. They now therefore appear as if they intend to keep possefsion of New York, and prevent our landing. Tis supposed they have not lefs than 4000 men between Hellgate and New York, with a considerable quantity of Artillery. It is supposed we shall land somewhere about Haerlem, and by taking a position acrofs the Island, which is narrow in that part, endeavor to cut off all that part of the Rebel army between us and New York, for if some ships go up the North River at the same time it will be almost impofsible for any of them to escape. The Island in that part affords some very advantageous positions, which would enable us to prevent those near New York from escaping to Kingsbridge, or receiving any afsistance from thence. The destruction or Capture of a considerable part of the Rebel army in this manner, would be attended with numerous advantages, as it would imprefs the remainder with a dread of being surrounded and cut off in every place where they took post, would encrease their discontent, and probably be the means of breaking up the whole of their Army, and reducing the Colonies to submifsion. It is in our power at any time to drive them from New York, and take posfefsion of it, but if we attacked them there, they might set fire to it, and once more slip out of our hands. It is of very material consequence to prevent them from burning the town, which will no doubt afford quarters to a considerable part of our Army during the ensuing winter, and be made the principal Depot of Stores, and harbour for our Shipping.

10th Sep — Thick weather

Another Battery was constructed last night at Hellgate, and 4 12 prs were brought up to it this Morning.

There was some firing on each side this day at the Batteries at Hellgate, but as that on our side is not continued with energy, it appears as if we only intended to amuse the Rebels, and take off their attention from some more material object.

Many flatboats came up with last night's tide to Hellgate. The Ships did not come up.

At daybreak the 1st and 2nd Battalions of Light Infantry embarked in flatboats (which came last night with the flood tide through Hellgate undiscovered by the Enemy) and landed on Montresor's and Buchannan's Islands, nearly opposite Haerlem. They met with no opposition except from one fellow, who staid to fire three shots at the boats, by which two men were wounded, (both by one ball). There were not more than 20 Rebels on the Islands, who retired and made their escape as soon as they saw our people landed. The possession of these Islands facilitates the landing of the Army on York Island, and will protect the boats which may have occasion to pass through Hellgate, or come down from Flushing or Whitestone. The Hessian Grenadiers and Jagers, who form a Corps under the Command of Col° Donop, moved from Bushwick this morning, and encamped near Hellgate.

The troops are ordered to have two days provisions ready dressed 'till further orders.

A Return was called for this day of the Number of Officers and Men, each Corps will have to embark.

Everything indicates a speedy movement of the Army.

5th Brigade — Number of Officers and Men, to Embark

	Offrs	S.	D.	R & F	Total
22nd Regiment	18	21	9	281	329
43rd	16	19	6	252	293
54th	20	15	12	280	327
63rd	17	18	7	250	292
Total	71	73	34	1063	1241

3rd Brigade	R & F
10th Regt	292
37th	307
38th	340
52nd	234
	1173

11th Sep^t

Two Battalions of the 1st Brigade paſſed over early this morning to the Islands, to support the Light Infantry and secure the poſts there. The Rebels appear numerous on the opposite shores, which probably made it necefſary to reinforce them.

A good deal of firing at the Batteries at Hellgate. The Rebels have thrown some of their Shells very well. We had some men wounded there.

A great number of the Country small Craft, are collecting at Flushing for the service of the Army.

John Winters, a Soldier of the 59th Regiment, who deserted laſt winter from Boſton and was taken in arms in the Rebel Service on the 27th Auguſt, was hanged this day in pursuance of the Sentence of a General Court Martial.

Two Soldiers of the 57th Regiment found Guilty of committing a Rape, have been sentenced to suffer death.

12th Sep^t — The two other Battalions of the 1st brigade paſſed over to the Islands.

The fire is ſtill kept up on both sides at Hellgate; but that of the Rebels slackens. We had four or five men wounded there this day.

The Brune frigate, came down the Sound, and Anchored above Montresor's Island.

Three Delegates from the Continental Congreſs came yeſterday, by permiſſion, to Staten Island, where it is said they had a Conference with Lord Howe. The businefs on which they came is not yet publickly known. It is reported that they demanded to be considered and treated as Ambaſſadors from Independant States. It is supposed, if this is true, that Lord Howe would have dismiſſed them immediately, as he certainly would not hearken to anything from people, who inſtead of coming with offers of compromise or submiſſion, presumed to insiſt on the acknowledgement of their Independency as a preliminary article.

The Delegates were Benjamin Franklin, John Adams, and ——Rutledge.

13th Sep^t   The Rebel Delegates returned yeſterday. Whatever they have offered has been rejected.

A good deal of firing towards New York this Evening.

The Commander in Chief acquainted the Army, in orders this Evening, that an attack upon the Enemy being shortly intended, he reminded them of their evident superiority on the 27th August, by charging the Rebels with their Bayonets, even in Woods where they thought themselves invincible; that, they now place their security in slight breastworks of the weakest construction, and which are to be carried with little lofs, by the same high spirited mode of attack. He therefore recommends to the troops an entire dependence upon their Bayonets, with which they will ever Command that succefs which their bravery so well deserves.

The Army ordered to draw two days fresh provisions tomorrow, which they are to use that day and the next, and keep their Salt provisions ready drefsed.

The troops are all in the highest health and spirits, and one may venture to say that their behavior when they attack the Enemy will fully answer the General's expectations. A Frigate arrived this day from Quebec, and brings letters of the 12th August. When she left Quebec, the last accounts from General Carleton's Army were, that they were at Chamblée, St. John's, La Prarie, Montreal, and Trois Rivieres and employed in building vefsels to pafs the lakes, and making other preparations to attack the Rebels. They did not expect to get over the lakes 'till about the end of September. There were about 700 Indians with the Army, who were very impatient to attack the Rebels. The 8th Regiment remained at the Upper posts in Canada, undisturbed.

14 Sept

Four Frigates pafsed the Town yesterday Evening, notwithstanding all the fire of the Enemy's Batteries, and came up the East River about 3 miles above New York. Altho the Rebels fired very briskly at them from several Batteries, they received no damage of consequence, and had but one man killed. The ships did not fire a Shot.

Tis thought the Army will move this night, as everything seems ready for putting the General's design in execution. We have no doubt of succefs, as from the abilities of the General, and the bravery of the troops, seconded by the operations of the Ships of War, everything may be expected.

It is reported that the fleet with the 2nd Division of the Hessian troops, has been seen off the Coast. If this is true, it is pofsible the movement of the Army may be suspended for a day or two, in order that they may land and join in the Attack.

NEW YORK ISLAND

15th Sep^{tr}

Orders were given laſt night for the four brigades encamped in the Environs of Newtown, to ſtrike their tents at 2 o'Clock this morning, load their baggage, form at the head of their Encampments, with their blankets and two days provisions, and wait for orders. Some other preparatory movements were also ordered, and executed.

At 4 this Morning the Brigade of Guards marched to Newtown where they waited for orders. In this situation we all expeƈted to have received orders to proceed towards Hellgate, and either to have embarked there or at some place farther to the right, in order to make a descent on that part of New York Island opposite; but were much surprized at receiving orders to march towards Bushwick.

At 6 oClock the left Column of the Army began its march in the following order; — 42nd Regiment (which had been poſted in the Environs of Bushwick) at the head, 33rd Regiment, Park of Artillery, Brigade of Guards, 2nd brigade, 3rd brigade, 4th brigade (from Bedford) and a brigade of Heſsians (from Genl De Heiſter's Corps at Brooklyn), 5th brigade, and 6th Brigade. This Column marched from Newtown through Bushwick, and at 8 in the Morning drew up in a Column of Battalions at Bushwick point. The 42nd and 33rd embarked immediately on board Six transports, which had paſsed the town, and came up the River yeſterday, in order to facilitate the landing the troops on the Island.

The Column on the right was composed of the British Light Infantry and Grenadiers, the Heſsian Grenadiers, and Jagers, and marched very early from the neighbourhood of Hellgate, to the head of Newtown Creek, where at 6 o'Clock they began to embark in 60 flat boats. When embarked they rowed down the Creek, and lay on their Oars at the mouth of it, until all was ready.

Early this morning the five ships of War, vizt, The Renown 44 Guns, Phoenix 44, Orpheus 28,   28, and Rose of 20, took their Stations along the shore of New York Island, from Kipps's bay near Turtle bay on the right, to the point behind Mr John Watts's house on the left, and about 200 yards from it. They anchored with their broadsides to the shore.

We could observe from Bushwick point, that the Rebels had made an Entrenchment along the Shore from Corlder's hook up to Turtle bay, with a few intermiſsions, and that they seemed to expeᶜt the troops would land at Turtle bay, having drawn moſt of their men that way.

About 10 o'Clock the flatboats began to row from the mouth of Newtown Creek, and afsembled aStern of the 6 transports at Bushwick point, in four Divisions. During this time The Guards embarked in flatboats which were prepared for their reception. The whole when afsembled, amounted to about 30 flatboats with troops, besides several Launches and other Craft, with some Light Artillery, Mantelets, Intrenching tools, Ammunition, &c. &c.

A little before 11, upon a signal given, the five Ships of War opened their fire upon the Entrenchments, on the shore, and the adjoining woods. This fire was continued until the Boats began to move, and the troops to land. Very few of the Rebels showed themselves, and those only in the moſt secure places.

The Rebels, who judged from what they saw of the movement of the Boats and Ships, that the troops would land at Turtle bay, observing the boats row from Newtown Creek, and afsemble at Bushwick point, immediately conceived they were going to land on the flat grounds near the town, and therefore marched several Battalions with their Colours flying into their line and works on that side, and made every appearance of an obſtinate defence; but they were deceived, for as the wind and tide set ſtrongly up the River, the boats were under the necessity of afsembling at Bushwick point, in order to be able to fetch the intended place of landing, which was Kipps bay.

At 12 o'Clock, everything being ready, the boats put off from Bushwick point, having on board three Battalions of Light Infantry, four Battalions of British, and 3 Battalions of Hessian Grenadiers, The Hefsian Jagers, and the Brigade of Guards: — under the immediate Command of Generals, Howe, Clinton, Lord Cornwallis, Vaughan, Mathew & Leslie, and Colᵒ Donop. They rowed over in 4 Divisions. This was a grand, and moſt intereſting sight. The boats ſtarted off in four Columns, and pafsing under Cover of the Ships, which continued their fire, reached Kipp's bay, to the right of the Ships, in about half an hour, and immediately landed there, without firing or receiving a Shot. Parties were inſtantly sent forward, who took pofsefsion of the ground in front and flanks. As soon as the troops were formed, they advanced to Murray's hill, (or Ingleberg) an advantageous piece of ground about $3\frac{1}{2}$ miles on the great Road from New York to Kingsbridge. The Hefsian Grenadiers who landed on the left met with a few of the Enemy in Mr Watts's

Disposition of Boats, &c for the reception of two Brigades, 15th Sep. 1776

Brigades	Corps	Com-panies	No. of Men	No. and nature of Boats	No. of Men in each
3rd brigade	10th Reg^t	8	259	1 Flat boat	49
				3 Batteaux	70
	37th	8	323	3 Batteaux	73
				1 Galley	104
	38th	8	295	4 Batteaux	74
	52nd	8	260	1 Batteaux	74
				1 Galley	120
				1 Gun boat	43
				1 Launch	27
5th brigade	22nd Reg^t	8	262	5 Flat boats	52
	43rd	8	231	4 Flat boats	57
	54th	8	234	4 Flat boats	58
	63rd	8	260	5 Flat boats	52

N. B. Similar dispositions were made for all the brigades and Corps that pafsed the River in Boats; and as the Officers of the Navy in each Boat, knew what Corps, and the No. of men he was to take on board, the whole was conducted without confusion.

orchard who fired on them, by which 2 Hefsians were killed and about 10 Wounded: but they paid dearly for this, as did some others who came forward soon after, with an intention of surrendering themselves, as the Hefsians killed about 60 of them, and took a few prisoners. On the right, a few ftragglers fired on the British Grenadiers, by which Genl Vaughan was wounded slightly in the thigh. He was the only person of the British hurt this day.

The Rebels who were posted in the works to our left of the Ships, seeing the boats, after they had put off, go up the River, began to march out of their works, with an intention as we supposed (who could see all their motions from Bushwick point), to go and oppose their landing; but they never showed themselves afterwards, except in making the best of their way towards McGowan's pafs. We could also see those troops which at first made a shew of opposing ours in landing at Turtle and Kipp's bay, going off as fast as they could, the moment they ascertained that the landing would be made at those places.

The boats, after landing the first Division, returned as quick as pofsible for the others, and this was continued with such dispatch and diligence, that the whole of the Troops, with their artillery, were landed at Kipp's bay about 5 o'Clock in the afternoon.

General Howe made a movement with the greatest part of the troops towards Haerlem, and took post for the night with his right at McGowan's house, or pafs, about 7½ miles from New York, extending his left acrofs the Island, to the North River.

The 5th brigade, upon intelligence received that the Rebels had abandoned New York, was sent to take pofsefsion of it. Brigadier General Smith who Commanded the 5th brigade and with whom I am, as Major of brigade, began to move from the 3 mile stone about 6 in the Evening, and began from thence to place the troops in and near the houses along the Main road from thence to New York, and they were actually distributed in this manner, until part of the 22nd Regiment reached that part called the Bowery, which was not completed until 7 in the Evening. As I was well acquainted with all this part of the Island, I represented to the General, that by stationing the Troops acrofs the Island, by means of two different roads which were near him, and placing the right of the Brigade upon the road along the Shore of the North River, and the left extending towards Coerlaer's hook, or Mr Styvesant's house, he would effectually prevent any of the Rebels who remained in New York, from escaping thence during the night, which they would otherwise most certainly do by the North River road. But as he is slow, and not inclined to attend to whatever may be considered as advice, and seemed more intent upon looking out for comfortable quarters for himself, than preventing the retreat of those who might be in the town, upon my urging the matter

with some earnestnefs and undertaking to conduct and post the
22nd on the North River road, he grew angry, and said I hurried
him, and that he would place the brigade as he thought proper;
upon which I was silent: and he proceeded to put the Regiments
into the houses and Barns on each side of the road from the
3 mile stone, to within a short distance of a redoubt the Enemy
had made at the North end of the Town, called (as we afterwards found,) Buncker's hill. He then went very quietly and
took up his quarters at Mr Elliott's house, about 2 miles from
New York. The consequence of this disposition was, that many
of the Rebels who had not time to make their escape by daylight, and concealed themselves in the town, finding the North
River road unguarded, made their escape that way; and as
the left of Genl Howe's line did not extend to the Shore of the
North River until towards morning, they joined their com-
panions who had taken post on the heights near Morris's house.

A considerable body of the Rebels finding they were likely to
be cut off from Kingsbridge as soon as the Army landed, made
the best of their way to New York, and crofsed the River to
Paulus hook, in great confusion. Some were drowned in attempting to pafs on rafts. Had our ships been able to anchor in
that part of the River they would have been prevented. Another body of them, as soon as they found the troops had landed,
made directly acrofs the Island to the North River shore, and
marching along, made their escape before General Howe could
intercept them.

The Rebels left a great quantity of Cannon, Ammunition,
Stores, provisions, tents, &c. &c. behind them, and abandoned
those immense works which had cost them infinite labour and
pains, without making the least attempt to defend one of them.

About 70 men were killed, and about 200 taken prisoners.
The nature of the ground from the place where the Army first
drew up, which is in most parts covered with wood, and thick
brush, saved many of them, as from the uncertainty of the
numbers on the Island, and their having made no attempt to
oppose the landing, it became prudent to advance with caution.
One brafs 6 pr and one 5½ Inch howitzer were taken.

16th Septr — While the Army was on the march yesterday
Morning three Ships of War pafsed the town up the North
River. They received a good deal of fire from the Battery at
Paulus hook, but without any damage.

The 5th brigade is ordered to do the duty in and near New York. Major General Robertson is appointed to Command in the town.

The Rebels have abandoned everything they had in New York. The works they have made, in and about the town, are truly aſtonishing for their numbers and extent. Many of the Rebels who were unable to make their escape yeſterday, are now in the town, and as they have changed their drefs it is extremely difficult to discover them. Moſt of the loyal Inhabitants have fled, or been carried away from the town, so that numbers of the houses are empty.

During laſt night, information was given to Lt Col^o Campbell of the 22nd Regiment, who was moſt advanced towards the town, that some of the Inhabitants were carrying off Powder and other Stores from the Magazine in Buncker's hill Redoubt, which was near him; he immediately detached an officer & some men who took poſt in the Redoubt and prevented further depredations.

Early this morning the Rebels set fire to a Sloop, and sent her down the North River with the wind and tide, in hopes of her damaging some of the ships anchored there; but she went over to the Jersey shore near Hoobuck, where she burnt out and sunk, without having come near any of our ships.

This Morning as the Light Infantry were extending their poſts to the left, they fell in with a body of the Rebels, who retreated before them, when some of the Companies pursuing them into the adjacent woods without proper precautions or support, they fell in with a considerable body of them without expeƈting it, and were rather severely handled by them. Had not some of the troops which were neareſt at hand advanced with the utmoſt expedition and drove the Rebels back, those Companies muſt have been cut off.

The lofs on our side in all, was about 100 men. Major Straubenzie of the 17th, Capt Matchel of the 15th, & Lieu^t Mackenzie of the 42^d, were wounded in this affair.

This was an unfortunate businefs, and gave the General a good deal of concern, and nothing was intended or gained by it, and we were obliged, from the nature of the ground, to bring the troops back to their original position. The Rebels left about 30 killed upon the ground, and muſt have had many wounded.

The Rebels have now taken poſt on the heights near Morris's house, about 9 miles from New York, a very advantageous position, where they are again Fortifying themselves. Their right is on the North River, and they extend to Haerlem, which is in front of their left, and occupied by them. They have a Corps encamped at Paulus hook.

The 1ſt brigade of British Infantry continue on Montresor's and Buchannan's Islands opposite Haerlem. The 71ſt Regiment remains near Hellgate, to keep up the communication that way with Long Island.

General De Heiſter remains encamped near Brooklyn with part of the Heſsian troops.

17ᵗʰ Septʳ — General de Heiſter's Corps marched this morning and encamped near Hellgate on Long Island, or the ground on which the Brigade of Guards was Encamped.

The Camp Equipage and Baggage of the Army has not yet been brought over from Long Island, owing to the difficulty of transporting so many Waggons and horses. Moſt of the troops therefore remains without tents, but they have made Wigwams or other shelter for themselves. Some Corps lie in Barns which are near their poſts.

Detail of the Guards — New York. 17ᵗʰ Septʳ 1776

Guards	C	S	S	C	D	P
Main Guard	1	2	3	3	2	50
Prison	1	2	3	3	2	50
North Ferry	.	1	1	1	1	30
New Barracks	.	1	1	1	1	30
Vauxhall Battery	.	.	1	1	.	12
Church Battery	.	.	1	1	.	12
Harrison's brewery	.	.	.	1	.	6
Fort George	.	.	.	1	.	6
Provision Store	.	.	.	1	.	6
Major Genˡ Vaughan	.	.	1	.	.	6
Total	2	6	11	13	6	208

The following account of the attack on the Rebel Army on Long Island on the 27ᵗʰ Augᵗ, and of some of the subsequent movements, was published by The Rebels in a New York paper, dated 2ⁿᵈ Sepᵗ.

"Accounts from the Ministerial Army on Long Island since our last are as follows, viz[t]. — There was little done on Monday on either side, but that night about 11 o'Clock the English troops in three divisions, taking three different roads, and the advantage of the night, almost surrounded the whole of our out parties; who, tho' encircled by more than treble their numbers, bravely fought their way through the Enemy, killing great numbers of them, and brought off some prisoners. The New York first Battalion behaved with great bravery. Lord Stirling's brigade sustained the hottest of the Enemy's fire. It consisted of Col[o] Miles's two Battalions, Col[o] Atlees', Col[o] Smallwood's, and Col[o] Hatche's Regiments: they were all surrounded by the Enemy, and had to fight their way through the blaze of their fire. They fought and fell like Romans! L[t] Col[o] Barry of the Pensylvania Musquetry, was shot through the head as he was giving orders to, and animating his men. The major part of Col[o] Atlee's and Col[o] Piper's Regiments are missing. Doctor Davis and his Mate were both taken prisoners as they were dressing a wounded person in the Wood. Col[o] Miles is missing (a truly amiable character) and supposed to be taken. The Generals Stirling and Sullivan are thought to be prisoners. General Parsons with 7 men came in on Wednesday morning, much fatigued, being for ten hours in the utmost danger of falling into the Enemy's hands. Our killed wounded and missing are imagined to be about 1,000: but for our encouragement the missing are hourly coming in.

"General Grant of the British troops, from good intelligence is among the killed. His hat with his name on it, was found near the dead body. The bullet had gone through and through the hat, and carried some of his grey hairs with it. Thus fell the hero who boasted in the British house of Commons, he would march through America with 5000 men, having only marched 5 miles on Long Island with an Army of four times the number.

"Our out guards have retired to the main body of the Army within the lines. The British Army have two encampments about a mile from our lines, and by their Manoeuvres 'tis plain they mean to attack us by surprize and Storm our entrenchments. Our men show the greatest bravery, and wish them to come to action. The firing continued yesterday all the day.

"The Alarm was so great last Tuesday (occasioned by the attack of the British troops) the day appointed for fasting,

humiliation, and prayer in this State, for imploring the divine
afsistance in forming the Government, that the Churches were
not opened, nor public worship performed.

"From the best accounts we learn, that the force of the
Ministerial Army on Staten and Long Islands are about 23,500
men. Marines unknown. The fleet consists of the following
Ships, The Asia & Eagle of 64 Guns, the Roebuck & Phoenix of
44, one Bomb, and about 20 Frigates and Sloops of War. They
have also about 300 sail of transports, Store-ships, and prizes.

"A Retreat from Long Island having been resolved on, the
same was effected on Thursday night and Friday morning, with
regularity and good order, without being observed by the
Regulars. On Friday and Saturday, Mitten, or Governor's
Island was evacuated. Our men brought off everything of consequence, notwithstanding a very hot fire from two men of War,
two batteries on Long Island, and one on Red-hook. In a few
hours after the retreat of our men from Long Island, the Enemy
appeared and fired upon several boats in the River; and we hear
the Light-horse have been alongshore in the Sound from whence
they have taken all the Cattle from 3 miles below Flushing,
where there was not a man to oppose them."

The following is a Copy of a letter from Mr Washington to
The Commanding Officers of Regiments in the Rebel Army,
and was taken from an original, signed by him —

New York, 4th Septr 1776

"Sir

Whether you do not get the orders with that regularity which
is to be wished, or whether (which is hard to suppose) you do
not attend to them, I will not undertake to determine, but it is
a melancholy truth, that returns, efsentially necefsary for the
Commanding officer to govern himself by, and which might be
made in an hour after they are called for where care and order
are observed, are obtained with much difficulty. Nor can I help
regretting, that not only regular returns, but that orders, in
instances equally important, should be so little attended to.
I therefore addrefs myself to you in this manner, requesting in
exprefs and peremptory terms, that you do without delay, make
out, and return to the Adjutant General's Office, immediately,
an exact State of the Regiment or Corps under your Command;
and that the like return be given in every Saturday at orderly
time without fail.

"I also desire in equally exprefs terms, that you do not suffer the men of your Corps to ftraggle from their quarters, or be absent from the Camp without leave and even then, but few at a time. Your own reputation, the safety of the Army, and the good of the Cause, depends, under God, upon our vigilance and readinefs to oppose a crafty and enterprizing Enemy, who are always upon the watch to take advantages. To prevent ftraggling, let your Rolls be called over three times a day, and the delinquents punished. I have one thing more to urge, and that is, that every attempt of the men to plunder houses, orchards, Gardens, &c. be discouraged; not only for the preservation of property, and sake of good order, but for the prevention of those fatal consequences which usually follow such diabolical practices. In short, Sir, at a time when everything is at ftake, it behoves every man to exert himself. It will not do, for a Commanding Officer of a Regiment, to content himself with barely *giving* orders; he should see (at leaft know) they are executed: he should call his men out frequently, and endeavor to imprefs them with a juft and true sense of their duty, and how much depends upon Subordination and discipline. Let me therefore, not only Command, but exhort you and your Officers, as you regard your reputation, your Country, and the Sacred cause of freedom, in which you are engaged, to a manly and vigorous exertion at this time, each ftriving to excel the other in the respective duties of his department.

"I truft it is unnecefsary for me to add anything further, but relying with the fulleft confidence, that these, and all other articles of your duty, you will execute with a spirit and punctuality becoming your Station,   I am, Sir,

Y^r Moft humble Servant

G. Washington

Colonel Gay"

18th Sept^r — The Commander in Chief's sentiments upon the conduct of the troops on the 15th & 16th Inftant, was signified in the orders yefterday in the following terms.

"The Commander in Chief entertains the higheft opinion of the bravery of the few troops that yefterday beat back a very superior body of the Rebels: and he desires to return his beft thanks to the Battalions, & to the officers and men of the Artillery, that came to their support with that expedition which so strongly marks the prevailing spirit in this Army, and which, if properly tempered, must always insure succefs to His Majesty's Arms: — but, at the same time he finds himself under the necefsity of disapproving a want of attention in the Light Companies pursuing the Rebels without that proper discretion to be observed where there are not troops to support.

"The General has also much satisfaction in taking notice of the steady behavior and activity of the Troops under the Command of Lt General Clinton, who made good the descent on this Island on the 15th Instant."

Major General Robertson, Commanding at New York gave out the following orders this day.

"The troops who may do duty in, and about New York, are hereby informed, that not only the best, but the greatest number of the Inhabitants of this Province, are Loyal, good, Subjects: — lately they have been persecuted for publishing their sentiments, and the fear of death has forced many to disguise them.

Soldiers whose valor has freed a people from the worst kind of Slavery, will be careful that no act of theirs prevent the enjoyment of all the blefsings that attend British liberty.

No person is to take anything that does not belong to him, under pretence that it is Rebel property. None but the Commander in Chief has a right to give judgement on this subject; and if a Military man had a right to condemn, he would commit a crime in appropriating the confiscation to his own use, and will be considered as guilty of a breach of the Commander in Chief's orders against plundering.

Endeavors are using to get reasonable markets established: this design, equally to the advantage of the troops and Inhabitants, would be baffled, if the Gardens, &^{c}. were permitted to be destroyed. No Soldier is to pull roots, or enter Gardens, without the owner's leave."

The Army is now Encamped, and is posted as follows. The three Battalions of Light Infantry, four Battalions of Grenadiers, 33rd, & 42nd Regiment, three Battalions of Hefsian Grenadiers, and the Jagers, with some Artillery, from the 1st Line, in front, with their right at McGowan's house, on the road to Haerlem, and their left at Jones's house on the North River.

The 3rd, and 4th brigades of British and Stirn's brigade of Hefsians, form the 2^d Line — The right towards Hellgate, and the left to Col^o De Lancey's house.

The 2nd and 6th brigades form a third line, near the public house called The Dove, about 5½ miles from New York. At this house, The Park of Artillery is placed.

The Guards are encamped at the 5 mile stone. The 5th brigade is encamped in the Environs of New York. The 22nd Regiment near Corlear's hook, facing the East river, the 54th and 63rd, near Judge Jones's house, facing the Country; and the 43rd near Lispenard's house, facing the North River.

The 1st brigade, with part of the 71st Reg^t remains on Buchannan's Island, with a post of 100 men on Montresor's Island. The remainder of the 71st Reg^t are near Flushing, and Jamaica, in which Neighbourhood are the 17th Dragoons, & Major Rogers's Corps.

General De Heister with the Hessian troops under his Command are near Hellgate on Long Island. The two New York Companies at Bedford and Brooklyn.

Staten Island is occupied by a Hessian brigade, and Col^o Dalrymple's Corps.

19th Sept^t I heard Lord Dunmore say at table this day, that Lee, had declared in a public Company, when General Amherst's coming to command in Chief in America, was the subject of Conversation, that he would rather Command against Genl Amherst and 27,000 men, than against General Howe with 17,000, So high an opinion did he entertain of the abilities of the latter.

The Rebels are extremely busy in fortifying their position near Col^o Morris's house; and are making Batteries, Lines, and Abbattis, without end. The position is certainly a very good one, naturally, but they are adding much to its strength.

Many deserters come in from them daily. Each Regiment of the brigades of the 2nd Line are making fascines, by order, at the rate of 100 each, per day.

The Rebels having left a great quantity of old straw in their encampments, and in the houses which they occupied as hospitals, it was all burnt this day by order of The General, in order to prevent infection.

A great number of flat boats were brought up to Greenwich on the North River last night.

The Rowbuck of 44 Guns came down the North River this Evening, and in passing Paulus hook, was fired at from thence — only 3 shot struck her, but she received no material damage.

The other ships remain up the River in a line with our advanced poſt.

20ᵗʰ Sepᵗ — A little after 12 o'Clock laſt night a moſt dreadful fire broke out in New York, in three different places in the South, and windward part of the town. The Alarm was soon given, but unfortunately there was a brisk wind at South, which spread the flames with such irresiſtible rapidity, that not-

Detail of the Guards, New York. 20ᵗʰ Septʳ 1776

Guards	C	S	S	C	D	P
Main	1	2	3	3	2	50
North ferry	.	1	1	1	1	30
New Barracks	.	1	1	1	1	30
Naval Stores	.	1	1	3	1	36
Prison	.	1	1	1	1	24
Bridewell	.	.	1	1	.	9
Jail	.	.	1	1	.	9
New Hospital	.	.	1	1	.	12
Vauxhall Battery	.	.	1	1	.	12
Church Battery	.	.	1	1	.	12
Harrison's brewery	.	.	.	1	.	6
Fort George	.	.	.	1	.	6
Provision Store	.	.	.	1	.	6
Wood Store	.	.	.	1	.	6
Buncker's hill Redoubt	.	.	.	1	.	3
Major Genˡ Vaughan	.	.	1	.	.	6
Total	1	6	13	19	6	257

withſtanding every aſsiſtance was given which the present circumſtances admitted, it was impoſsible to check its Progreſs 'till about 11 this day, when by preventing it from croſsing the Broad-way at the North part of the town, it was ſtopped from spreading any further that way, and about 12 it was so far got under that there was no danger of its extending beyond those houses which were then on fire. It broke out firſt near the Exchange, and burnt all the houses on the Weſt side of Broad Street, almoſt as far as The City Hall, & from thence all those in Beaver Street, and almoſt every house on the Weſt side of the town between the Broad way and the North River, as far as The College, amounting in the whole to about 600 houses, besides several Churches, particularly Trinity Church, the principal one in town.

On its first appearance two Regiments of the 5th brigade went into town, and some time after, a great number of Seamen from the Fleet were sent on shore under proper officers by order of Lord Howe, to give assistance. About daybreak the Brigade of Guards came in from Camp, but from the absence of the regular Firemen, the bad state of the Engines, a want of buckets, and a Scarcity of Water, the efforts of the Troops and Seamen, tho' very great, could not prevent the fire from spreading in the manner it did. The first notice I had of it was from the Sentry at Genl Smith's quarters at Mr Elliot's house, who called me up about 10 Clock and said New York was on fire; on going to the window I observed an immense Column of fire & smoke, and went and called Genl Smith, who said he would follow me into town as soon as possible. I dressed myself immediately and ran into town, a distance of two miles, but when I got there the fire had got to such ahead there seemed to be no hopes of stopping it, and those who were present did little more than look on and lament the misfortune. As soon as buckets & Water could be got, the Seamen and the troops, assisted by some of the Inhabitants did what they could to arrest its progress, but the fresh wind, and the combustible nature of the materials of which almost all the houses were built, rendered all their efforts vain.

From a variety of circumstances which occurred it is beyond a doubt that the town was designedly set on fire, either by some of those fellows who concealed themselves in it since the 15th Instant, or by some Villains left behind for the purpose. Some of them were caught by the Soldiers in the very act of setting fire to the inside of empty houses at a distance from the fire; many were detected with matches and combustibles under their Clothes, and combustibles were found in several houses. One Villain who abused and cut a woman who was employed in bringing water to the Engines, and who was found cutting the handles of the fire buckets, was hung up by the heels on the spot by the Seamen. One or two others who were found in houses with fire brands in their hands were put to death by the enraged Soldiery and thrown into the flames. There is no doubt however that the flames were communicated to several houses by means of the burning flakes of the Shingles, which being light, were carried by the wind to some distance and fall-

ing on the roofs of houses covered with Shingles, (which is most
generally the case at New York,) and whose Inhabitants were
either absent or inattentive, kindled the fire anew. The
Trinity Church, a very handsome, ancient building, was perceived to be on fire long before the fire reached the adjacent
houses, and as it stood at some distance from any house, little
doubt remained that it was set on fire wilfully.

During the time the Rebels were in possession of the town,
many of them were heard to say they would burn it, sooner than
it should become a nest for Tories — and several Inhabitants
who were most violently attached to the Rebel cause have been
heard to declare they would set fire to their own houses sooner
than they should be occupied by The King's troops.

No assistance could be sent from the Army 'till after daybreak, as the General was apprehensive the Rebels had some
design of attacking the Army.

It is almost impossible to conceive a Scene of more horror and
distress than the above. The Sick, The Aged, Women, and
Children, half naked were seen going they knew not where, and
taking refuge in houses which were at a distance from the fire,
but from whence they were in several instances driven a second
and even a third time by the devouring element, and at last in a
state of despair laying themselves down on the Common. The
terror was encreased by the horrid noise of the burning and
falling houses, the pulling down of such wooden buildings as
served to conduct the fire, (in which the Soldiers & Seamen were
particularly active and useful) the rattling of above 100 waggons, sent in from the Army, and which were constantly employed in conveying to the Common such goods and effects as
could be saved; — The confused voices of so many men, the
Shrieks and cries of the Women and children, the seeing the fire
break out unexpectedly in places at a distance, which mani-
fested a design of totally destroying the City, with numberless
other circumstances of private misery and distress, made this
one of the most tremendous and affecting Scenes I ever be-
held.

The appearance of the Trinity Church, when completely in
flames was a very grand sight, for the Spire being entirely
framed of wood and covered with Shingles, a lofty Pyramid of
fire appeared, and as soon as the Shingles were burnt away the
frame appeared with every separate piece of timber burning,

until the principal timbers were burnt through, when the whole fell with a great noise.

20th Sep^t — The 3rd Battalion of Light Infantry, and the 2nd & 6th brigades received orders laſt night to be in readineſs to march this Morning at 6 oClock. They were to have made an attack on Paulus hook this morning, under cover of the fire of three Ships of War, and were to have been commanded by Lord Percy. But the fire laſt night put a ſtop to the attempt for the present.

21 Sept^r — The troops mentioned yeſterday as intended for an attack on Paulus hook, were to have marched again this morning at Six, for that purpose, but the wind not permitting the Ships of War to come up to their Stations, the attack was poſtponed.

22nd Sep^t — The Army continues in the same position.

400 men began to work this morning at McGowan's house, where we have begun to conſtruct some works for the defence of our right.

The 3rd Battalion of Light Infantry, the 2nd & 6th brigades, and Stirn's brigade of Heſsians, marched from Camp at 9 o'Clock this morning to Greenwich, where part of them embarked in the flatboats, in order to croſs the River & make an attack on Paulus hook; but the wind being unfavorable for the Men of war to come up to cover the attack, it was thought adviseable to poſtpone it, especially as it appeared by the Rebels' firing at some ships in the River, that they ſtill had some Cannon there. The troops therefore disembarked and returned to Camp.

As the Rebels saw plainly for some days paſt that it was intended to attack the poſt, they ſtruck their Camp there yeſterday, and sent off moſt of their baggage and some of their Cannon. It is therefore probable that if the troops had rowed acroſs the River, they would have retired in time to have secured their retreat acroſs the Neck.

A person named Nathaniel Hales, a Lieutenant in the Rebel Army, and a native of Connecticut, was apprehended as a Spy, laſt night upon Long Island; and having this day made a full and free confeſsion to the Commander in Chief of his being employed by Mr Washington in that capacity, he was hanged at

11 o'Clock in front of the Park of Artillery. He was about 24 years of age, and had been educated at the College of Newhaven in Connecticut. He behaved with great composure and resolution, saying he thought it the duty of every good Officer, to obey any orders given him by his Commander in Chief; and desired the Spectators to be at all times prepared to meet death in whatever shape it might appear.

23rd Sept — A Regulation stating the numbers of horses and Waggons allowed for the Army, was given out this day, and the General has signified to the Army that he expects the strictest obedience will be paid to it, as not only the immediate situation of the Country, but the future operations of the Army make it indispensibly necefsary.

At 1 oClock this day, the 3rd Battalion of Light Infantry, and 2nd and 6th Brigades, marched to Greenwich in order to embark for the attack of Paulus hook. Three Ships of War came up at the same time, and anchored off the principal Battery, at which they fired a few shot, but none of the Rebels appearing, the 57th Regiment only received orders to embark; which they did and soon after landed without any opposition. They immediately took pofsefsion of the Peninsula, and all the Rebel works thereon, in which they found 2 32 prs, and forty Casks of biscuit. The pofsefsion of this post secures the principal anchorage in the North River, and renders the communication with the North part of the town, by water, safe.

The Rebels retired to Bergen heights about two miles distant, where they have formed a Camp; but they keep a post in a Redoubt on their side which Commands the Neck. As soon as the 57th landed, the other troops returned to their Camp.

A party of the Rebels, consisting of about 200 men, under the Command of two Majors, made an attempt this morning to surprize the Detachment posted on Montresor's Island. They came down Haerlem River in five large boats, a little before daybreak, conducted by two fellows who had deserted from the Brune Frigate Stationed near, and a fellow who had formerly been a Servant to Captain Montresor, and knew the Island perfectly. The two first had informed them that we had not above 20 men posted there. Our Detachment which consisted of a Captain and 100 men, having discovered them approaching, orders were given to suffer them to land, and then, before they

Regulation of Horses and Carriages for The Army. 23ʳᵈ Sep. 1776

	Horses	Waggons
Lieuᵗ General	.	3
Major General	.	2
Brigadier General, or Colonels, Commanding Corps	.	1
Aides-de-Camp	2	.
Majors of Brigade	2	.
Adjutant General	4	
Deputy adjᵗ General	3	1
afsiſtants	2	
Deputy Qrmſtʳ General	4	
afsiſtants	2	1
Baggage of each British Regiment	.	4
Do each Heſsian Regiment	.	6
Field officers Commanding Regiments	3	.
Majors	2	.
Officers under the Rank of Field offʳˢ Comdᵍ Regᵗˢ	2	.
Each Staff Officer	1	.
A Company of Heſsian Chaſseurs		1

Each Waggon to have two Horses

The Horses for the General officers is not regulated, the General being persuaded they will not have more than are absolutely necefsary for their service.

24ᵗʰ Sepᵗ — The Eſtablishment of the Brigade of Guards being the same as the Heſsians, the same number of Waggons (6), to be allowed to each Battalion.

Captains of the Guards, as Field officers of the Line, are, as such, to be allowed forage for two horses.

could put themselves in order, to rush suddenly on them with Bayonets fixed. The Detachment were prepared for this, and suffering them to come on, one of the Boats had reached the Shore, and the men landed, when the eagernefs of some of the 71ˢᵗ Regiment prevented their total deſtruction, for not obeying the orders given they rushed forward as soon as the firſt boat had landed, and began to fire, on which the other boats pulled off from the shore, and fired on our people, by which two of the 71ˢᵗ were killed. One of the Majors and 13 men were taken prisoners; and some were killed and wounded. They muſt have had several killed & wounded in the boats, as they received the fire of the detachment within 20 yards of the Shore, which was continued on them as long as they were in sight. They rowed off in great confusion.

Some of the prisoners whom I conversed with told me they were called out of their tents in the middle of the night by their

Serjeants, and told to take their arms: and that they were soon after embarked in the boats, without knowing where they were going, or for what purpose.

Regulation of forage to be issued by The Commissary General

For Dragoon horses — officers & men. 14 lb⁸ Hay, 10 lb⁸ oats, or,
                                        7 lb⁸ Indian Corn
For Waggon horse   12 lb⁸ Hay, 8 lb⁸ Oats, or,
                                        5 lb⁸ Indian Corn

No forage to be drawn but for Effective horses

24ᵗʰ Septʳ — We are now constructing a Chain of small Redoubts acrofs the Island, in front of our firſt Line; from McGowan's house on the right, to Mʳ Jones's house on the North River. The Island at that part is not above 1400 yards over, and the position is a very good one. When these Redoubts are finished, a small body of troops may defend the position from an Enemy advancing from Morris's house.

The Rebels are busy in fortifying their position near Morris's house.

Great numbers of the Rebels desert to us daily, and among them are some officers. Near 80 deserters came in one day lately, by which we may judge of the very great desertion in the Rebel army, as there can be no doubt that much greater numbers leave them to return to their own homes, and to other places in the Country.

25ᵗʰ Septʳ — Major General Prescott, who was taken prisoner by the Rebels laſt year in Canada, joined the army laſt night, being exchanged for General Sullivan, who was taken the 27ᵗʰ Augᵗ laſt. General Prescott has been 16 weeks in close confinement in three different Jails, and very ill treated. He was laſt confined in Reading Jail with common Malefactors, and the moſt notorious Villains.

Captain Balfour of the 4ᵗʰ Regᵗ, Aide de Camp to the Commander in Chief, is going home in a few days with his dispatches.

26ᵗʰ Sepᵗ — The 1ˢᵗ Battalion of Light Infantry advanced laſt night from McGowan's house, as far as Haerlem, from whence they drove the Rebels poſted there with little or no opposition. As it is a poſt which cannot be kept in the present situation of the Army, and otherwise of no material consequence, they abandoned it, and returned to Camp at daylight without any lofs.

Early this morning a Detachment of 100 men from the 57th Regiment advanced from Paulus hook, and took pofsefsion of a Redoubt which the Rebels occupied beyond the Causeway. The Rebels abandoned it on the approach of our people, who had only one man wounded.

The Rebels have a Camp of near 4000 men on Bergen heights, and altho it is naturally an exceeding ſtrong poſt, they are fortifying it with great assiduity.

27th Septr — The Rebels fired a few Cannon shot at our poſt in the advanced Redoubt from Paulus hook, which was returned from two pieces of Cannon we had there. They have an advanced poſt at a Mill within about 500 yards of the Redoubt.

A great number of transports and Storeships have come up into both the Rivers within a few days, and are unlading, Stores, Coals, Baggage, &c. &c.

All quiet at our advanced poſts.

Many deserters came in.

The General having considered the inconveniences that may arise to Captains not having horses in the course of aćtive Service, allows one horse to each Captain of Infantry, notwithſtanding the reſtrićtion so absolutely necefsary upon forage in the present ſtate of this Country.

28th Septr — Fine weather

The Army in the same position.

A Soldier of the 57th Regiment deserted laſt night from Paulus hook. The Rebels fired a few Shot at our advanced poſt there.

A Servant of Mr Alsop, one of the New York Delegates to the Continental Congrefs, came in from the Jersies a few days ago. He says that many of the Delegates have left the Congrefs since their declaration of Independence, that they are in great confusion, and much difsatisfied with each other. He says he met near 4000 of the Southern people on their way home from the Army; that the Country people in general are tired of the War, and wish that things were returned into their former Channel.

By the moſt authentic accounts which we receive of the State of their Army in this neighbourhood, it is extremely sickly, and many desert; so that the numbers of the Militia of the Northern Colonies who are daily coming in, are scarcely sufficient to make up their lofses by death and desertion.

29th Sept^r — Cold day & inclining to Rain

We have no authentic accounts yet of the operations of the Army in Canada.

Some deserters came in, who say the Rebels are constantly employed in fortifying and strengthening their position on the heights near Col° Morris's; and that their Army was under arms all last night, and until daybreak, in expectation of being attacked by us. I believe they may be easy on that head, for I am of opinion Gen¹ Howe will never attack them in front in their present position. He certainly intends something very different, if we may judge from his fortifying the narrow part of the Island so strongly, and other preparations which are making for a movement.

The works which the Rebels have made at different times in and near New York, are really astonishing for their number and extent. The shore of the Island, from Hellgate on the East River, quite round, by the town, up to Bloomingdale on the North River, an extent of near 14 miles, is fortified at almost every accefsible part; and there is hardly a height without a Redoubt or a Battery on it. They also made a Line, with Redans, and Redoubts at proper distances, quite acrofs the Island from Richmond Hill, the late residence of Gen¹ Haldimand, on the North River, to Corlear's hook on the East River.

This line faces the Country and has several Redoubts advanced from it. The works in town, particularly those in and about Fort George, must have cost them an immensity of labour, as almost all the Earth of which they are made, must have been brought there by land or Water from the outskirts of the town. The Sods have been brought from some of the adjacent Marshes. The Parapets are high and very thick, with numerous traverses, & other works to prevent Enfilading and the effects of Shells. The narrow part of the top of the Embrazures are covered with strong planks and Sods, to prevent the men at the Guns from being exposed to the fire from the Men of war's tops.

It must have discouraged their men greatly, to have abandoned those immense works, which they had constructed with so much labour and pains, without making the smallest effort to defend one of them. The giving up the Idea of defending New York against such a fleet and Army as we could have brought against, especially after we had taken pofsefsion of Brooklyn, was a wise measure; for had they remained to defend it, every man engaged in that defence must inevitably have been taken.

A large and Strong Redoubt on Murray's Hill, (or Ingleberg) would have been of more service to them than half the works they made at New York, as it is an advantageous piece of ground, and a Commanding situation, and in some measure commands the landing place at Kipp's bay. If they had had such a Redoubt there, we should not have effected the landing so easily on the 15th Sept^r, nor have been able to advance to McGowan's without having taken it.

The following Gentlemen having offered their services to raise a Brigade of Provincials, of three Battalions of 500 men each for the Service of His Majesty, and the supprefsion of the present unnatural Rebellion, The Commander in Chief has made the following appointments.

Oliver De Lancey Esqr, Brig^r Genl and Col^o of the 1st Battalion

John Harris Cruger Esqr — Lt Colonel
Captain   Green, late of the 40th Regiment, — Major
2nd Battalion —
George Bruerton Esqr — Colonel
Stephen De Lancey Esqr — Lt Colonel
Thos Bowden Esqr — Major
3rd Battalion —
G. Ludlow Esqr — Colonel
Richd Hewlett Esqr — Lieu^t Col^o
A. Menzies Esqr — Major
A. Campbell Esqr — Major of Brigade

30th Sep^t — The weather inclining to be cold.

300 men from the Guards, and the 2nd & 6th Brigades, began to be employed this day in making Cartridges for the use of the Army.

Several ships are going in a few days to Halifax to bring Coals for the use of the Troops during the ensuing winter.

By the arrangements which are now making, some movement of consequence appears to be intended soon. The greateft afsiduity is used in completing the works which are conftructing acrofs the Island near McGowan's pafs. It is probable the movement will not take place until they are finished.

Scarce a day pafses that several deserters do not come in from the Rebels. They all agree that the Rebels are discontented, and tired of continuing so long in Arms, especially since the misfortunes they have suffered since we landed on Long Island. They are ill clothed, and must suffer exceedingly for want of good warm clothing when the severe weather sets in.

1st Oct^r   The Mornings and Evenings are now cold; but the middle of the day very fine and clear.

Many of the Transports have received orders to get in readiness for Sea, and to prepare to receive troops on board, on the shortest notice.

2nd Oct^r — The Grenadiers and other troops composing the first Line, moved from their position this morning and took up the ground of the 3rd & 4th Brigades of British, and Stirn's brigade of Hessians; which Brigades marched forward and took up the ground of the 1st Line. The Light Infantry cantoned in the farm houses and Barns near Bloomingdale. It is probable from this movement, that the three brigades now advanced, are to remain in that position, when the rest of the Army moves.

Two Soldiers who were tried by a General Court Martial for a Rape, and were sentenced on the   to suffer death, have been pardoned, in consequence of the intercession of the injured party.

As it is apprehended that some Villains may be employed by the Enemy to burn the remainder of New York, in which a great quantity of Stores, Ammunition, Provisions, Baggage, &c. is now deposited; it is probable, that whenever the Army moves, the 5th brigade will be left in order to furnish the necessary Guards and protect the town. The Guards now amount to above 250 men daily.

There are now about 1000 Rebel prisoners confined in New York.

The following, (taken from the Newport Mercury of the 30th Septr 1776) is the account published by The Continental Congress, of the Message sent them by Lord Howe; and of the interview between him and a Committee of Congress, on the subject of an accomodation —

"The following is the purport of the Message sent from Lord Howe to Congress by General Sullivan.

"That though he could not at present treat with the Congress, as such, yet he was very desirous of having a conference with some of the Members, whom he would consider for the present only as private Gentlemen, and meet them himself as such, at such place as they should appoint.

"That he, in conjunction with General Howe, had had full powers to compromise the dispute between Great Britain and America, upon terms advantageous to both; the obtaining of which had delayed him two months in England, and prevented his arrival at this place before the declaration of Independency took place.

"That he wished a compact might be settled at this time when no decisive blow was struck, and neither party could say they were compelled to enter into such agreement.

"That in case Congrefs were disposed to treat, many things which they had not yet asked, might, and ought to be granted them; and that if, upon the conference, they found any probable ground of an accomodation, the authority of Congrefs must be afterwards acknowledged, otherwise the compact could not be complete."

Extract from the Minutes
Chas Thompson, Sec^y.

"In Congrefs, 5th Septr 1776 —

"Resolved: That General Sullivan be requested to inform Lord Howe, that this Congrefs being the representatives of the Free and Independent States of America, cannot, with propriety, send any of its members to confer with his Lordship in their private Characters, but, that ever desirous of establishing peace on reasonable terms, they will send a Committee of their body to know whether he has any authority to treat with persons authorized by Congrefs for that purpose, in behalf of America and what that authority is: and to hear such propositions as he shall think fit to make respecting the same.

The members of the Committee chosen were, Mr Franklin, Mr John Adams, and Mr E. Rutledge.

The Committee who were appointed to wait on Lord Howe, having returned to Congrefs, made their report in the following words —

In obedience to the order of Congrefs, we have had a meeting with Lord Howe. It was on Wednesday last on Staten Island opposite to Amboy, where his Lordship received and entertained us with the utmost politenefs.

His Lordship opened the conversation by acquainting us, that tho' he could not treat with us as a Committee of Congrefs, yet, as his powers enabled him to confer and consult with any private Gentlemen of influence in the Colonies, on the means of restoring peace between the two Countries, he was glad of the opportunity of conferring with us on that subject, if we thought ourselves at liberty to enter into a conference with him in that Character. We observed to his Lordship, that as our businefs was to hear, he might consider us in what light he pleased, and communicate to us any propositions he might be authorized to make for the purpose mentioned: but that we could consider ourselves in no other Character but that in which we were placed by the order of Congrefs. His Lordship then entered into a discourse of considerable length, which contained no explicit proposition of peace except one, vizt, that the Colonies should return to their allegiance and obedience to the Government of Great Britain. The rest consisted principally of afsurances that there was an exceeding good disposition in the King and his Ministers to make that Government easy to us; with intimation, that in case of our submifsion they would cause the offensive acts of Parliament, and the Instructions to Governors to be reconsidered; that so, if any just causes of complaint were found in the Acts, or any errors in Government were perceived to have crept into the Instructions, they might be amended or withdrawn.

We gave it as our opinion to his Lordship, that a return to the domination of Great Britain was not now to be expected. We mentioned the repeated humble petitions of the Colonies to The King and Parliament, which had been treated with contempt, and answered only by additional injuries; the unexampled patience we had shewn under their Tyrannical government, and that it was not until the last act of Parliament which denounced war against us, and put us out of The King's protection, that we declared our Independence. That this declaration had been called for by the people of the Colonies in general; that every Colony had approved of it when made and all now considered themselves as Independent States, and were settling, or had settled their Governments accordingly; so that it was not in the power of Congrefs to agree for them that they should return to their former dependent State. That there was no doubt of their inclination to peace, and their willingnefs to enter into a treaty with Britain that might be advantageous to both Countries. That though his Lordship had at present no power to treat with them as Independent States, he might, if there was the same good disposition in Britain, much sooner obtain fresh powers from thence for that purpose, than powers could be obtained by Congrefs from the several Colonies to consent to submifsion. His Lordship then saying that he was sorry to find no accomodation was likely to take place, put an end to the conference.

Upon the whole it did not appear to your Committee that his Lordship's Commifsion contained any other authority of importance than what is exprefsed in the act of Parliament, vizt. that of granting pardons, with such exceptions as the Commissioners shall think proper to make, and of declaring America, or any part of it, to be in The King's peace, upon submifsion. For as to the power of inquiring into the State of America, which his Lordship mentioned to us, and of conferring and consulting with any persons the Commifsioners might think proper, and representing the result of such conversations to the Ministry, who (provided the Colonies would subject themselves) might after all, or might not, at their pleasure, make any alterations in their former Instructions to Governors, or propose in Parliament any amendment in the acts complained of, we apprehend any expectation from the effect of such a power, would have been too uncertain and precarious to be relied on by America had she still continued in her state of dependence.

In Congrefs — 26th Sep^t 1776

Resolved: — That 88 Battalions be inlisted as soon as pofsible, to serve during the present war, and that each State furnish their respective quotas in the following proportion, Viz^t.

	Battalions
New Hampshire	3
Mafsachusett's Bay	15
Rhode Island	2
Connecticut	8
New York	4
New Jersey	4
Pensylvania	12
Delaware	1
Maryland	8
Virginia	15
North Carolina	9
South Carolina	6
Georgia	1
Total	88

20 Dollars bounty to each Non-Commifsioned Officer and Soldier who shall Inlift to serve during the War, unlefs sooner discharged by Congrefs.

The Expence of Arms, Clothing, &c. to be deducted out of the
20 Dollars.

Lands to such as serve till the Close of the War, or are discharged, or killed —

Colonel	500	Acres
Lᵗ Colonel	450	"
Major	400	"
Captain	300	
Lieutenant	200	
Ensign	150	
Non-Commifsᵈ Officer & Private	100	

3ʳᵈ Oᶜᵗʳ 1776 — Arrived The Daphne, 20 Guns Captain —
with 11 sail of transports under her Convoy, having on board
the 16ᵗʰ Regiment of Light Dragoons in 11 weeks from Falmouth. One transport brig of the Convoy is mifsing. The
Regiment has loft 46 horses during the pafsage. They met with
three violent gales of wind during the voyage, so that the reft of
the horses are Sickly and out of condition.

The fleet with the 2ⁿᵈ Division of the Hefsian troops, three
British Regiments, and Recruits for the Army, were to have
sailed a day or two before them from Plymouth, amounting
to about 90 Sail, under Convoy of three Ships of War.

A Packet sailed from Falmouth the day before them.

Preparations are making for the movement of a very considerable part of the Army by water, as many of the transports
have been getting ready, and some part of the heavy Artillery,
and other matters are put on board. The Bridge Mafter has
received directions to prepare materials for a Bridge. It is not
improbable that an attempt may be made upon Philadelphia.
This is far from being impracticable. The transports may convey the troops in a very short time to Amboy, and the Troops
might be conveyed from thence in boats to Brunswick, which is
not above 40 miles from Philadelphia. But it is generally supposed the expedition is intended againft Rhode Island or some
considerable port or place to the Eaftward. Certain it is that
the object is of magnitude; and we are in expectation that it will
close the Campaign with succefs.

The Phoenix and Roebuck went up the North River this
afternoon, and anchored about 4 miles above the town.

4th Oct^r — The Phoenix and Roebuck weighed and went higher up the River this morning.

The 16th Light Dragoons disembarked, and went into quarters in New York. Their horses look very indifferently, and it will be some time before they are in proper Condition for service.

5th Oct^r   A number of pieces of Light artillery were brought from New York this morning, and placed in the Park of Artillery near The Dove.

The object of the next movement of the Army, which will certainly take place shortly, is (as indeed it should be) quite a Secret. Most people think Rhode Island is the place, as the harbour is a very fine one for our large ships, the Island very defensible, and the Rebels have but a small force there. It may therefore be intended to make that place the right of our Winter quarters.

As the position the Rebels have taken upon this Island is too strong to be attacked without considerable lofs, the movement of a large Corps to Rhode Island would oblige them to divide their force, and pofsibly, with the Combined operations of this army, and that under General Burgoyne from Canada, oblige them to abandon their position and retire into New England.

6th Oct^r — Orders were given this day for the 2^d & 6th brigades to march tomorrow to Bedford, and the next day to Jamaica, where they are to put themselves under the Command of General de Heifter. It is uncertain how much farther these brigades are going, but it is conjectured towards the Eaft end of the Island, to which part the Rebels have lately sent over some parties, who have carried off the Cattle and plundered the Inhabitants. Tis said a letter was found yefterday on Long Island, directed to the officer Commanding the Rebel troops there, from Mr Washington, acquainting him with an intention of making an attack on that Island as soon as some other arrangements have taken place. Some persons imagine that the movement of the two brigades is in consequence of this information. I am rather of opinion that they are intended to co-operate with the reft of the Army in the attack which is projected againft the Rebels.

7th Oct^r — The 2^d and 6th brigades marched from their encampment at 7 o'Clock this morning to New York, where they embarked in flatboats which landed them at Brooklyn ferry, from whence they marched to Bedford.

The 17ᵗʰ Dragoons are now afsembled at Flushing on Long Island. The 16ᵗʰ Dragoons remain on this Island.

The greateſt part of the Rebels who were encamped on Bergen heights, have moved from thence within these few days. A very small Corps remains there.

The 57ᵗʰ Regiment continues at Paulus hook.

A Soldier of the 40ᵗʰ Regiment deserted laſt night. Brigadier General Sir William Erskine is appointed Quarter Maſter General of this Army.

8ᵗʰ Oĉtʳ   A Council of War was held at Headquarters this day, at which all The General officers, and Lord Howe attended. They did not break up till near 4 o'Clock. From the orders which were afterwards given for the 2ᵈ & 6ᵗʰ Brigades to be in readinefs to embark on the shorteſt notice, and for some other arrangements, it is supposed the General's plan of the intended operation was laid before them, and determined on.

The Grenadier Company of the 42ᵈ Regiment, and the two Grenadier Companies of the 71ˢᵗ Regiment, have hitherto formed the 4ᵗʰ Battalion of Grenadiers. As the two laſt Companies are sickly, that Battalion is now broke up, & the 71ˢᵗ Companies ordered to join their Regiment. The 42ᵈ Company is ordered to join the 3ʳᵈ Battalion.

I am pretty well convinced that the intended attack will be direĉted againſt that part of the Rebel Army poſted on this Island and at Kingsbridge; for however terrifying an attack on the Jersies, or towards Philadelphia would be to them, yet it would by no means be prudent to divide our Army so much, and run the risque of having any considerable part of it defeated. The grand point in view is certainly to beat and disperse this their principal Army, which if once effeĉted, little more will remain to be done; as they never will be able to assemble another Army fit to oppose The King's troops.

From the discontent which prevails in the Rebel Army, and among the people in general, and the dangerous situation in which they will find themselves as soon as General Burgoyne makes any progrefs through the Country towards Albany, it is highly probable that, if the intended plan is crowned with moderate succefs, we shall have very little more trouble with the Rebel Army, and that they will never make another stand of any consequence.

Several Transports sailed for Halifax. They are to return loaded with Coals for the use of the Garrison during the ensuing winter.

Six days provisions ordered to be issued to the Troops to-morrow; and it is strongly recommended to the Commanding officers of Corps not to suffer any part of them to be wasted.

9th Octr — At half past 7 in the morning The Phoenix, Roebuck, and Tartar, weighed anchor, and having the advantage of the flood tide, and a brisk Southerly wind, stood up the North River, followed by three or four small tenders. As soon as the Rebels perceived them under way, they beat to arms and manned all their batteries on each side of the River. About 8 o'Clock they began to fire very briskly at the Ships from both sides, but par-ticularly from the batteries near Kingsbridge and immediately opposite. The Ships fired but little, and in about 3/4 of an hour had entirely passed those batteries without receiving any dam-age that could be observed by us. In their passage up, while we could see them, they drove about 20 sail of small craft before them, some of which they took. About 10 o'Clock they were again fired on by Some of the Batteries up the River, but as they were then out of our sight, it was not known what the conse-quence was.

This movement is certainly connected with the general plan for the attack of the Enemy, and points out clearly that our operations are intended against Mr Washington's Army on this Island.

A Soldier of the 38th Regiment deserted this Morning from the advanced post beyond McGowan's house.

10th Octr — A Deserter came in this morning, who says that the Enemy are very numerous near Colo Morris's and at Kings-bridge; said to amount to between 35, and 40,000 men. That before the ships went up the River, they were very busy in erecting Barracks at those places, but that as they cannot now get anything down by water, they have been obliged to desist. They daily expect an attack to be made on them, and are con-tinually employed in erecting new works and strengthening their position. They are sickly, and but ill provided with Cloth-ing.

The Troops were this day ordered to drefs four days provisions toMorrow Evening.

A great number of Horses for the use of The artillery, have been embarked, within this day or two; also Waggons, Portable bridges, and other matters requisite for the movement of a large body of the Army in the Country. Great numbers of Sloops, Schooners, Pothangers, and other small craft, came up the East River today; and there were some movements among the Frigates. Things seem to be advancing fast towards the Execution of the General's plan; and by the dispositions which are making, it appears that almost all the troops, excepting the 3rd, 4th, and 5th Brigades of British, are to be employed in the more active part of the intended operation. Those three brigades will probably be left for the defence of this Island, and eventually to attack the Enemy on this side.

A very laudable secrecy prevails as to the real object of the Expedition, or the place where the attack is to be made. It is obvious however that the great object of the Campaign is to strike at Washington's Army and disperse it. How that is to be effected, a short time will shew. The Commander in Chief seems to have considered everything with great attention, and to have made every previous arrangement, and provided every means for ensuring succefs to the Army; and as his plan is to be put in execution by troops of known bravery, and zealous in the cause of thier Country, the most brilliant succefs, and advantageous consequences may be expected.

11th Octr — The Artillery of The Park, struck their tents at 3 o'Clock this afternoon, and marked immediately to Turtle bay, where they embarked. Some pieces of light artillery, with a proportion of Ammunition, &c., were put on board Gunboats; the remainder and the baggage on board Transports which had been brought up for their reception.

At 3 o'Clock all the Gunboats, flat boats, Batteaux, Launches, &c., &c., came up from the harbour, and drew up on the shore at Turtle bay. They amounted to about 150. Several Armed vefsels and transports weighed from Bushwick point at the same time, and came up with the flood tide.

The Majors of brigade and orderly officers having received directions to attend at 5 in the afternoon at the Dove for orders, the orders they received at that time were, that the Troops under orders for march (which were the whole of The Army

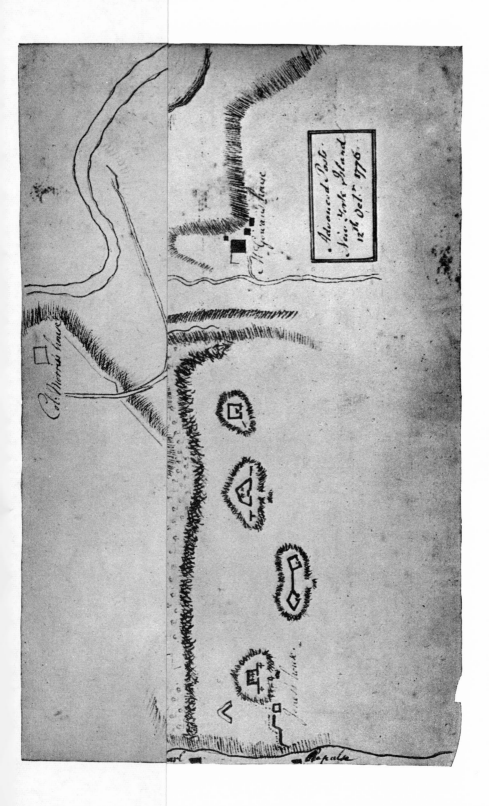

Advanced Post.
New York Island.
12th Octr 1776.

except the 3rd, 4th, & 5th brigades of British Infantry, and Stirn's brigade of Hefsians) should strike their tents at 6 in the Evening, put their baggage on board, and be ready to march immediately. It was also ordered, that as soon as the Troops move against the Enemy, Lieutenant General Clinton should Command the first Division, consisting of the Light Infantry, Reserve, Hefsian Grenadiers & Chafseurs; Lieu^t Genl Earl Percy to Command on York Island & posts depending; and that the patroles of the advanced posts should be very alert in securing all suspected persons. In consequence of those orders, the Army (except the brigades abovementioned) struck their tents at 6 o'Clock, sent their baggage to Turtle bay, and remained on their ground waiting for further orders.

12th Oct^r — Frost last night. The first this Season.

The troops marched from thier ground at 10 o'Clock last night, and soon after began to embark at several places in the East River, particularly Turtle-bay, Marston's wharf, General Howe's quarters, and other wharfs up that way. Many of the troops went in transports, but the principal part in the Boats, Sloops, and Schooners. About 4 this morning they began to move with the tide, and pafsed up the East River and through Hellgate with great rapidity, and without any other accident than the lofs of a Gunboat, in which were a Detachment of artillery with 3. 6 p^{rs} by which 4 men of the artillery were drowned and the guns lost. This accident was occasioned by the vefsel getting into one of those dreadful Eddies with which that place abounds, and being thrown on an adjacent rock. Having pafsed Hellgate, the whole proceeded up the Sound with a fair wind, and at 12 at noon landed at a place called Frog's point in West-Chester County, without any opposition. The Rebels had a post of an officer and 30 men there, who, as soon as they found the troops were going to land, took to their heels without firing a Shot. We hear that Genl Howe advanced two miles into the Country after landing, and encamped on the ground he intended, without meeting with any opposition.

The Rebels on this Island were much alarmed when they perceived the movement of the troops, and got under arms and manned all their works as soon as pofsible. A body of about 6000 men marched down towards Haerlem, expecting that an attack would be made thereabouts, but they were much surprized when they observed the troops were gone further up.

They continued in their works all day; and we could observe them constructing new ones in several places. They appear to expect an attack on this side.

A Deserter came in this day who says the Rebels have been under arms ever since they observed the ships and Boats in motion, expecting an attack, but entirely at a lofs to know where it would be made.

Lord Percy commands on this Island, having under him tne 3rd and 4th brigades, who occupy the posts in the right of the Line, from McGowan's; Stirn's brigade of Hefsians (about 1500 men) who extend from The North River to the left of the British — and the 5th brigade, incamped near New York. The 57th Regiment remains at Paulus hook. A Soldier of the 38th deserted this day. The 16th Dragoons remain in New York.

The Deserter who came in today says, the Rebel Army is computed to amount to between 35, and 40,000 men.

13th Oct^r — The 1st brigade which was encamped on Buchannan's Island went with the Army yesterday, and were replaced by 300 of the 71st Regiment. The 17th Dragoons also went with the Army.

A Squadron of the 16th Dragoons pafsed over to Long Island this morning to replace the 17th Dragoons.

A great many transports and other vefsels went through Hellgate yesterday Evening to the Army.

Several transports with Hefsian troops from Staten Island, came into the Eaft River in order to proceed to the Army, but the wind being unfavorable, they were obliged to anchor off Bushwick point.

Some ships, part of a fleet of 21 sail with Recruits from England arrived this day.

Very few of the Rebels appeared in their lines during the course of the day. There are as yet no indications of their moving, but it is probable they will soon take another position, for if Genl Howe can get upon their Communications, he will render thier means of subsiftance so very precarious, that they will have no alternative but a speedy retreat. I am confident they will not attack his Army, nor will they venture to attack our position on this Island: — and if the Ships of War in the River keep a good look out, it will be almoft impofsible for any considerable number of them to retreat to the Jersies.

A Soldier of the 40th Regiment deserted.

14th Oct^r   We have not learnt anything certain of the motions of the Army under Gen¹ Howe. Tis said he is repairing some bridges which the Rebels broke down, before he can advance further into the Country.

The Rebels were discovered yesterday making a bridge of boats over Haerlem River below Morris's house. They have some works opposite to it on the West Chester side. It appears this bridge is intended to facilitate their communication with West Chester County.

Our position on this Island is very strong. A Chain of Redoubts from McGowan's house to the North River, with an almost impenetrable Abbatis in front of them, covers our front. The Pearl & Repulse frigates at anchor in the North River, covers our left flank, and The Fowey of 24 Guns, is in the mouth of the Creek on our right which runs up towards McGowan's house.

Three deserters came in from the Rebels.

We were somewhat alarmed yesterday morning on receiving information that the Rebels had landed on Staten Island. Colonel Dalrymple of the 14th Reg^t who commands there applied for a Reinforcement of Troops, and a Regiment was to have been sent to him in case of necefsity; but Lord Percy having sent an officer to learn the real state of affairs there, it appeared, that on the march of The Hefsian brigade, a few Rebels had come over, and burnt four or five houses. As they did not appear to be in any considerable force, no troops were sent.

15th Oct^r — Arrived The Perseus frigate, from England, with about 20 Sail of Victuallers under Convoy, in 11 weeks pafsage. These ships have brought out about 400 Recruits. The Perseus took a Rebel privateer of 8 Guns off the Coast, and brought her in with her.

The transports with The Hefsians attempted to go up the East River last Evening, but there being little wind, & it being very dangerous to attempt going through Hellgate with those large vefsels, with the tide only, they were obliged to come to an anchor again.

The Rebels still keep their position opposite to us; but the Deserters say they are under great apprehensions of being cut off.

Lord Howe is gone with The Army. Lord Shuldham Commands the fleet during his absence.

16ᵗʰ Octʳ — We have no particular accounts from the Army under Genˡ Howe. They remain on Frog's Neck from Whence the road to Kingsbridge crofses a Creek, the bridge over which the Rebels have deſtroyed. Tis said the troops are repairing it. I am of opinion there muſt be some other obſtacle to prevent the Army from advancing than the deſtruction of a single bridge.

The Transports with the Hefsians have not yet been able to pafs through Hellgate. They therefore remain at anchor near the Battery there.

Lieuᵗ Bristow of the 16ᵗʰ Dragoons going forward yeſterday Evening to the advanced poſt in front of McGowan's to satisfy his curiosity, was fired at by some lurking Rebels and wounded in the leg by a Musket ball. One of the Sentries was wounded in the leg also by a BuckShot.

Lord Percy immediately ordered 2. 6 pʳˢ and two Howitzer shells to be fired at their Guard. By a deserter who came in laſt night we were informed that they had one man killed by a Shell.

Nothing is so improper and imprudent as for officers or others belonging to an Army to go forward to the advanced poſts and Sentries unlefs they have businefs there. It frequently occasions the lofs of men who are there on duty, answers no purpose but the satisfying an idle curiosity, and sometimes occasions unnecefsary alarms. It is generally forbidden in moſt Armies; even where it is not usual for the advanced Sentries to be fired upon. In this Army it should be prohibited, as the Enemy opposed to us take every opportunity of getting a shot at a Sentry.

The Deserter who came in says the Rebels have about 4000 men about Morris's heights, and that they are in hourly expectation of being attacked.

By the accounts from Staten Island, the Rebels have landed near 1200 men there, have burnt some houses, and done other damage. Captain Stanton of the 14ᵗʰ Regᵗ who was poſted at Richmond with a Detachment of about 60 men, has, it is said, been obliged to retire from thence with some lofs.

The 22ⁿᵈ Regiment is under orders to go from hence to reinforce the troops there, if there should be occasion.

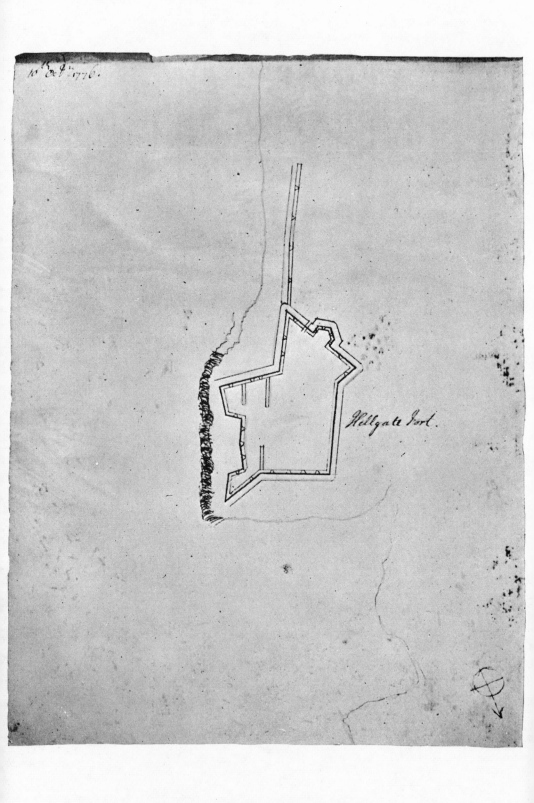

10 R Oct 1776.

Hellgate Fort.

As it is said the Fleet with the 2ᵈ Division of the Heſsian Troops have been spoke with off Sandy hook, and within sight of the land, it is probable they will come in very shortly; and if some of them are landed at Staten Island, it will not only clear the Island effectually of those fellows, but serve to refresh the troops after their voyage.

General Lee is expected to join the Rebel Army with some troops from the Southward, about the 19ᵗʰ Inſtant.

The chief ſtrength of the Rebel Army at present consiſts of Natives of Europe, particularly Irishmen: — many of their Regiments are composed principally of those men, and they are in general much better able to go through the fatigues of a Campaign, and live in the manner they at present do, than the Americans. They certainly have much more spirit, and in some measure make it a common cause with them for the sake of a present subsiſtence, Clothing, & plunder; and the prospect of acquiring some property, and becoming men of some consequence, in case they are succeſsful. The leaders of the Rebellion hold up to them these flattering prospects, and at the same time magnify the dangers they are exposed to if conquered; and aſsure them, that few of the Old-Country people, as they call them, can expect mercy. Among so many ignorant people these things have great weight. It would be good policy to endeavor by every means in our power to undeceive them and detach them from the cause and support of Rebellion by full promises of pardon to such as surrender within a certain limitted time.

17ᵗʰ Octʳ — Some hours heavy rain laſt night. Thick weather inclining to rain all day.

A good deal of firing heard towards the Army this morning.

The Recruits lately arrived for those Regiments which are with the Army under General Howe, went through Hellgate this morning in Flatboats.

The ships with the Heſsians cannot go through for want of a proper wind. Several ships with Horses and Waggons are detained for the same reason.

The Senegal Sloop of War got through this Morning with much difficulty; she touched the Shore several times, but at laſt effected the paſsage with much labor and danger.

A Deserter came in who says the Rebels are extremely apprehensive of being attacked on this Island, and are continually employed in adding to the ſtrength of their positions.

18th Oct[r] — A good deal of firing towards the Army.

The Rose of 20 Guns went through Hellgate this Morning without any difficulty, having a fine wind, & favorable tide. The transports with the Hefsian brigade, from Staten Island, which have waited so long for a favorable opportunity, went through without any accident, and proceeded to join the Army.

A Signal this morning at Staten Island for a fleet, supposed to be that with the Hefsians. In the Evening 7 ships came up to New York, in one of which arrived Major Donkin of The Welch Fusileers, who confirms the account of its being the fleet so long looked for, with about 7000 troops; out 14 weeks, & all arrived safe, under Convoy of The Diamond, Ambuscade, and another Frigate.

19th Oct[r] — By the accounts from the Army under Gen[l] Howe, he has found it necefsary to change his position. He accordingly embarked yesterday morning with the greatest part of the Army from Frog's-point, and made good a landing at a place called Hunt's point, where he took post after a slight opposition, in which L[t] Col[o] Musgrave, Cap[t] Evelyn, & L[t] Rutherford were wounded, & about 30 men killed & wounded from the fire of about 60 men, who concealed themselves behind a Stone wall 'till the troops were on the point of landing, and then, giving their fire, took to their heels.

The position Gen[l] Howe has taken is represented to be very advantageous, and tending to hem in the Rebel Army in such a manner, that they must be reduced to the necefsity of fighting him, or laying down their arms. I am afraid we are rather too sanguine in this matter, and that the Rebels will either find means of crofsing the North River into Jersey, or slip away from him to the Northward.

Those more immediately opposed to us on this Island, seem inclined to move off, and Lord Percy has made the necefsary dispositions for prefsing upon their rear as soon as they are discovered to be in motion.

The greatest part of the last Fleet from England came up from Sandy hook this afternoon.

20th Oct[r] — The Remainder of the fleet came up. The whole amounts to about 120 sail, and the reinforcement of troops to between 7, and 8000 men.

The Rebels were observed to be very busy this day in transporting Cannon, Baggage, &c, acrofs the North River to The Jersey shore under Fort Conſtitution. Very few of them appear in their works near Morris's house, nor are there any tents remaining there in our view. They ſtill keep an advanced poſt on the road opposite ours. It is evident they are preparing to go off, and we are all apprehensive they will once more slip out of our hands; to prevent which every pofsible exertion should now be made. If Gen¹ Howe has shut them up on his side, they have no retreat but acrofs The North River to Jersey; and I fear we cannot at present cut off their communication with that Province, which is open to them by means of Fort Washington on this Island, and Fort Conſtitution on the opposite shore, which from their ſtrength and elevated situation, & the number of heavy Cannon & Mortars in them, cannot be approached or damaged by our ships of War. Boats may therefore pafs and repafs, particularly during the night, without danger or molestation. The pofsefsion of Fort Conſtitution, would infallibly cut off their retreat, but it is extremely difficult to approach that place so as to attack it with advantage. I am convinced the Rebel Army will not venture to attack ours.

21ˢᵗ Octʳ   Two deserters came in laſt night, who say that the Rebels are certainly going from this Island, as they have already removed moſt of their heavy Cannon, Mortars, & tents; and very few men remain in their lines opposite to us.

Arrived a Packet from England in .   weeks. She had a smart engagement with a Rebel Privateer off the Coaſt, in which the Captain of the Packet was killed, & some men killed & wounded. The Rebel attempted to board her but was beat off with considerable lofs, and at laſt obliged to sheer off. Tis supposed the Privateer muſt have loſt near 40 men.

The Frigates that Convoyed the laſt fleet from England, brought in with them two Privateers which they took at Sea.

Tis said that the Hefsian troops lately arrived are to go up the North River the firſt opportunity; but I cannot believe the report, as it would be difficult for them to pafs the Rebel Forts and batteries, and there is no good landing place on either side for several miles, particularly on the Jersey shore where only their presence could have any good effect: and even should they effect a landing there, the communication with them would be extremely precarious.

22nd Oct^r   Greatest part of the Hessian troops lately arrived, went up the East River and through Hellgate this morning in flat boats to join the Army with General Howe, as did all the officers, Recruits, and other men with Arms belonging to the British Regiments with him.

Major General Vaughan, having recovered of the wound he received on the 15th September last, also went to join the Army.

About   German Recruits for the British Regiments arrived in the last fleet, but as they are not yet armed or Clothed, those belonging to the Regiments with General Howe remained in the Barracks at New York, the others joined their respective Regiments. They are but indifferent Recruits, and have been very sickly during the passage.

The Rebels seem to have given over any thoughts they might have had of attacking our troops upon Staten Island. Everything is now quiet there, altho the Rebels are in possession of the Southern part of the Island.

Deserters come in daily, who all agree that there remains but a small number of their troops on this Island.

23rd Oct^r — The flat boats which went up with the Hessians yesterday returned this day. 'Tis expected the remainder of these troops will go up the first opportunity. At present the wind blows too hard.

A Soldier of the 38th Reg^t attempting to desert last night was discovered by one of the advanced Sentries, who fired at him, broke his leg, and brought him back. The wound was so bad, that his leg was taken off soon after.

A Deserter came in last night, who says the Rebels have not above 500 men on this Island, and that for some days past they have been employed in transporting their sick, which are very numerous, to the Jersey shore.

We know nothing certain relative to the operations of the Army under Genl Howe. 'Tis said he has taken the post he intended, and that the Rebel army must soon be greatly distressed thereby. Some of Major Rogers's Corps have been severely handled within a day or two, by a party of The Rebels. This Corps is composed principally of Rebel deserters. Major Rogers is the person who made himself famous as a Partisan during the last War in this Country.

Some of the Captains of The Navy who attended for the Regulating of the boats and vessels when they went through

Hellgate with the Army the Morning of the 12th Instant, have since declared that it was a most hazardous enterprize to go through a Channel of that dangerous nature with such a fleet, and before it was daylight. What made it still more dangerous was, that an unexpected fog came on early in the morning, which prevented them in a great degree, from seeing the boat and buoys which had been previously fixed to mark the proper channel. It was too late when the fog came on to postpone the movement; the troops and everything necefsary were embarked, and the wind and tide answered exactly; therefore notwithstanding the hazard it could not be delayed. I dare say at the moment the Army began to move the General and Admiral would have compounded for the lofs of one or two hundred men. Fortune however favored the bold: — only one boat, having on board an officer and 25 Artillery men and 3 6 prs was sunk. All but 4 men and the guns were saved, which was more than could have been expected. Everything else got safe through that dangerous pafsage, where at all times, except at high & low water, the tide runs with the utmost rapidity, forming dreadful whirlpools, and at half tide roaring over the mafses of Rocks which project into, or rear up their broken heads in the middle of the Channel. In one place if the Stream catches a boat or vefsel, it is drawn into a kind of whirlpool or Eddy, where it is carried round several times with great violence, and then if not sucked in, is thrown on the adjacent rocks, and dashed to pieces. One boat with a Detachment of Grenadiers was caught into this place, and after some turns round was thrown upon the shore, but fortunately the men got out safe, and soon after got into another boat and followed the Army. This pafsage is thought extremely dangerous by those who are best acquainted with it, and who take every advantage of winds, tides, and other circumstances. When I was formerly quartered at New York, I frequently went out as far as Hellgate to see vefsels go through, especially when there were any which carried topsails, and the Pilots were generally under much apprehension when they had such vefsels under their charge. Those men were in the utmost astonishment to see Ships of War of 44 Guns, Frigates, Transports full of troops, Horses & Waggons, and flat boats with troops and artillery, attempting and accomplishing so difficult an undertaking, with such a trifling lofs. To any other nation the obstacles would have seemed insurmountable.

Since the Army went through, I have frequently seen large transports go through Stern foremost, with all sails set and filled, the strength of the tide overcoming the power of the wind upon the sails. Some officers of the Navy say this is the safest way, as the ship has better and more certain Steerage.

24th Octr   Ten persons came over from Jersey last night, who say that part of Washington's baggage has been carried over the N. River lately; that there are about 2500 men of the Rebels near Fort Constitution; and that if a body of our troops was to appear on that side, the Inhabitants would declare for The King.

In consequence of the intelligence given by two deserters who came in last night, and said that the Rebels would certainly go off from near Morris's house early this morning, a party of an officer and 20 men was sent out a little before day break, with directions to advance and obtain information of the situation of the Enemy, and whether they really were in motion. The officer found that they had drawn their advanced post further back, but that they still occupied their works in considerable force.

'Tis said that the transport with part of the 16th Dragoons on board, which separated from the fleet and has been missing some time, has been taken by the Rebels.

A Report prevails that the Rebels have been defeated near Ticonderoga by the Army from Canada.

If that army does not soon get over the lakes and advance towards Albany, the severity of the approaching season will prevent it from effecting anything of consequence until next Spring. It has been said that if that Army, after leaving a sufficient force in Canada to secure the several posts there, had embarked, come down the St Lawrence, and made a descent on some part of New England, or attacked Rhode Island, it would have rendered more service to the cause than by anything which it can effect on its present line of operation.

25th Octr
This being the anniversary of The King's accession at 1 o'Clock all the Ships of War in the harbour, and those in the different Stations in both Rivers, fired a Royal salute.

A Soldier of the 57th Regiment deserted yesterday from Paulus hook.

As the Rebels seem determined to remain in and defend their position near Kingsbridge, 'tis said Gen¹ Howe is making the neceſsary preparations to attack their works, and that for this purpose a numerous train of heavy artillery is collecting. All the German Recruits now at New York are to go up to the Army tomorrow to aſsiſt in drawing Cannon to the batteries, and other neceſsary duties which may be performed by men without arms.

26ᵗʰ Octʳ — The Lark, Frigate arrived yeſterday with 25 sail of Victuallers from Cork, but laſt from Halifax. These ships have brought out a great many officers, & between 4 and 500 Recruits for the British Regiments.

The German Recruits did not go up to the Army as was ordered, but Captain Campbell's Company of New York Provincials went up from Brooklyn, in their stead.

By accounts from the Army it appears that Gen¹ Howe made a movement yeſterday, and encamped at a place called Whiteplains, by which position Mʳ Washington's Army will be so much ſtreightened, that he will be under the neceſsity of taking some decisive step very shortly. One may venture to say he will not attempt to attack General Howe's Army; but that if there is a poſsibility of a Retreat, he will go off. In so doing he muſt give our troops a great advantage over him, & may suffer very materially. Gen¹ Howe has cut off from the Rebel Army a considerable Magazine of provisions, Stores, and Clothing, the loſs of which, particularly the latter, muſt diſtreſs them greatly.

Gen¹ Clinton advanced two days ago with a Corps of near 2000 men to reconnoitre the Enemy's position, on which occasion he drove in several of their advanced poſts, killed some of the Rebels, and took 18 Prisoners. A Company of Heſsian Chaſseurs lately arrived, following some of the Runaways with too much precipitation, were unexpectedly fired upon by a party of the Enemy, and had five men killed, and an officer and four wounded.

Major Rogers, with some of his Corps, made an excursion lately as far as Bedford in Connecticut, where he released and brought off 6 or 8 officers and men of the Navy who were prisoners there. He was joined within these two days by a Company of 120 men, raised secretly in Connecticut by one of his old Captains.

Naval Force on Lake Champlain Summer 1776

British Fleet

1 Ship	18 12 pounders
1 Schooner	14 6 Do
1 Do...	12 6 Do
1 Radeau .... 6 24 p^{rs} 12 12 p^{rs} 4 8-Inch Howitzers, all brafs
28 Gondolas, One each, 24, 18, or 12 p^{rs} & 1 8-Inch Howitzer

Rebel Fleet

1 Schooner ⎫	
3 Gallies ⎬ burnt or taken	
8 Gondolas ⎭	
1 Sloop	12 Guns
6 Schooners	8 Do each
2 Gallies	
2 Gondolas	

Taken from a Rebel officer's account.

The account of the defeat of the Rebels in Canada, is confirmed from several quarters. The Subftance is, that the Rebels having for near 8 months paft, given their whole attention to providing such a force of armed vefsels on Lake Champlain as should be superior to anything Genl Burgoyne could bring againft them, conceived at laft that they were in no danger of being defeated there. Genl Burgoyne however was equally afsiduous in conftructing and afsembling a force sufficient to attack them on the Lake; and having, by the indefatigable exertions of Lieu^t Schanks of the Navy, by whom it was firft suggested, had a vefsel fit for the purpose, taken to pieces in the St Lawrence, she was conveyed into the Lake and there put together again, and mounted with 18. 12 p^{rs}. With this vefsel, and others of inferior force which were built on the Lake, he attacked the Rebel fleet on the 11th Inftant, and entirely defeated it. The lofs of the Enemy has not yet been particularly mentioned, but the immediate consequence of the Victory was, the advance of the Army to Crown-point. This victory will probably be followed by further succefses and advantages, as Genl Burgoyne will now meet with but little difficulty in advancing as far as Albany, from whence a Junction with this Army may be effected before the close of the Campaign; or if thought more conducive to the succefs of the general plan, he may move to his left, and fall upon the back of the New England Provinces. From present appearances the deftruction of Washington's Army seems extremely probable; and if that Army is destroyed or dispersed, the subjugation of the American Colonies, may be said to be nearly effected; for it is highly improbable they will be able to assemble another army in the field able to face that of Britain.

The cautious conduct of Gen¹ Howe in all the operations of this Campaign is generally approved of; and altho many are of opinion that he should have followed up the advantage he gained on the 27ᵗʰ August, and either on that day, or the following, attacked the Rebels in their lines at Brooklyn, yet it must be allowed that it was extremely proper in him to consider what fatal consequences might have attended any check which the Army might have received in the first action of the Campaign. He has therefore conducted every enterprize in that cautious, circumspect manner, which, altho not so brilliant and striking, is productive of certain and real advantages, at the same time that very little is set at stake. Great Britain has at an immense expense, and by great exertions, assembled an Army from which the Nation expects an entire suppression of the Rebellion, it would therefore be the heighth of imprudence in the Commander in Chief, by any incautious or precipitate conduct, to give the Rebels any chance of an advantage over it.

27ᵗʰ Octʳ — Lord Percy received orders last night from Gen¹ Howe, to advance early this morning from the Lines near McGowan's, with the Troops there under his Command, and try how the Enemy felt in their lines opposite: — and if he found it practicable to move on to Morris's house, or as far as he could on the way to Kingsbridge. In consequence of these orders, the 22ⁿᵈ Regiment marched at 4 this Morning from New York to join & reinforce those under Lord Percy, and at day break the troops marched out from the Lines in two Columns, the first composed of the British on the right, under the Command of Major General Jones, and the Second of the Hessians on the left under Colonel Hackenberg. The advanced Guard was Commanded by Lieuᵗ Colᵒ Mawhood. Upon the appearance of the Columns, the Rebels retired from all their advanced posts, and drew all the troops which they had at hand, into that part of their Lines nearest to Morris's house, leaving only some detached parties in the works nearest to us. The Hessian Column advanced to the point of a height which projects within about 400 yards of the Right of the Rebels works, and from thence

Cannonaded all who appeared; but as the Rebels kept close under their works, and their Cannon were no other than the Battalion guns, no great effect was produced. The British Column advanced a good way into the plain beyond Haerlem, and a disposition was made for advancing from thence against some of the most advanced works of the Enemy, and then to penetrate the principal Lines; but this design was soon after laid aside on observing that the Rebels were continually reinforced from the works behind, so that there were not less than 3000 men in them; and it appeared that if we drove them from those most advanced we could not keep possession of them if the Enemy brought any guns into those behind which were upon higher ground, and Commanded them. The troops therefore remained in the position they had first taken, and there was some firing between the advanced parties. In the Evening the Rebels brought two pieces of Cannon forward, and fired upon the British Column, which was answered from two guns upon our right which were well served and pointed.

The Repulse & Pearl Frigates went up the North River with the tide when the troops advanced, in order to flank the Enemy, but the fire from Forts Washington and Constitution obliged them to return to their former stations. Indeed as the Rebels did not abandon their works on their right, their going higher up would have answered no good purpose. The Rebels struck the Ships several times, but they did them no other damage than wounding one man on board the Repulse.

Several transports came down through Hellgate this morning; and in the course of the day all the officers and Recruits lately arrived belonging to the Regiments with Gen¹ Howe went up to join the Army.

Much firing heard towards the Army all day; so that we are in hopes of hearing in the Morning that the General has been able to intercept Mr Washington.

The troops under Lord Percy remain in the position they took this morning.

We had 4 or 5 men wounded in the course of the day by the skulking fire of the Rebels. They must also have lost some men.

28th Octr —

The Rebels made no particular movement last night, nor did they molest our advanced posts, except by firing a few shots at the Sentries. Our troops remained in the same position last night and this day. The Rebels have fired from one only piece of Cannon today. They have moved it several times from one place to another.

Not more than three or four hundred Rebels have appeared to day in their advanced works; but we have no doubt they are numerous in all the woods & cover near their Lines, and that they wish us to attack them. It does not however appear to be the intention of Lord Percy to advance further, unlefs some change in the disposition of the Enemy makes it adviseable to do so. It is now probable that this movement is intended to divide the attention of the Rebels, to alarm them for this part of their position, and to facilitate the succefs of some general attack making by the Commander in Chief. If he succeeds we are here ready to seize any advantage which may offer. If it is the intention of the Corps pofted near Morris's house, to pafs the N. River, they judge right in endeavoring to keep us as diftant as pofsible from the place of their embarkation, as by sacrificing a few men left in their moft advanced works, they may be enabled to pafs the River in the night without being discovered. Mr Washington is certainly endeavoring to retire by his left along The N. River, and to get into the Mountainous part of the Country which lies higher up. The Objeƈt of General Howe is to prevent his escaping that way; and if he succeeds therein, Washington muft return towards Kingsbridge, and endeavor to pafs the River into Jersey under proteƈtion of The Forts; which muft be a very difficult and dangerous measure. The situation therefore of the Rebel Army is at this time extremely critical, and their fate depends on the succefs of their operations within a few ensuing days.

Some Cannonading heard towards the Army this morning. About 12 we observed a great Smoke towards Kingsbridge.

Many transports came through Hellgate today. A Soldier of the 57th deserted from Paulus hook laft night. This is the third man who has deserted from that Regiment since it has been pofted there; two of them while Sentry on the advanced poft. On enquirey I find their advanced Sentries are pofted singly, which is highly improper. Sentries on the advanced pofts, should always be double. They are more confident, observe with more certainty what pafses, and prevent desertion. When there are two Sentries on an advanced poft, one of them, when they observe anything with which it is necefsary the Guard should be acquainted, can come back to acquaint the Guard with it, while the other remains at the post. It would be highly improper for a Single Sentry to call out to the guard when he observes anything particular, or to leave his post to give the information. There is nothing in which the generality of Officers in this Army appears so deficient, as in the manner of disposing of, and instructing the Sentries of an advanced post.

29th Oct^r

Remarkable fine weather. — Nothing could have been more favorable for the operations of the Army, than the weather we have had of late. There has been very little rain since the troops landed on this Island.

A fleet of above 60 Sail went out of the harbour under convoy of The Resolution, Armed ship. They are principally empty Victuallers, and store ships, bound to England & Ireland.

Lord Percy drew back the Troops about Sunset yesterday, to their Encampments. Tis supposed this Movement was taken in consequence of information received from Gen¹ Howe. The 22ᵈ Regiment returned about 9 at night to their encampment at New York.

Our loss in this excursion was 3 men killed and 5 wounded.

Gen¹ Howe's Army made a move yesterday; with an intention of getting more on Mʳ Washington's left.

A Corps of Troops from the left of Gen¹ Howe's Army advanced on the 27ᵗʰ towards the heights beyond Kingsbridge, by which movement they prevented a Corps from this Island, which was on the march under Gen¹ Lee, from joining Washington. Lee then returned with that Corps to support the Lines against Lord Percy.

30th Oct^r

It appears by some accounts received from the Army that on the 28ᵗʰ Instant an attack was made by the 2ᵈ brigade upon a considerable body of Rebels who were posted on some heights which the General found it necessary to possess. The brigade carried their point notwithstanding an obstinate resistance, in which we had several officers and above 100 men killed and wounded. The loss of the Rebels is said to have been very great.

The officers are said to be Captains Gore, 49ᵗʰ, & Deering 28ᵗʰ, and Lᵗ Eagle 35ᵗʰ killed. Lieuᵗ Colᵒˢ Carr 35ᵗʰ, Walcott 5ᵗʰ, Capᵗ Massey 35ᵗʰ, & Lᵗˢ Jocelyn & Roberts 49ᵗʰ wounded.

There was another attack yesterday, in which it is said we have gained some further advantage over the Rebels.

In pursuance of orders received last night from Gen¹ Howe, the 4ᵗʰ Brigade marched from McGowan's early this morning to Hellgate, where they embarked in boats, and went up to join the Army.

Accounts are said to have been received this Evening by Lord Percy, that a Corps of Hessians had stormed and taken a Fort called Fort Independence near Kingsbridge; that Gen¹ Howe had taken the Enemy's magazines near White plains, and had so effectually cut off Washington's retreat to his left, that the Rebel army was marching with all speed to take post on this Island, with a view of retiring acrofs the River into Jersey.

If this proves true a short time must determine the fate of the Rebel Army. It is now that our ships of War should use all pofsible means, and run all risques to prevent them from pafsing the River.

General Howe has notified to the Army His Majesty's having been pleased to grant certain Bounties to such officers as may lose an eye or a limb, and to Widows and orphan Children of such as may be killed, in Action.

For the Regulation, allowances, and other particulars, see Appendix.

31ˢᵗ Octʳ

Heavy rain all last night, and 'till 10 this Morning.

The situation of the two armies is now so critical, that we may hourly expect to hear of an Action.

The pofsefsion of Fort Independence is of considerable importance.

1ˢᵗ Novʳ. 1776

Several deserters came in from the Enemy, who say that our troops have pofsefsion of Kingsbridge, and that the communication between the troops on this Island and the Continent is cut off. They also say that Gen¹ Howe has taken pofsefsion of some considerable Magazines at Whiteplains town; and that Gen¹ Washington has declared he will now put everything upon the issue of a Battle.

The movement of the troops under Lord Percy on the 27ᵗʰ October, was of material service to Gen¹ Howe, as it divided the attention of the Enemy, and obliged them to keep a considerable

Corps in their works to prevent us from gaining their right flank. Our whole lofs on the 27th & 28th amounted, by the returns given in, to 4 men killed, and 6 wounded. Three of the latter were Hefsians.

2nd Novr— Cold day, and fresh wind at S. W.

Accounts from the Army say that Genl Howe intended to attack the Rebels in their works yefterday Morning, and that the Army was in motion for that purpose; but when the advanced parties approached them, they found them abandoned. 72 pieces of Cannon, (all spiked) were found in them. The Army is said to be in pursuit of the Enemy.

The Rebels have abandoned Morrifsania in Weft-Chefter County, and all the pofts they had on that side of Haerlem Creek between it and Kingsbridge.

The Fowey, came down yefterday from her Station at the mouth of Haerlem Creek, and anchored in the harbour. She is appointed to Convoy a large fleet of transports, victuallers, and other vefsels which are to sail for England in a short time. The Mercury replaced her in Haerlem Creek.

A Frigate went up the N. River this morning.

3rd Novr

General Knyphausen with Six Hefsian Battalions which had taken poft on the heights near Kingsbridge lately, pafsed over to this Island yefterday, without a Shot being fired at him, and encamped on the high grounds near Fort Washington. This movement completely cuts off all communication between the Rebel troops on this Island, and those under Genl Washington.

The Rebels having abandoned Morrifsania, and all that part of Weft Chefter County, that part of the 71st Regt which was encamped on Montresor's Island, pafsed over this day, and encamped at Morrifsania.

The Repulse Frigate, having been relieved by the Emerald, came down the N. River this morning, and anchored in the harbour.

Orders were given this day by Lord Percy for each Regiment to make 1000 fascines, with 4 Pickets to each immediately. It is imagined they are intended for the conftruction of Batteries againft Fort Washington.

In the several attacks lately made on the Rebels by the troops under Genl Howe, very few prisoners have been taken.

The Soldiers generally made use of their Bayonets. The 17th Dragoons are said to have behaved remarkably well, and to have taken several Batteries. Preparations have been making for some time past by the Barrack Master General in New York for the reception of such troops as may be quartered there during the ensuing winter. Many of the public buildings have been and others are fitting up for Hospitals; such as The College, The Bridewell, The Workhouse, The new Hospital, and some of The Meeting houses and Churches.

It is probable the quarters of the Army this winter will be, from the East end of Long Island, round by West Chester County, to Kingsbridge, this Island, & Staten Island, including Paulus-hook. Which will include the whole of Long Island, York Island, & Staten Island. It appears rather too late in the Season to attempt Rhode Island, altho the posfesfion of that Island would be extremely advantageous, by affording quarters for a considerable body of troops, securing an Excellent harbour for large ships, and in a great measure commanding the entrance of The Sound.

The first object at present is the reduction of Fort Washington, and thereby the complete posfesfion of this Island: after which Gen¹ Howe will probably detach a considerable part of the Army to the Southward, where operations may be carried on with advantage during the winter, or else penetrate into Jersey, and endeavor to enlarge the quarters of the Army in a Province abounding with Provisions, fuel, and other necefsary supplies. The extension of our quarters will also give the Loyalists an opportunity of declaring themselves, and circumscribe the resources of the Enemy.

A man named Diamond, who says he was Ensign and Adjutant, and acted as Major of brigade in the Rebel Army, deserted yesterday from their advanced post. He says the Rebels remaining on this Island amount to about 2000 men, who, if they are obliged to abandon their advanced works, are to retire into Fort Washington, and defend it to the last extremity, having therein two Months provisions, many Cannon, and plenty of Ammunition. He says there are great difsentions in the Rebel Army, everybody finding fault with the mode of proceeding, and the inferior officers, even Ensigns, insisting that, in such a cause, every man has a right to afsist in Council, and to give his opinion. They are much distrefsed for Clothing. The people from the Southern Colonies declare they will not go into New-England, and the others that they will not march to the South-ward. If this account is true in any degree, they must soon go to pieces.

4ᵗʰ Novʳ

Nothing particular from the Army. It is said that Washington is again entrenching himself, and General Howe preparing to attack him, or oblige him to move again.

By the information received from Deserters we learn that the Rebels have not lefs than 5000 Sick at Hackinsack and that neighbourhood, in Jersey. If we could spare a Corps of 4 or 5000 men to land in Jersey, and cut off the communication with those at Fort Conftitution, that poft would probably fall into our hands, and deprive those on this Island of any retreat.

It is expected that some ships of War will go up the N. River the firft fair wind, in order to diftrefs the Enemy, and render their communication with the Jersey shore more difficult.

Four Rebel officers, well drefsed, came with a flag of truce this Morning to our advanced poft in front of McGowan's. They were very desirous of speaking to Lord Percy, and one of them earneftly desired leave to come in for that purpose; but as that could not be permitted, they delivered some letters to Lord Percy's Aide-de-Camp, the purport of which was, that they were desirous of sending in some money to the prisoners confined in New York.

5ᵗʰ Novʳ

A Packet containing several letters from Washington to the Congrefs, and other persons, was brought in laft night, and delivered to Genˡ Robertson by a person who said he saw them lying on a table in a house at Trenton, and who, taking advantage of the absence and carelefsnefs of the person entrufted with them, put it in his pocket, and got off undiscovered.

Mʳ Washington in some of the letters, complains much of the want of discipline in his Army, and the great deficiency of good and careful officers; prefses much to have an adjutant General appointed who is fit for the Station and capable of executing the duty of it, having no person with him qualified for it: recommends new modelling the Army, and appointing officers to succeed to vacancies if they are men of abilities, without regard to Seniority: and advises them to afsemble a body of troops in

Jersey to prevent us from taking post there. There are many other matters mentioned in those letters which shew the undisciplined and disordered state of the Army, the knowledge of which will be of much service to Gen[l] Howe.

Washington mentions that he is employed in sinking vessels and other things in the N. River to obstruct the navigation of it, and prevent our ships of War from passing up and down. He confirms the account of the defeat of their fleet on Lake Champlain, and says that Gen[l] Carleton commanded the British force.

Transports sufficient for the reception of near 15,000 men on the shortest notice are now almost ready in the harbour of New York; and are victualled, watered, and nearly ready to proceed to Sea. Their destination is not known, but it is generally imagined an Expedition against some place of consequence is intended. The preparation of these vessels may be with a view to deceive and alarm the Enemy, and by putting them under apprehensions for places at a distance, prevent them from sending reinforcements to Washington's Army. If it is intended to send troops from hence, it by no means follows that because transports for 15000 men are prepared, so many will embark. This may also be done in order to deceive the Rebels. The putting provisions on board the transports for 15,000 men for several weeks, may be done in order to secure them against accidents; for were they deposited in Storehouses, & the town accidentally or wilfully set on fire, the Army might be distressed for want of them. On board the ships they are safer than on shore, and as easily issued to the troops when wanted.

As the Rebels have good intelligence of what we are doing, it must alarm them when they are informed that so large a fleet is ready to put to Sea, and has nothing to do but take the troops on board, which might be done in a few hours. The uncertainty where the Storm would fall, must keep a considerable part of the Country in a state of constant preparation, occasion much expense, and harrass the Country people by being kept away from their families and employments.

The Rebel Army must suffer greatly as soon as the severe weather sets in for want of proper Clothing, of which they are now in the greatest need. It is a fact that many of the Rebels who were killed in the late affairs, were without shoes or Stockings, & Several were observed to have only linen drawers on,

with a Rifle or Hunting shirt, without any proper shirt or
so Waistcoat. They are also in great want of blankets. The
weather during the former part of the Campaign has been so
very favorable that they did not feel the want of those things,
but in less than a month they must suffer extremely if not supplied with them. Under all the disadvantages of want of confidence, Clothing, and good winter quarters, and constantly
harrassed by a victorious and incensed Army, it will be astonishing if they keep together 'till Christmas.

6th Novr

The Pearl, Frigate, and two Navy Victuallers got under way
about 3 o'Clock yesterday afternoon from their anchorage near
Jones's house on The North River, and notwithstanding a very
heavy fire from the Rebel Forts and Batteries on both sides,
they got up as far as the mouth of Spikendevil Creek near
Kingsbridge, without having received any apparent damage.
They came to an anchor there, as the tide was spent. They are
going with provisions for the three ships of War stationed
higher up.

Four deserters came in this morning. They say but one shot
struck the Pearl. By their account the Rebels have about 2000
men on this Island.

Orders were received today from Genl Howe, directing that
no more boats or vessels should go up the East river. It is conjectured from this order that the Rebels have got possession of
some of the projecting points of land on the left shore of The
Sound.

It is now said that Genl Howe has given over any further
pursuit of Washington's Army, which has retired into the strong
Country in the neighbourhood of   , and that he is
returning towards Kingsbridge.

The 7000 fascines which were ordered to be made by the
Seven Battalions near McGowan's, have been ordered to be
deposited near Jones's house on the N. River, from which it is
probable that the intention is to force the Rebel lines, and erect
Batteries against Fort Washington, the reduction of which will
ensure the capture of the 2000 men who remain on this Island.
If Genl Howe's Army is marching down towards Kingsbridge,
that Fort must be taken, as it commands the North part of the
Island, and prevents a communication with him. It is probable
the General will attack that part of the Rebel troops stationed

on the Jersey side near Fort Conſtitution, and if they defend
that Fort, besiege it. The reduction of these Forts will give us
the uninterrupted paſsage of the River, and prevent the Rebels
on this side under Washington from communicating with those
in Jersey.

It is thought probable that the transports which are now
ready in the harbour may be employed in conveying a considerable part of the Army up the North River towards Albany, in
order to forward the operations of the Army under Genˡ Carleton, and aſsiſt in dispersing the Rebels opposed to him before
the winter sets in. This does not appear impracticable. There
is no danger of any Ice in the River till January, and it is navi-
gable for transports and large veſsels within 30 miles of Albany.
The very appearance of an Army coming upon their backs,
would probably oblige the Rebels to retire. Moſt persons however are of opinion that the fleet is deſtined for the Southward.
Admiral Sir Peter Parker is to Command. The Carcase Bomb
is ordered to go with it.

Many officers are ſtill of opinion that the Expedition is intended againſt Rhode Island, as being the Beſt harbour for the
Ships of War.

7ᵗʰ Novʳ

The weather has with little exception, been very fine ever
since we landed on this Island. There has been a slight froſt at
night for this fortnight paſt, but it disappears as soon as the Sun
rises. For the laſt 8 or 10 days there has been a hazy kind of
weather, altho the Sun shone clear during the middle of the day.

No wind for some days paſt, so that if it was intended to send
any number of ships up the North River, it could not have been
effected.

Genˡ Howe's Army is at present at Phillipsburg, a house
about 6 miles from Kingsbridge, and nearly on the bank of the
N. River.

It appears that part of the Rebel troops have advanced again
as far as New Rochelle. Moſt of the transports and other veſsels
which had been up in that part of the Sound, came down today,
and anchored near Montresor's Island.

Our next operation will probably be againſt Fort Washington, in order to clear this Island entirely of the Rebels; and it is
likely that Fort Conſtitution will be attacked at the same time,
to prevent any of them making good their retreat that way.

8ᵗʰ Novʳ

Orders were iſsued this Morning for the 3ʳᵈ, & 5ᵗʰ brigades to prepare for immediate Embarkation. We are entirely ingnorant of our deſtination. It is said that 2500 men (which is about the numbers the above mentioned brigades can take into the field) are to embark in 11 transports, and go up the N. River, to land on the Jersey side. Tis said that 10,000 men are deſtined for some other service (supposed to go to the Delaware or farther to the Southward) under the Command of General Clinton.

Transports allotted for the reception of the 3ᵗʰ and 5ᵗʰ Brigades of British Infantry
At 1½ Tons pʳ maⁿ

Regiments		Men	Ships	Tons	Total Tons
3ʳᵈ	10ᵗʰ	407	Isabella .... 410 Emprefs 251		661
	38ᵗʰ	412	Grand Dutchefs of Rufsia .. 303 Sea Venture............... 299		602
	52ⁿᵈ	353	Saville .... 355 Antelope 207		562
	37ᵗʰ	359	Eagle .... 344 Susanna 240		584
5ᵗʰ	22ⁿᵈ	414	James & William .... 393 John 229		622
	54ᵗʰ	440	Grand Duke of Rufsia....... 672		672
	63ʳᵈ	390	Amity's Admonition .... 410 John & Bella 194		604
	43ʳᵈ	370	Royal George .... 352 Earl of Oxford 231		583

Majʳ Genˡ Jones, & Brigʳ Genˡ Smith } Earl of Effingham

The transports which anchored yeſterday near Montresor's Island, came through Hellgate and anchored in the harbour.

General Howe's Army are said to have been yeſterday at Dobbs's ferry on the N. River, which is about 10 Miles above Kingsbridge. We heard a great Cannonade in that quarter this Evening, but as the weather was thick we could not ascertain from whence it proceeded.

We expeɕt every day that something will be undertaken againſt Fort Washington.

9ᵗʰ Novʳ   The transports were allotted this day for the reception of the 3ʳᵈ and 5ᵗʰ brigades. There are 15 Ships for the Eight-Battalions, and one for the two General officers. The

Ships are all in the North River, are victualled for 3 Months, and are ready to take the troops on board.

The object of the expedition remains a profound secret.

The firing heard yesterday was from the Rebels; who had brought two pieces of Cannon out of Fort Washington and fired at the advance posts of Gen¹ Knyphausen's Corps. Gen¹ Knyphausen has got one of the Companies of Hessian Chasseurs with him, who annoy the Rebels greatly.

Gen¹ Howe's Army has approached nearer to Kingsbridge, and is said to be encamped near the 17 mile Stone from New York.

A report prevails that the Fort at Ticonderoga has been blown up, by a shell falling into the Magazine.

10th Novʳ 1776.

The same kind of hazy weather which we have had for some time past continues. The Sun shines clear during the middle of the day, and the air is mild. Slight frosts at night, and very little wind.

Came in 7 sail of Victuallers from Cork in 9 weeks. They have brought some Recruits.

Some firing towards Kingsbridge and the North part of the Island.

General Howe having sent for Lord Percy on some particular business, the Command of the troops in the Southern part of this Island, devolves on The Hessian Major General Stirn.

Everything is ready for the Embarkation of the 3rd and 5th Brigades, and part of their heavy baggage is on board. The destination remains a secret.

It is not supposed we are going to Rhode Island, as the passage there at this season is rather dangerous and tedious, occasioned by the prevalence of the Northerly winds, particularly off the end of Long Island, which makes it difficult to beat up so far. The transports and Frigates indeed, might go through Hellgate and the Sound, but none of the two decked ships can go that way, nor the Grand Duke of Russia transport of 672 Tons, and as they must go by Sandy hook and the back of Long Island, and the fleet wᵈ by this means be seperated. In the opinion of many the chief expedition is intended for the Delaware, and the other up The North River to attack Fort Constitution, or to proceed farther up to hasten the retreat of the Army opposed to General Carleton.

Preparations appear to be making for an attack on Fort Washington.

11th Nov^r

Near 200 sail of Veſsels went out this day for England and Ireland under Convoy of The Fowey and Active. The Greyhound also went out with them. She is to see them 100 leagues to the Eaſtward and then return.

Some firing towards Fort Washington.

Gen¹ Knyphausen is erecting some works on his side againſt Fort Washington, chiefly for Mortars. The Enemy continue to fire at them. A deserter who came in says they have got 18 pieces of Cannon and two Mortars in the Fort, and are determined to defend it to the laſt extremity.

Gen¹ Washington's Army is now poſted principally near the banks of the North River; some part of it as high up as Fishkills. By this position it appears as if his object was to prevent our moving upwards againſt the Northern Army, or to march into Connecticut should Gen¹ Howe move that way. It will be impoſsible for him to interrupt us in our operations againſt Fort Washington.

Information has been received that some Heſsian Soldiers who were taken prisoners in Auguſt laſt on Staten Island, were immediately carried to Philadelphia, where at firſt The Congreſs voted that they should be sold as Slaves, but they soon after changed their opinion, and endeavored to gain them over by good treatment. They provided a good table for them at a Tavern in Philadelphia, and made them the moſt liberal offers of money and lands for themselves and friends, if they would give up their Country and become Settlers. The men have to all appearance, rejected and despised those offers, and the Rebels have now directed them to be sent back; and tis said they are now at Elisabeth town for that purpose. General Robertson is of opinion that the men have been gained over by the Rebels, whose intention it now is to send them among their Countrymen, that they may endeavor to persuade them to desert. It may be so, and their officers, who are in general well acquainted with the characters and dispositions of their men, will soon be able to find out whether they are inclined to liſten to their infamous proposals. Should they come back, it will be prudent to keep a ſtrict watch upon them in order to discover if they attempt to corrupt their fellow Soldiers. I do not think they will. No Hefsian Soldier has deserted yet.

The report of the blowing up of Ticonderoga gains ground. It is also said that the Rebel Army is retiring from that part of the Country towards Albany.

There was a report to day that The Province of Connecticut has withdrawn itself from the Rebel confederacy, and accepted of The King's pardon. There certainly are a great variety of opinions among the people of the Country, and many difsentions. The troops belonging to the Northern Colonies have an aversion to going Southward of this Province.

Lord Percy returned today from Gen¹ Howe's Army. It is imagined his businefs there was to settle with the General the plan of operations against Fort Washington.

12ᵗʰ Novʳ — Rain from 4 o'Clock yesterday afternoon 'till 11 at night. High wind all night at N. and until 1 this day. Fine clear day, with sunshine, but Cold.

Some firing of Cannon and small arms this morning near Fort Washington.

A Soldier of the 52ⁿᵈ deserted last night.

A flag of truce went out this day from McGowan's, by permifsion of Lord Percy, with letters from Colonel Miles, the Senior officer of the Rebel Prisoners confined at New York, to Gen¹ Washington, representing in strong terms the distrefsed state of the prisoners for want of clothing and other necefsaries, and desiring he will order clothing to be sent to them, or endeavor to get them exchanged. He also complains of the great sicknefs and mortality among the prisoners, and of their scanty allowance of provisions.

With respect to their provisions they have no real cause of complaint, as they are served with the same kind of provisions ifsued to The King's troops, at two third allowance, which is the same as given to The King's troops when on board Transports. They certainly are very Sickly, owing to their want of Clothing and necefsaries, salt provisions, confinement, foul air, & little exercise. They are confined principally in the Churches, Sugar houses, and other large buildings, and have the liberty of walking in the yards. But they are such low spirited creatures, particularly the Americans, that if once they are taken sick they seldom recover.

Their situation is really dreadful, and their dirty, unhealthy, and desponding appearance enough to shock one. If they do not send them Clothing and necefsaries soon, they muſt suffer greatly from the severity of the weather.

13ᵗʰ Novʳ — Clear fine weather. Slight froſt. Wind N. W.

The Army made a movement Yeſterday, and again this day, nearer to Kingsbridge. The General seems now determined to take Fort Washington immediately. Several shells were thrown at it this day from the works on the N. part of the Island; and a Battery of 4–12 pʳˢ has been completed, and is ready to open upon it. The troops on this side are prepared to join in the attack, as soon as everything is in readinefs, which it is expeᑍed will be in a few days.

The Situation of Fort Washington is very ſtrong, as it Commands all the adjacent heights. It is said to be a regular Pentagon of considerable size, with some outworks.

General Clinton came to New York today from the Army. He is to have the command of the troops going on the Expedition, and Sir Peter Parker is to Command the Fleet. Tis now generally supposed we are going to the Delaware.

The troops under orders for this Expedition are, a Battalion of British Grenadiers, one of Light Infantry, the 3ʳᵈ, 4ᵗʰ & 5ᵗʰ Brigades of British Infantry, two Brigades of Hefsians, Donops Corps, a Detachment of 17ᵗʰ Dragoons, & a Detachment of Artillery.

14ᵗʰ Novʳ — Fine weather

Part of Genˡ Howe's army is within 3 miles of Morrifsania. The reſt near Kingsbridge.

From the dispositions which are making it appears there will be a general attack on all the Rebel Lines and outpoſts on this Island, from whence they will be driven into Fort Washington. If the report of their numbers is accurate (about 2000 men), it will be impofsible for them all to find shelter in the Fort.

Four thousand fascines which have been made by the 5ᵗʰ Brigade, have been put on board the transports.

15ᵗʰ Novʳ — Fair, mild weather

Above 30 flatboats went up the North River laſt night as far as Kingsbridge. They pafsed the Rebel's forts undiscovered. It appears from this that the General is determined to land a body of troops as soon as pofsible on the Jersey side, and perhaps with a Corps from New York, invest Fort Constitution. Their force on that side is said to be between two and 3,000 men. They have few or no troops assembled in any other part of that Province or in Pensylvania.

Nothing further transpires relative to the object of the intended expedition, nor is it yet quite certain what Number of troops are to embark. From the general appearance of matters, it is probable, that the moment Fort Washington is taken, General Howe will land a body of troops in Jersey from the right of his Army, and after taking Fort Constitution penetrate into that Province towards Philadelphia. If, at the same time, a force was landed at Amboy, and a fleet with troops sent into the Delaware, Pensylvania would be attacked by three Columns, which must infallibly penetrate to Philadelphia, route the Congress, and establish the left of our line of quarters in that City.

Numberless advantages would arise from the execution of this plan, which does not appear difficult to effect, as the Rebels have very few troops that way, and it would be impossible for them to receive any succours from Washington's Army, or that above Albany time enough to prevent our arrival at Philadelphia. The appearance of a formidable force in Pensylvania, where the measures of Congress are now much condemned, would induce numbers of the deluded inhabitants to seize the favorable opportunity of returning to their Allegiance, and the enjoyment of their former ease, peace, and happiness. Many of the leading men in Congress might also take the opportunity of making their peace by an early submission. If anything of this nature should happen, the strength of the Rebellion is at an end, and Washington's Army would disperse.

Accounts are said to be received that Gen¹ Burgoyne has advanced on this side of Ticonderoga, and that the Rebel Army, under Gates, is retiring before him. It is probable, that immediately after taking the two Forts, some troops will be sent up the N. River, to hasten Gates's retreat.

The Works are carrying on against Fort Washington, but the natural strength and situation of the ground renders it difficult to advance them with effect.

16ᵗʰ Novʳ

When I went to Lord Percy's quarters this Morning at an early hour for orders, I found that His Lordship and the troops under his Command at McGowan's had advanced to assist in the Attack of Fort Washington; I therefore followed him, and remaining with him untill the Fort was taken, had an opportunity of witnefsing some of the operations of the day. The attack commenced at Day break by a violent Cannonade from all our Batteries, during which the different Columns were brought forward, and having received their respective orders, the signals were given, and the attacks were attended with such complete succefs, that notwithstanding their numerous Lines, works, and batteries, in the most advantageous situations, the Rebels were driven on all sides, and by one o'Clock as many of them as The Fort would hold were driven into it, and the remainder into the ditch, and an unfinished outwork. The troops being drawn round the Fort at a proper distance the place was immediately summoned, about 3 oClock they surrendered, and about 4 o'Clock they marched out, amounting to about 2300 men, and were conducted to Haerlem. The 3rd brigade of British and Stirn's Brigade of Hefsians, advanced from our lines early in the Morning, and proceeded as far as the 9 mile Stone with very little opposition, and then formed in line about 200 yards from a Line of works which the Rebels occupied in considerable force. The troops were in this position when I joined them, and I found the orders were to remain in that position until firing was heard from near Morris's house, where an attack was to be made from the West Chester side by the 42d Regiment. While we lay waiting for this attack we heard a very severe fire of Musquetry beyond Fort Washington, and some firing at other points. As soon as the 42d Regiment commenced thier attack, the Rebels in the Lines opposite Lord Percy began to abandon them, and to run towards the Fort; they were instantly pursued by the two brigades, until they got within 600 yards of The Fort, where the Rebels threw themselves into a small wood, and our people pursuing too eagerly received a heavy fire from thence which checked them a little. The 42d having carried thier point pursued those who opposed them, and some of those who fled before Lord Percy, quite to the shore of the North River, where they took a good many prisoners.

Lord Howe was with Lord Percy's Corps, and close up to Morris's house about the time of the attack there. He was unattended by any Officer or Servant, and myself and another officer afsisted in opening a part of a line of Abbatis to make way for him to get forward. Soon after the Fort surrendered,

I went into it, and having seen Lord Percy, and received the orders for the 5th brigade, I returned to New York. Gen[l] Howe met Lord Percy before the place surrendered, at the 11 mile Stone, which is very near the Fort. He crofsed over Haerlem Creek with the Light Infantry.

17th Nov[r]

The following is a more circumstantial account of the attack of Fort Washington. —

General Howe having made every necefsary arrangement for the attack of Fort Washington, and erected Batteries on all the heights which were within reach of it, ordered the place to be summoned on the 15th. The Commanding Officer was informed that it is was impofsible for them to hold out or to escape, and afsured of the General's determined resolution to take the place at all events; he was also afsured that if he was so obstinate as to persist in defending it, the Garrison must expect to be put to the Sword. He however talked in a high strain, & rejected all terms whatever; confiding in the strength of his situation. In consequence of this it was determined to make a general attack upon all the Enemy's works round the Fort yesterday, and to Storm the Fort itself. The attack commenced accordingly at day break, with a furious Cannonade from all the Batteries which were within reach of the works, but particularly from those on the heights on the West Chester side opposite Col[o] Morris's house, and from those along Haerlem Creek as far as the Enemy's posts reached.

The Disposition of the several attacks was nearly as follows — General Knyphausen, with the Hefsian brigades under his Command, was to advance from Kingsbridge, and drive the Enemy from their advanced posts, and then to take post on a hill which was within half Cannon shot of the Fort, with his right to the N. River. The Brigade of Guards were to crofs Haerlem Creek, and join Gen[l] Knyphausen's left. The 1st Light Infantry were to crofs the Creek on the left of the Guards; the 2d Light Infantry in another place on the left of the 1st, and the 42[d] Regiment to pafs it under Col[o] Morris's house. All these were separate attacks, and to be supported by other troops. Lord Percy, with the 3rd brigade of British Infantry, & Stirn's brigade of Hefsians were to advance from the Lines at McGowan's, drive the Enemy from their most advanced posts, & wait, with his left to the N. River, until he heard or saw that

the troops which were to crofs Haerlem Creek, had gained the
summit of the hill. Every Column was then to push forward,
force all the Enemy's pofts, and unite as near as pofsible to Fort
Washington. This was executed on every side with succefs,
and the Rebels were in a short time drove in on all sides. General Knyphausen's Column, having very difficult ground to get
through, which was occupied by the principal force of the
Enemy, met with considerable resiftance, but after a very smart
fire of Musquetry, which continued for about 35 minutes, the
Hefsians carried their point. The 42ᵈ also met with some resiftance, and sustained a heavy fire, from between 2 and 300
Rebels ftrongly pofted near Morris's house, while they were
rowing acrofs and getting out of the boats; but as soon as the
Highlanders had landed they pushed the Rebels up the precipice
with great bravery, notwithftanding all the disadvantages they
laboured under, and pursuing them acrofs the Island with their
bayonets, took above 100 prisoners close to the North River
shore. The Guards and Light Infantry drove all before them.
A considerable body of the Rebels remained behind a Line and
in some Redoubts opposite Lord Percy's Corps, but as soon as
they heard the firing near Morris's house, which was in the rear
of thier left, they took to thier heels, and altho they had other
lines and Redoubts in thier rear, ftrengthened by Abbatis,
which we expected they would have defended, they never
ftopped 'till they got into, and on the Glacis of, the Fort. They
were immediately and briskly pursued over all their works by
the two brigades, for near two miles, and the ardour of the
troops was only checked by a smart fire which the moft advanced received from some Rebels who had thrown themselves
into a small wood very near the Fort, from which also some
shots were fired. The 10ᵗʰ and 52ᵈ Regiments having outrun the
Hefsians, had a few men killed & wounded by this fire. The
two brigades then drew up in line under cover of a small copse,
and some rocks, within half Cannon shot of the Fort, into which
the Rebels had been driven from all their pofts. The troops
from all sides having got close up to the Fort, the Rebels, in
momentary expectation of being Stormed, and finding they were
so much crowded in the Fort that they could not pofsible defend
it, beat their Drums, and soon after sent out to desire terms;
General Knyphausen, who at that time Commanded, demanded that they should surrender at discretion, and they

desired half an hour to consider of it. In the meantime Genl Howe, who had paſsed Haerlem Creek after the Light Infantry, came up, & sent to inform the Commanding officer that he insiſted they should surrender immediately, without any other terms than a promise of their lives, and their baggage, which after some hesitation they agreed to. This was about 3 o'Clock, and about 4 they marched out, amounting in all to about 2300 men. They left their Arms, & accoutrements in the Fort, and were sent under the Escort of the 10th & 52^d Regiments to Haerlem.

About 200 prisoners were taken before the surrender; of which, 104 were taken by the 42^d Regiment. The loſs of the Rebels in killed and wounded is not yet ascertained, but it muſt have been considerable.

There are about 90 officers among the prisoners, among whom are Colonels Magaw and Cadwallader. The former Commanded, who says there were only 2200 men on the Island in the Morning, but that a Reinforcement, the numbers of which he was not acquainted with, came over during the attack. It is said Mr Washington was on the Island in the Morning, but made his escape in a small boat a short time before our troops came up to the Fort.

There were found in the Fort and some adjoining batteries, 34 pieces of Cannon, of different Calibres, and 2 5½ Inch braſs Howitzers, also several Stands of Colours, a great quantity of ammunition, and about 14 days provisions for their numbers on the Island.

Immediately after the Fort surrendered the Rebels fired several Cannon shot from Fort Conſtitution at our troops which were neareſt the N. River. They were 32 p^{rs} and the shot came quite home. But no person was hurt by them.

The 2^d Battalion of Light Infantry took poſseſsion of The Fort. It is an irregular Pentagon, well situated, with a small outwork, or Covert way in front of the entrance. The Baſtions have two Embrazures in each face, and one in each flank. The whole is of Earth, without any fraize or pallisade; but there is good Abbattis round it. As it is situated on very rocky ground, there is hardly any ditch, as they have not blown any part of the Rock to form one. There would therefore have been no difficulty in Storming it; and if General Howe, after having summoned it the 15th, had not given orders that the troops were

Return of The loss of The King's Troops, in the Attack of Fort Washington.
16th Nov' 1776

Regiments, or Corps	Killed					Wounded						Missing		Total
	C	S	S	D	R & F	FO	C	S	S	D	R & F	St	R & F	
British														
17th Light Dragoons											1			1
2nd Light Infantry			1		3				2	1	7			14
Royal Artillery					1		•				1			2
4th Regiment													1	1
10th	1				3						5			9
15th					1						1			2
23rd									1					1
27th													3	3
28th											1			1
38th											6			6
42nd			1		8			3	4		66			82
52nd								1	1				1	3
71st											1	1		2
New York Company													1	1
German														
Chafseurs					6			1			5			12
Köhler's Grenadiers					6		1		1		33			41
Du Corps					2						1			3
Hereditary Prince											2			2
Wutginau	1	1	1		13			2	3		59			80
Ditfourth											2			2
Donop											1			1
Losberg					5			1			17			23
Knyphausen	1				6	2		1	5		58			73
Stein		1			1						1			3
Rall				1	2			1			3			7
Wiesenbach											4			4
Hayne		1			2			1	4		21			29
Brenau					2				3		23			28
Waldeck Regiment					6						16			22
Total	3	3	3	1	67	2	1	11	24	1	335	1	6	458

only to drive the Rebels into the Fort; there is no doubt but they, (especially the Hefsians, who were extremely irritated at having loſt a good many men in the attack) would have gone on, and taken it by afsault. The Carnage would then have been dreadful, for the Rebels were so numerous they had not room to defend themselves with effect, and so frightened they had not the power. Indeed after having rejected the offers made them

on the 15th, they had no right to expect the mild treatment they
met with: — but in this instance, as well as in every other since
the commencement of the Rebellion, the British humanity has
been conspicuous.

Many are of opinion that if Gen¹ Howe had treated the Garrison of Fort Washington with the severity which might have
been inflicted upon them by the laws of War, it would have
struck such a panic through the Continent, as would have prevented the Congress from ever being able to raise another Army.
They say we act with too much lenity and humanity towards
the Rebels, and that 'tho it is praiseworthy, and might be supposed to be the most likely means of bringing them back to a
sense of their duty, yet it will prove bad policy in the end: for
they now oppose us as long as they have the power, and when
they fall into our hands, instead of being treated as Rebels taken
in Arms against their Sovereign, they find they have nothing
more to dread than the common sufferings of prisoners of war.
Altho the humanity hitherto shewn to the Rebels has not had
the desired effect, I hope it may in the end; and I am of opinion
it is right to treat our Enemies as if they might one day become
our friends. Humanity is the characteristic of the British
troops, and I should be sorry they should run the risque of for-
feiting what redounds so much to their honor, by one act of even
necessary severity.

Part of the troops employed yesterday, returned in the Evening to their former encampments. The 37th Regiment, and some
Hessian Battalions remained near the Fort, where General
Knyphausen remained in the Command. Gen¹ Howe returned
to his quarters at De Lancey's Mills.

18th Novr 1776

The 3rd Battalion of Grenadiers, the 3rd Light Infantry, and
two Brigades of Hessians, marched from the Army this morn-
ing, and at 2 o'Clock encamped near New York. The 1st Brigade of British Infantry marched also this Morning from the
other side of Kingsbridge; and at McGowan's house received
the Rebel prisoners taken at Fort Washington, from whence
they escorted them to the several places appointed for their
confinement in New York; after which they encamped near the
town. The Rebel prisoners were in general but very indifferently clothed; few of them appeared to have a Second shirt, nor
did they appear to have washed themselves during the Cam-

paign. A great many of them were lads under 15, and old men: and few of them had the appearance of Soldiers. Their odd figures frequently excited the laughter of our Soldiers.

The 1st brigade to come to do the duty at New York in place of the 5th brigade, which, with the 3rd, that is expected to encamp near the town toMorrow, is shortly to embark.

The Rebels fired several 32 p^{rs} this day from Fort Constitution at our people in Fort Washington; they also threw some 13 Inch shells, which fell and burst near the Fort, but without doing any damage.

19th Nov^r — Remarkable fine weather

The 3rd brigade came and encamped near the town.

The troops now encamped near New York, and which are expected to embark on the intended Expedition, are, The 3rd Battn. of Light Infantry, 3rd of Grenadiers, 3rd and 5th Brigades of British, and Losberg's & Schmidt's brigades of Hessian Infantry.

The 1st brigade is encamped near, and doing the duty of the town.

Great part of The Field artillery came into town today.

20th Nov^r — A good deal of rain last night. Fine mild day.

The 1st and 2^d Battalions, of Light Infantry, the Grenadiers, Guards, and other Corps of the Reserve under the Command of Lord Cornwallis, struck their tents last night at 9 o'Clock, and about daylight this morning passed The North River in flatboats, and landed on the Jersey shore about 5 miles above Fort Constitution without opposition. Tis said the Rebels have been withdrawing from Fort Constitution for these two last days.

A fleet arrived yesterday from the Southward, having, as is said a part of the 6th Regiment on board from Antigua, & some Companies of the 14th from St Augustine in Florida.

The Rebel officers who have been taken prisoners lately, are suffered to walk about in every part of this town on their parole, and in their Uniforms. This gives great disgust to all the Loyalists. At such a time as this, and when there are full 3000 prisoners in the town, in places of no great security, I think it is rather imprudent to give these fellows so much liberty, and allow them to go about in all places without any restraint. They publickly avow their principles, and instead of appearing sensible of the crime they have committed, seem to glory in the cause in which they are engaged. Our treating them so well, and keeping so many of them in a town of such great consequence as this is, may be attended with fatal consequences. It is perfectly easy for them to set fire to the remainder of the town; and as we know they would not scruple to commit an act of that nature, especially as they know the greatest part of our Stores and provisions are now deposited in it, we should not put it in their power to do what might distress the Army in a very great degree.

21st Nov^r

The troops that landed in Jersey yesterday, marched immediately towards Fort Constitution which they had found had been very recently abandoned by the Rebels, who retired further into the Country in the most precipitate manner; leaving behind them, 2 brass and one Iron, 13 Inch Mortars, and several pieces of Cannon, brass & Iron, some of which they had drawn some distance from the Fort, but finding our troops were advancing, they abandoned them, as also their tents, baggage, Stores, provisions, &c. &c. Our troops pursued them so rapidly, that about 8 or 10 were killed, and about 70 taken prisoners when the accounts came away. This is now the time to push these rascals, and if we do, and not give them time to recover themselves, we may depend upon it they will never make head again. A body of troops landed at this time at Amboy, might, in conjunction with those already in Jersey, push on to Philadelphia, with very little difficulty.

Quarters for a considerable part of the Army will now probably be taken in Jersey. At least we may stretch as far as Brunswick, which will include an extensive tract of Country, and afford quarters and supplies for a large force.

The troops under orders for the Expedition, are one troop of the 17th Dragoons, 3rd Battalion of Light Infantry, 3rd Grenadiers, 3rd & 5th brigades of British, Losberg's and Schmidt's brigades of Hessians, and two Companies of Artillery. Most of the two Decked Ships of War, are also under orders. General Clinton is to have the Command of the Army, and Admiral Sir Peter Parker of The Navy. It is generally supposed that Rhode-Island is the object. The officers of the Navy say it is not too late to go there, and as it seems necessary to secure a good harbour for the large ships during the Winter, that place, which has an Excellent one, and generally free from Ice, naturally offers as the object of the intended Expedition; — which will probably sail very soon.

22ᵈ Novʳ — Rain laſt night, and moſt part of this day

Came in a fleet of 9 sail, laſt from Cork with provisions, and about 400 Recruits on board. Came in also a transport with two Companies of the 6ᵗʰ Regiment, which had parted from the fleet to which she belonged, a few days before they came in. She was attacked off the Hook by two small privateers, but beat them off.

The heavy baggage of the two Heſsian brigades going on the Expedition, was put on board the transports allotted for them.

The accounts from the Troops in Jersey are, that they have taken large magazines, belonging to the Rebels, of provisions and ammunition, 4 braſs, and 2 Iron Mortars, 18 pieces of Cannon, and a quantity of baggage. The Rebels are retreating towards the Delaware with the utmoſt precipitation. Our troops are at Hackinsack. Tis said the 4ᵗʰ brigade were ordered to paſs over to Jersey this day.

Nothing certain transpires relative to the object of the intended Expedition. The succeſs we have met with in Jersey, may poſsible make some alteration in the deſtination of the troops under orders for Embarkation.

23ʳᵈ Novʳ — Rain laſt night

General Howe came to New York laſt night.

Arrived a fleet from England, & Cork, under Convoy of the Mermaid, with Recruits and provisions.

Part of the troops for the Expedition are to embark to-Morrow.

Part of our troops in Jersey have advanced as far as New-bridge. The Rebels hardly appear. They are retreating towards Philadelphia, which place, it is said, they intend to fortify.

24ᵗʰ Novʳ   Heavy rain laſt night. A soft warm day.

The 3ʳᵈ and 5ᵗʰ brigades Embarked this morning, on board the transports allotted for them.

The 3 Regiments of the 6ᵗʰ brigade moved down towards Haerlem this day.

Captain Gardiner, Aide de Camp to General Howe is going home in a few days in the Packet, with his dispatches.

Distinguishing Vanes of the transports ordered to receive the British Troops for the Expedition

Corps	Ships	Vanes
Light Infantry ...	{ Mercury / Argo	} Red — Main Top Mast-head
Grenadiers	{ Rachel & Harry / Hunter	} Red — Fore T. M. head
10th Regiment	{ Isabella / Emprefs	} White, 1 Red ball Main &c.
38th	{ Grand Dutchefs of Rufsia / Sea Venture	} White, 1 Red ball — Fore
52d	{ Saville / Antelope	} White, 3 Red balls — Fore
37th	{ Eagle / Susannah	} White, 3 Red balls — Main
22d	{ James & William / John	} White, 2 Red balls — Main
54th	Grand Duke of Rufsia	White, 1 Blue ball — Main
63rd	{ Amity's Admonition / Three Sisters	} White, 1 Blue ball — Fore
43rd	{ Chambre / Earl of Oxford	} White, 2 Red balls — Fore
General Clinton...	Sovereign	Red, 2 White balls — Main
Lord Percy	Briton	Red, 3 White balls — Main
Generals Prescott, & Smith	} Earl of Effingham	Red, 1 White ball — Main

{ New York Harbour
24th Novr 1776 }

NEW YORK HARBOUR

25th Novr Remarkable warm weather these two last days. Cloudy, and Wind S.

The Grenadiers and Light Infantry, and the two Hefsian brigades embarked.

The 2nd brigade pafsed over to Jersey to join the troops under Lord Cornwallis.

Some vefsels arrived from England.

26th Novr Rain most part of the day.

A Ship arrived yesterday Evening from London. She sailed the 1st October, at which time no account had been received of the operations of this Army since it left Staten Island.

Some firing heard towards Elisabeth town today.

By accounts received from Canada it appears that General Carleton, finding the season too far advanced, had drawn the Army back to Montreal, Quebec, &c., leaving garrisons at St Johns, and Chamblee. As he has a very ſtrong force on the Lake, he will be able to advance without any interruption next Spring, as soon as the Ice breaks up. The Rebels had so many armed veſsels on the Lake this Summer, that he was obliged to employ the greateſt part of the Season in building a fleet of sufficient force to enable him to attack that of the Enemy; so that before he could defeat them it was too late to begin his march towards Albany, which place if he could not have reached, his return to Canada would have been extremely hazardous.

27th Nov^r
Moſt of the transports with troops on board for the Expedition, went out of the N. River to day, and anchored between Governor's Island and Redhook. The large ships are gone down to Gravesend bay.

It is ſtill uncertain where we are going; but Rhode-Island is now generally supposed to be our deſtination; and that The Frigates and transports will go through the Sound, and the two decked Ships round Long Island, and rendezvous off the E. end of Long Island.

28th Nov^r
The transports with the troops came up with the tide, and anchored in the Eaſt River between Corlaer's-hook and the town. The two decked ships, and the large transport with the 54th Regiment on board, are gone down to Sandy hook. It is now pretty evident that we are going to Rhode Island.

Major General Prescott, Capt. Welsh, his aide de Camp, & Brigadier General Smith, together with Major of brigade Baker and myself, embarked this day on board The Earl of Effingham, which ship has been allotted for those two Generals, with their Suite and baggage.

Two horses have been embarked for Each General Officer, one for each Aide de Camp, & Major of brigade; & one for Each Field Officer and adjutant.

The following general order was given out this day —

"The Detachments of the Royal Artillery and 17th Dragoons, the 3rd Battalion of Light Infantry, 3rd Battalion of Grenadiers,

3rd and 5th brigades of British, and two brigades of Hefsians (Losberg's & Schmidt's) as well as all other officers and Soldiers now embarked under the Command of Lieu^t Genl Clinton, will receive their orders from him."

EAST RIVER. N. YORK

29th Nov^r

The Earl of Effingham came down the N. River this morning about 10 o'Clock with the Ebb tide, and with the next flood went up the East River, and anchored off Bushwick point. Greatest part of the Expedition fleet is now at anchor in the E. River between Turtle bay and Bushwick point. About 60 sail are afsembled. The Frigates which are Convoy us, pafsed through Hellgate some days ago, and are waiting for us in the Sound.

The large ships, vizt Asia, Chatham, Centurion, Renown, Experiment, & Preston with some Frigates, and the transport with the 54th Regiment, went over the Bar, and put to Sea this Morning with a fine wind at N.

Rhode Island is certainly our object, at which place it is said there are some Rebel Frigates, and a great quantity of Goods and Stores.

30th Novr Rain all last night, and most part of this day, attended, during the night, with a strong wind at N. E.

The transports here cannot move until the wind and weather are more favorable.

It is probable the fleet under Sir Peter Parker, came back to Sandy hook last night; if not, they must have stood away to the Southward.

LONG ISLAND SOUND

1st Dec^r

The Expedition fleet weighed anchor at daybreak, with a fine wind at S. went all safely through Hellgate, and at 3 in the afternoon anchored near Whitestone, & not far from Frog's-point. Here we found the Brune, Mercury, and Kingsfisher, appointed, with some others not yet joined, to Convoy us. Some of the ships which did not leave New York yesterday, came down this Evening. Commodore Hotham, who Commands this part of the fleet, hoists his broad pendant on board the Brune.

No accident happened to any of the Ships in paſsing through Hellgate, notwithſtanding the extreme narrownefs and difficulty of the paſsage, and the rapid tide which sets through. The day being very clear and fine, the appearance of so many large ships going through such a narrow and dangerous paſsage, in a line ahead, with all their sails set, and with considerable velocity, afforded a grand and pleasing sight. In some places a ſtone might have been thrown on either shore.

The tide, at some times, runs 7 or 8 knots an hour in this paſsage, and I have several times seen large transports paſs through with a contrary wind, Stern foremoſt, with all sails set.

During the time the army has been on New York Island, very few accidents have happened, considering the great number of veſsels which have paſsed through this dangerous Channel. They have frequently touched the Rocks, but no ship has been loſt. The beſt time to go through is at the beginning of the flood tide, and near high water, as then the ſtrength of the Current is much abated. It is safer to go from New York into the Sound, than the contrary. Before the arrival of the Army at New York, it was very uncommon for any veſsel drawing above 10 or 12 feet water, to attempt going through this paſsage.

Fresh wind this Evening at N. W.

2ᵈ Decʳ   Fresh wind at E. with rain.

The fleet remains at anchor near Frog's point.

The Earl of Effingham and some other ships changed their births, and anchored further in round the point, in order to be out of the ſtrength of the Tide.

A hard gale of wind during the latter part of the day, at S. attended with rain.

The Maſters of Ships received orders, sealed up, to be opened in case of separation.

3ʳᵈ Decʳ   Hard gale of wind all laſt night from the Southward, with very heavy rain. It was so very dark laſt night, that we could not diſtinguish the water out of the quarter Gallery windows.

We are under some apprehensions for our friends who are gone round Long Island.

Calm this morning, but thick weather, with rain. The laſt of the ships belonging to our fleet came down from New York laſt night. The whole is now aſsembled, and consiſts of about 70 sail of veſsels.

4th Dec^r — The wind being fair this morning, the signal for
weighing was made about 11 o'Clock, and at 2 in the afternoon
almost the whole of the fleet was under way with a light wind at
N. Towards Evening the wind came round to the Westward,
and freshened; and about Sunset the whole was well in company, making all the sail they could, under Convoy of The
Brune, Rose, Carysfort, and Kingsfisher. The Mercury remained at Whitestone, waiting for an Hospital ship which had
not arrived from New York.

This Evening, just as it grew dark, our ship being among the
headmost in the fleet, we had an opportunity of viewing a most
beautiful Seapiece from our Cabbin windows. The fleet was
going down the Sound before the wind, those ships which sailed
the worst having all their sails set, the others such as were necessary to keep them in their respective Stations. The Sun having
set from under some very thick clouds, a Streak of a reddish
colour between those clouds and the horizon, shewed the fleet
aStern of us, and just discernable. The perspective was very
fine: in the farthest distance we could perceive some of the
Sternmost ships, with their Mast heads and Top Gallant Sails,
reaching about half way up the red streak: — according as the
ships were situated nearer to us, less of them appeared; in some
only their Topsails, in others nothing more than thier Courses.
But the principal object in the piece was the Brune Frigate; this
ship had nothing more than her three topsails set, and she was
exactly at that point of distance in which no part of her could be
seen but her lower masts and rigging, her Hull being below the
horizon, and her sails above the red streak. What was seen of
her had a singular appearance. The stillnefs of the Sea added
much to the beauty of the piece, which would have afforded an
uncommonly fine subject for a Painter.

5th Dec^r   The wind increased considerably last night, and we
went above 6 knots an hour under topsails only. It blew very
fresh this morning at N. W.

At day break being nearly off Seabrook, we saw Sir Peter
Parker's Squadron at anchor under the Long Island shore, with
thier yards and top masts struck. At Sunrise Commodore Hotham saluted him with 13 Guns, which was soon after returned
with the like number. Immediately after this, out fleet stood
over to the Connecticut shore, and about 12 oClock anchored
off Seabrook, which stands on the Mouth of Connecticut River.

The last ships of the fleet were at anchor by 3 o'Clock. Fresh wind at N. W. Soon after our fleet appeared, Sir Peter Parker's Squadron began to set up their yards and topmasts. About 12 o'Clock they weighed, and about Sunset they anchored near us.

The above Squadron consists of the Chatham, Asia, Preston, Centurion, Experiment, Renown, Emerald, Sphynx, and ; — also the Grand Duke transport, with the 54th Regiment on board.

The wind abated towards night.

Some of our ships are anchored within less than a mile of the Shore. Very few people appear there. Many Cattle and Sheep are feeding along shore, and every thing appears perfectly quiet. In the Evening some few people, who seemed to be attracted by curiosity alone, came down to the shore, without arms.

A Signal having been made in the afternoon on board The Admiral, for all Masters, they returned soon after with a paper containing the order of Sailing to be observed by the Fleet. See the opposite page.

Form of Sailing of the fleet under the Command of Sir Peter Parker. Chatham, off Block Island, 2d Decr 1776

Chatham

Experiment . .	{ Lieut Knowles's, Transports Lieut Parry's, Transports }	*Asia*

Renown

Emerald	{ To repeat Signals, as Com- mander in the 3rd post }	*Brune*
Sphynx	{ Lieut Dickenson's, Transports Lieut Sutherland's Ships }	*Centurion*

Preston

A Man of War will be ordered to bring up against any Battery that may be at the entrance of the harbour, that the Transports may pass under her cover.

Besides the ships of War mentioned in the form of Sailing, the Carysfort, Mercury, Rose, & Kingsfisher are with the fleet, and are employed in Cruizing, or other services.

Lieut Knowles's transports have on board The Light Infantry, Grenadiers, and 3rd brigade.

Lieut Parry's, the 5th brigade,

Lieu^t Dickenson's — The Hefsians, and
Lieu^t Sutherland's, the Light Dragoons, The Artillery, Stores,
&c. &c.

6th Decr 1776

The fleet weighed this morning at 7 o'Clock, Wind E; but
having the advantage of a strong ebb tide, we worked, as far as
The Race, which is between Fisher's and Gardiner's, Islands. At
2 o'Clock, the tide being spent, the signal was made for anchor-
ing, which Was done by the whole fleet by half past 3 o'Clock.
The Race lies between Long Island, Gardiner's Island, Fisher's
Island, and The Main; and is occasioned by the narrownefs of
the Channel, which confining the great body of water that
comes out of the Sound, causes a great rippling on the Ebbtide,
in the narrowest part, and has the appearance of the water run-
ning over a reef. There is however above 20 fathom water on it.

The tide which flows in at Sandy hook and past New York, is
met at Whitest one by that which comes up the Sound from the
Eastward; from which place they return again. So that a vefsel
coming from New York as far as Whitestone with the flood tide,
has the advantage of the Ebb tide from thence down the Sound;
by which means the pafsage from New York to some of the
Ports in the Sound is made in a very short time.

The pafsage from New York is very entertaining, and the
many beautiful views on each Shore, but particularly that of
Long Island, which is in several places intersected by deep bays
and Inlets, make it extremely pleasing even at this season on the
year. In Spring or Summer the Views must be delightful.

From the place where we are now at anchor, we have a view of
the mouth of the Thames upon which river New London is
situated; and which we can see just over the W. end of Fisher's
Island. Several vefsels are plainly discovered at anchor in the
harbour, with their sails loose. We suppose some of them to be
Privateers, as many are fitted out from that place. Our Pilot
says there is not above 12 feet water on the Bar at high water.

We are now about 15 leagues from Rhode Island, to which
place, it now seems past all doubt, we are going. The Ships of
War are throwing overboard all uselefs lumber, and appear to be
clearing out in order to bring up against any batteries which the
Rebels may have to obstruct our entrance.

The Mercury Frigate joined the fleet this afternoon with the
Hospital ship which was left behind.

RHODE ISLAND HARBOUR

7th Dec^r

A fine fair wind all last night, and good weather; which continuing this morning, at 4 o'Clock the signal was made for the fleet to weigh, and at 5 the whole was under way, with a fresh wind at S. W. At 8 o'Clock saw Block Island, at 10 Point Judith, which is the S. E. point of Connecticut, and at 12 made the Light House on the S. point of Connonicut Island at the entrance of Rhode Island harbour. The Commodore soon after made the Signal to speak with The Experiment, Capt Wallace; and about 1 o'Clock that ship took the lead, and stood up the Western Channel, between Connonicut, and the Main, followed by the Chatham, and Asia, and then by the transports and other ships according to the form of Sailing given out.

No Enemy appeared on either side as we went up.

About 2 miles from the Light House, the Rebels had a Battery or Redoubt, with 4 Embrazures towards the Channel. But it appeared to be abandoned.

When the leading ships had got as far as the N. end of Connonicut Island, they hawled round the point to the Eastward, and steered down the Middle Channel towards Newport on Rhode Island, keeping near the Rhode Island shore. The rest of the fleet followed in order, and about 4 oClock the signal was made to anchor, which was done by the whole fleet at 5 in the afternoon, without the smallest accident, about 4 miles from Newport, between Dyer's Island, and Weaver's Cove, half a mile from the Shore, and immediately off Mr Stoddard's house. As the fleet turned round the N. end of Connonicut Island, we saw three large ships and a Brig, standing up the harbour at the back of Prudence Island, with all sails set. We at first took them to be some of our Frigates which had come up the Middle passage before us; but we soon found they were Rebel frigates, Commanded by Mr Hopkins, Commander in Chief of the Rebel fleet. They went up towards Providence. A Brig laden with Lumber and Poultry, which was too late in coming away from Newport, struck to the Chatham, who fired two shot at her.

No armed Rebels appear on the shore. A few appear on Tammany hill, about 2 miles from the town, where they appear to have a work thrown up, and on which there is a Beacon erected. The Rebel Colours are flying on the Batteries below the town.

As soon as the fleet came to an anchor, eight men came down to the shore near Stoddard's house, on which a boat was sent to them from the Experiment, which returned with four of them; the others rode back towards the town. It appears from this circumstance that the Rebels have no great force on the Island, and those who are there do not intend to make any resistance, & will probable retire before we land.

The passage of the fleet here, and the weather during that passage, has been as favorable as could have been wished, particularly during this day, when we had the most favorable wind that was possible, by which the fleet was enabled, without loss of time, to come in by a passage which it is probable the Enemy did not expect so large a fleet would attempt. The same wind served to bring us round Connonicut to our present anchorage without the smallest obstruction. We have by this means avoided those batteries which they no doubt have erected to defend the usual and principal entrance. We have now got above the town, and the Rebels must either abandon it, or fall into our hands.

Orders were given this evening for the Army to land toMorrow at daybreak.

RHODE ISLAND

8th Decr 1776

The Army landed this morning at Weaver's Cove near Mr Stoddard's house, in the following order —

The first Embarkation consisted of the Light Infantry, Grenadiers, and 10th Regiment, under the Command of Major General Prescott. As soon as they had landed, the boats returned for the three other Battalions of the 3rd brigade, which formed the whole of the 1st Division.

The 2nd Division consisted of Losberg's brigade, & Wutgenau's Reg^t under the Command of Major General Losberg.

The 3rd Division consisted of the 43rd, 54th, & 63rd Regiments of the 5th brigade, and the two other Hessian Regiments of Schmidt's brigade, under the Command of Brigadier General Smith: — All these Corps were landed in succession at the same place, and the whole of the Army was on shore by 3 oClock in the afternoon.

The first Embarkation under Genl Prescott, marched as soon as formed to the high road from Newport to Bristol ferry, a short distance from the landing place, and finding that the few of the Enemy who were on the Island, had retired in haste towards the N. end of it, he pursued them to the ferries, where he took a few prisoners, and a 9 p^r Cannon; and saved a great many Cattle & Sheep which they had not time to carry off.

The remainder of the 3rd brigade marched as soon as they landed and joined Genl Prescott. The 5th brigade and the two Hefsian brigades, were ordered to encamp near the road above Mr Stoddard's house.

The 22^d Regiment went down on their Transports under cover of some of the Ships of War, early this morning to Newport, and finding the Rebels had abandoned it, they landed, and took pofsefsion of it, and the Batteries.

It rained during the time the first Division were landing, but cleared up soon after, and proved a fine mild day.

It appears that the Rebels have driven off a considerable number of Cattle and Sheep belonging to the Inhabitants; and have removed most of their Cannon and Ammunition.

The Rebels have Batteries on the Main at Bristol Ferry, and Howland's ferry. They fired both round & Grapeshot from their Battery at Bristol ferry, at some of our advanced parties, but without any effect.

9th Dec^r

As the troops could not get their tents on shore from the transports last night, they were obliged to lie without any shelter, on a bleak hill, much exposed to the severity of the weather. The troops which advanced towards the ferries, were Cantoned in the adjacent houses & barns. Most of the tents were got on shore this morning and pitched.

Notwithstanding the Rebels drove off a great part of the Cattle and Sheep upon our first appearance on the 7th Instant, yet there still appears to be a good Stock on the Island, with plenty of forage.

The Rebels abandoned a well situated fort at the N. end of the Island yesterday, without attempting to defend it. It in some measure commands the pafsage to Bristol by the ferry.

A Corps of Safe Guards, consisting of an officer and 15 men from each brigade, under the Command of a Captain of the British, was formed yesterday, in order to afford protection to the houses and property of the Inhabitants.

Previous to landing the order on the opposite page was given out.

"General Orders.   On board His Majesty's Ship Chatham
                    Rhode Island harbour.   7ᵗʰ Decʳ 1776

"The General is certain that the officers Commanding Regiments will take the utmost care that the reputation thier courage has so justly given them during this Campaign, is not sullied by Marauding, or any other disorderly behavior. Want of discipline does not reflect lefs dishonor on a Corps, than deficiency in point of Spirit."

10ᵗʰ Decʳ   Very hard frost last night, and Ice an Inch and half thick this morning.

The Hefsian Regiment of Du Corps, marched into Newport this morning, where they are to be quartered. Three Battalions of British, and 5 of Hefsians remain encamped on the height above where the Army landed.

The Rebels have a Fort on their side of Howland's ferry, and have also some pieces of Cannon on a height above it, by which means they entirely command the pafsage; for the ground on our side, called Commonfence Neck, is flat land, intersected with Creeks, which extends near a mile from any part where we can establish a post. They have a Fort and Battery also on their side of Bristol ferry, and altho the ground on our side is higher and Commands that opposite, they keep their post, and fire occasionally at any person who appears within their reach. Indeed we have not attempted to dispofsefs them, nor should we derive any advantage from so doing.

11ᵗʰ Decʳ

The frost being very severe, the three brigades which are encamped, were this day ordered to go into Cantonments in the farm houses, but the order being received too late to admit of making the necefsary regulations, the movement was deferred until toMorrow.

The Chatham, Preston, and some other ships of War, went down to Newport this morning, and anchored off the town.

Capt Drummond, aide de Camp to Genˡ Clinton is going to England in a day or two, in the Mercury Frigate, with the General's dispatches.

12ᵗʰ Decʳ

Snow last night for some hours, which lay three Inches deep on the ground this morning. Cold raw weather all day.

The troops went into Cantonments this day. The whole is now Cantoned over the Island, except the 22ᵈ Regiment, and the Regiment Du Corps, which are quartered in Newport, and doing the duty there.

A Detachment of a Captain and 100 men of the 54ᵗʰ Regiment went over to Connonicut Island this Morning, to take possession of it, and protect the Inhabitants.

The Mercury sailed this morning for England, and The Kingsfisher in the Evening for New York.

13ᵗʰ Decʳ   Slight frost last night. Fine clear day.

The Rebels fire at our men from the height above Bristol ferry, whenever they see four or five of them together; but hitherto no person has been hurt. Indeed we have not had a man killed or wounded since we landed.

The Emerald Frigate is anchored in the passage between this Island, and Prudence Island; another Frigate is stationed above Prudence to prevent any vessel from passing between Connonicut and the Main; and two others are Stationed in the Eastern, or Sekonnet passage, to prevent any vessel from passing at the back of this Island. It is imagined the Rebel Frigates now at or near Providence, will endeavor to escape to Sea.

Orders given this day for all the Inhabitants to give in their arms.

The Inhabitants of this Island being principally Quakers, are exceedingly alarmed at the appearance of the Hessian troops, and under great dread of them. A Quaker told me today, that as the Rebels were now driven off the Island, he hoped the General would send all the Hessians on board the ships again.

14ᵗʰ Decʳ

The Regᵗ of Prince Charles, and that of Ditfourth, went into Newport this day, where they are to be stationed for the Winter. Barracks have been prepared and fitted up for the Regiments in Newport.

The Ships of War were placed today in the several Stations in which they are to continue during the Winter.

15ᵗʰ Decʳ   A very hard frost last night, with a Strong wind at N. W. The Cold was greater last night, by the accounts of the

Inhabitants, than any they experienced laſt winter. A Bottle of water under my bed froze entirely; and a bottle of Ink in a drawer in a Desk in the same room, was frozen up.

The wind continued very high all day at W. N. W. and the cold intense.

16ᵗʰ Decʳ   The weather rather milder today than yeſterday, with leſs wind. Very little Snow is to be seen on this or the other Islands, but it remains on the Continent, which ſhews that our situation is warmer than the neighbouring Country.

The 3ʳᵈ brigade marched into quarters in Newport.

Detail of the Guards in Newport. 16ᵗʰ Decʳ 1776

Guards	C	S	S	C	D	P
Main Guard	1	2	2	3	1	80
Long wharf	.	1	2	2	1	24
South end	.	1	1	1	1	21
North Battery	.	.	1	1	.	12
Provision Store	.	.	.	1	.	6
General's Guard	.	.	1	1	.	15
	1	4	7	9	3	158

A Field Officer of The day.
    The Duty taken alternately by British and Heſsians.

There is a hill about 7 miles from Newport, and on the Eaſtern side of this Island, Called Quaker hill (from there being a Quaker's Meeting house on it) from whence there is a very fine view of all the N. part of the Island, and of the adjacent Islands, and the Continent for many miles. The many fine and well cultivated Islands, and the beautiful bays and inlets, with the diſtant view of towns, farms, and cultivated lands intermixed with Woods, together with the many views of the adjacent waters, contribute to make this, (even at this bleak season of the year) the fineſt, moſt diversified, and extensive prospeĉt I have seen in America.

The Ships of War which are ſtationed in the different passages to watch the motions of the Enemy, are in such positions as to make it appear as if they were placed there only to add to the beauty of the Piĉture. In the beginning of Summer this muſt be a delightful view, and I should think hardly to be equalled in America, or any other Country.

17th Dec^r　　Hard frost, and cold wind at N.　Clear weather.

The 43rd, 54th, and 63rd Regiments of Genl Smith's brigade, changed their quarters this morning, and Cantoned in the houses at the N. end of the Island, taking the advanced posts opposite Bristol and Howland's ferries.

The Grenadiers and Light Infantry, which had hitherto occupied that part of the Island, fell back, and quartered within 3 miles of Newport.

Preparations are making for the movement of a Detachment of about 200 men by water.

Detail of the duty at the Advanced posts, Rhode Island, with the Number of Sentries from each.　17th Decr 1776

							Sentries	
Posts	C	S	S	C	D	P	Day	Night
At Bristol ferry house...................	I	I	I	I	I	34	4	11
Detached to the house at the point......	.	I	I	I	I	21	4	7
At the Town pond	.	.	.	I	.	6	I	2
At The Neck	.	I	I	I	I	21	2	7
At the road to Howland's bridge	.	I	I	I	I	18	2	6
Total	I	4	4	5	4	100	13	33

18th Dec^r　　Very cold weather and hard frost.

The Grenadiers and Light Infantry went into quarters in Newport.

A Prize taken lately by a Rebel Privateer, came into the harbour yesterday, not knowing the Island was in our posfesfion. She struck after a shot or two had been fired at her.

A man came in this day from Howland's ferry: He says the Rebels have about 2000 men on that side.

Their Fort near the ferry has 9 9 p^{rs} in it; and there are about 15 pieces of Cannon, from 4 to 24 p^{rs} in their Batteries above the Fort.

General Smith has the Command of all the troops Cantoned on the N. end of this Island.　His quarters are at Mr Collins's on the West road, about 5 miles from Newport.　I am in the house with him.

19th Dec^r　　Very hard frost, and cold wind at N.

The Rebels fired two 24 l^b Shot at our advanced post at Bristol ferry, but without any effect.

A Detachment of 200 men, British and Hefsians ordered to be in readinefs to embark under the Command of Lieu^t Col^o Gunning, 43rd Reg^t. They are going to Long Island with Six transports, to bring wood for the use of the troops in Newport.

20th Decr Hard frost.

The 54th Regiment pafsed over this morning to Connonicut Island, where they are to be quartered.

The Detachment under Lt Colonel Gunning embarked this afternoon.

The Hefsian Brigade of Schmidt, is at present under the Command of Brigadier General Hüyne; Major General Schmidt being at New York.

21st Decr It snowed for some hours laft night, and during the greateft part of this day, accompanied by a Strong wind at N. N. W. Very hard frost, and extremely cold. The Snow drifted much. It lay about 8 Inches deep, on a medium, at 3 o'Clock this afternoon.

There are a great number of Islands within the Bay in which this Island is situated. The Bay is called Narraganset Bay, and is included within Point Judith to the Weftward, and Seakonnet point to the Eaft.

Rhode Island, and Connonicut are the largeft and Inhabited; Prudence is the next in size, but has no Inhabitants on it. Dutch Island, and Fox Island lie in the Narraganset, or Weftern pafsage; Goat Island, Rose Island, and Coafters harbour (or Peft) Island, lie within Rhode Island harbour; Gold Island, and Dyers Island lie further up on the Weft side of this Island. Hope-Island, Despair-Island, and Patience Island, lie N. of Connonicut, and W. of Prudence. Hog Island lies to the W. of Briftol ferry; and Little-Island lies high up the Bay near the town of Providence. Hardly any of the smaller Islands are inhabited, but they are all cultivated.

22^d Decr Snow part of laft night. It lies 10 Inches deep on the ground. Clear cold day, with ftrong wind at N.

Permifsion has been to such of the Inhabitants as are recommended by the Commanding Officers in the respective Cantonments, to make use of their boats for catching fish, and to keep a Gun for killing wild fowl.

As it is extremely difficult for the Soldiers to move about during this Severe froft, without meeting with accident by falls;

200 pair of Creepers have been iſsued to such Corps as have not been already provided with them.

23ʳᵈ Decʳ   Hard froſt. The Snow continues to lie on the ground.

There was a change in the Cantonments of the troops ſtationed out upon the Island. The 43ʳᵈ and 63ʳᵈ Regimᵗ have taken up the Cantonments on the Weſt side, and The Heſsians those on the E. side of the Island.

The Rebels fired four shots this Evening from their Battery at Briſtol ferry. Two of them at the guard house, one at the house at the point, and one at the Emerald Frigate. One of those fired at the guard house went through both the officer's and men's guard room, but providentially did no mischief. Captain McKinnon of the 63ʳᵈ, who was on Guard had the moment before got up from the chair on which he was sitting, to go into the men's room, when the shot (a 24 pʳ) ſtruck the chair and broke it. The Shot fired at the house at the point, had very nearly ſtruck the Sentry. That fired at the Frigate fell short of her. The Rebels seemed to be intoxicated, as they came shouting and hallowing out of the Battery after each shot.

24ᵗʰ Decʳ 1776 — Hard froſt

The Rebels fired a shot at the ferry guard this morning, but it went over without doing any damage.

The advanced poſts of the British Regiments on the Weſt side have been reduced to a Subaltern, and 30 men, of which the Subaltern, a Serjᵗ Corpˡ Drummer and 18 men are ſtationed at the Ferry house, and a Serjᵗ Corpˡ and 12 men are detached to the house at the point. The Heſsians take the advanced poſts on the Eaſt side.

A Soldier of the 22ᵈ Regiment who was Sentenced by a General Court Martial to suffer death for committing a Rape since our landing on this Island, has been pardoned at the interceſsion of the injured party, and in consequence of his former good Character.

25ᵗʰ Decʳ   Froſty weather.

The Prize that was taken on her entering the harbour a few days ago, is one of a Coal fleet from Louisbourg to New York. She was taken by the Alfred Privateer belonging to Providence, and was sent in here by her not knowing the place was taken.

The Alfred took three other veſsels out of the same fleet, and she and them are daily expeƈted in.

26th Decᵗ   High wind at N. E. attended with heavy rain, from 8 this morning 'till 5 in the Evening. It blew extremely hard about 2 oClock. The Snow was nearly gone by the Evening.

Regulation eſtablished, for the present, for supplying the Troops at Rhode Island with Fuel & Candles —

A Brigadier General	2 Cords of wood pʳ week		
A Colonel	1½	Do	Do
A Lieuᵗ and Major, each	1	Do	Do
A Captain	½	Do	Do
Subalterns	¼	Do	Do
12 N. C. officers & Soldiers	½	Do	Do
Each Barrack Guard.................	half a foot pʳ day		

The proportion of Candles, is 2 lbˢ to a Cord of wood
No officer is to receive but in one Capacity
The Barrack Maſter is to supply the Hospitals at the rate of two Cords of wood, & 4 lbs of Candles, pʳ week
When Coals are delivered out, 12 bushels are to be received as equivalent to one Cord of Wood

The troops are now served with one days fresh, & Six days salt provisions per week. Fresh provisions and loaf bread is iſsued to all the Sick.

Orders have been given to be particularly careful of the Mills on the Island. As there is no ſtream of water in the Island, Wind Mills are used by the Inhabitants for grinding their Corn. There is a fulling Mill upon a very small run of water near General Smith's quarters, used for Fulling the Woolen articles made by the Inhabitants for their private use. These articles consiſt chiefly of Course Woolens for Women's petticoats, and Aprons.

27th Decʳ   Hard froſt laſt night and this day.

The Rebels have been tolerably quiet for some days paſt, and have not moleſted our advanced poſts.

28th Decʳ   Froſt, and some Snow.

A boat with a Lieutenant and 5 men belonging to a Rebel Privateer Sloop of 10 Guns, came on shore this morning on part of Brenton's neck. They were immediately seized by some of the troops quartered there, and brought to Headquarters. The vessel They belong to is off the point of the Eastern Main, and they were sent on shore by the Captain of her to obtain intelligence of the British, but did not know the town was in our posession. Orders were immediately sent to The Cerberus Frigate, which lay off Fogland Ferry in the Seconnet passage, to go in quest of her; and accordingly she slipt her Cable and went to Sea.

As the Alfred and her prizes are daily expected in, orders have been given to hoist the Rebel Colours upon the appearance of any vessels. The Ships in the harbour have struck their Colours, and the Commodores their broad pendants.

29ᵗʰ Decʳ   Hard frost.

There has been no arrival from New York since The troops landed here; so that we are totally ignorant of the operations of the Army under General Howe.

30ᵗʰ Decʳ   Frost. The Snow almost gone off.

The Redoubt constructed by the Rebels above Bristol Ferry, and abandoned by them, is ordered to be repaired and a Guard house to be erected therein for the accomodation of the advanced post. It is a much better situation for the advanced Guard than that they are now in, and the troops on duty will not be liable to accidents from the wanton firing of the Rebels on the opposite side.

31ˢᵗ Decʳ   Frost

The Cerberus has not yet returned from her search after the Rebel privateer that was off the Island a few days ago.

III

R. ISLAND

III

R. ISLAND

2nd June 1777

A Shower this Morning, which was very grateful after the heat of yesterday. Very fine day. Wind S. S. E.

The Kingsfisher sailed yesterday evening for New York.

A Brig taken by the Diamond, came in yesterday. She says she was chaced and brought to the Isis of 50 Guns, on the 31st May. There was a Sloop of War in company. On finding the Brig was a prize, they fired a gun and stood off. They would not communicate anything. The above ships are supposed to be part of the fleet expected from England.

3rd June   Fine weather. Wind S. E.

Three Soldiers of the 22^d Reg^t (all Germans) deserted last night.

A great Thunder-Storm this Evening. It began at 7 oClock, and continued till 11, with heavy rain, and frequent and very quick lightning. The rain will be of infinite service to the Country, as it was much wanted.

A Picquet of one of the Regiments on Windmill, is ordered to reinforce the advanced posts every evening 'till further orders.

4th June   Fine weather. Wind N. W.

This being the Anniversary of The King's birthday, 21 Guns were fired from the Park of Artillery at 12 o'Clock. The Ships of War fired at 1 o'Clock.

About 7 o'Clock this morning a Rebel Sloop weighed from Howland's ferry, and having a favorable wind she went to Sea. Seven shot were fired at her from the Redoubt at Fogland ferry, but without effect. She appeared to be Armed, and was full of men. It is surprizing the Commodore does not station a vessel in the Seconnet passage, to prevent those of the Enemy from going out in this manner. The Galley or an armed transport would be sufficient. The Diamond Frigate is now stationed near Dyer's Island; but as The Lark, and the Galley are advanced above her, she does not appear to be of any use there. She certainly would be of some service in the Seconnet.

At 12 oClock this day, a Privateer brig and an Armed Sloop came out of Providence River, and ſtood down the Bay. When they came as far as the N. end of Prudence the Brig went in by Warwick point, and the Sloop ſtood down towards our Galley, which was ſtationed ahead of the Lark near Papaſquaſh point. When she came within about a mile and half of her she fired a shot at the Galley, and then put about. The Galley immediately got under way and chaced her, but the Sloop having the advantage got off. The Galley then fired 2 18 prs at her, both of which fell short, on which she gave over the Chace and returned to her ſtation. When the Galley tacked the Sloop did the same, and kept plying back and forward in the bay till she was joined by the Brig, when they both made sail, and in the Evening returned towards Providence.

Several Sloops appeared in the mouth of Taunton River to day, and two of them came down to Howlands.

The Rebels fired a shot this morning at the relief of the guard at Briſtol ferry redoubt, which was returned by two from us, but without effect on either side.

It having been found this morning, and repreſented to General Prescott, that our battery at Fogland could not get so many shot at the Sloop which paſſed, as it could have done had the Guns been placed En Barbette, he ordered the Merlons to be taken down, which was completed by the Evening.

The Unicorn Frigate came in from a Cruize this day. She spoke with the Isis of 50 Guns, and the Swift Sloop off Block-Island yeſterday, bound to New York, having parted from their Convoy of 17 sail of Victuallers, &c, in a gale of wind. No particular news from Europe by the Isis.

5ᵗʰ June

A Rebel Sloop attempted to paſs the battery at Fogland this morning, in order to proceed to Sea; when the advantage of having the guns En Barbette was fully demonſtrated. Ten shot were fired at her before she came opposite the Redoubt, three of which ſtruck her, and damaged her so much that she was obliged to give up the attempt, and run into the bottom of the little bay behind the N. point of Fogland. She remained there till 6 in the Evening, when having a fair wind she went back to Howland's ferry. Our battery had four shot at her as she was going off, some of which fell very near her. Had the Battery been originally conſtructed in this manner, very few of the

Rebel vefsels would have been able to pafs, without being considerably damaged.

6th June   Fine weather.   Wind S. W.

The Rebels fired a shot this day at the Hefsian working party at Briftol ferry redoubt. It ftruck the inside of the Embrazure in which the 24 pr is placed, but did no damage. We returned them two shot.

7th —   A very hot day.   Little or no wind 'till the afternoon.

A Frigate has been seen off the mouth of the Seconnet pafsage all day, endeavoring to get into Newport. She appeared to have come from the Eaftward.

8th June   Fine weather.   Wind S. S. E.

We are very anxious at this time to have some accounts from New York, from whence we have not heard for near a Month. We are entirely [ignorant] of the operations of the Army under Genl Howe. Neither do we hear a syllable relative to the movements or operations of General Carleton's Army, upon the progrefs of which the succefs of the Campaign so much depends. By what we can learn from the Rebels, they are doing everything in thier power to afsemble a force sufficient to prevent General Carleton's Army from penetrating. As they muft be thoroughly convinced how very efsential it is to prevent, or retard his progrefs, I fear he will meet with many difficulties in his way to Albany. Every poft will be fortified, and every obftacle thrown in his way.

We hear The Centurion of 50 Guns is gone up Hudson's River as far as a place called Catskill. Her being ftationed there will prevent Washington's Army from receiving supplies from Albany and that Neighbourhood.

9th June   Fine weather.   Wind S. E.

The Country has a very beautiful appearance at present, and there is a fair prospect of our having plenty of every thing; except Beef and Mutton.

A Party of an officer and 50 men began to work this morning to throw down the Merlons of the 6 Gun Battery on Windmill hill, in order to give the Guns placed there, a better command of the adjacent ground. It certainly was extremely absurd to conftruct the battery originally with Embrazures, as the situation prevented an Enemy from bringing any guns againft it, and the trouble and expence of making them, during the severe weather in Winter was very great.

10th June   Thick fog from 12 last night 'till 8 this morning. Very fine day.   Wind S. E.

About half past 10 last night The Rebels made an attack upon the Subaltern's post on the road to Commonfence Neck. They had landed about 50 men in the bottom of a little bay between the two Necks; and having divided them into three of four parties, they advanced very silently towards the advanced Sentries, who, in consequence of the darknefs of the night, and their creeping up, did not perceive them, until they were within about 20 yards of them. The Sentry who first discovered them, fired his piece and retired to the Guard. The Rebels, finding they were discovered, rushed forward on all the Sentries, and got up to the Guard house just as the Guard was alarmed and turning out, and having nearly surrounded the house, they fired a good many shot at our men, by which one was killed on the spot, and three wounded, two of them mortally. Our men having recovered themselves a little, fired very very briskly on the Rebels, and in lefs than five minutes they were beaten off, and dispersed. As The night was so very dark, and the number of the Rebels then uncertain, our Guard did not venture to pursue them. The Picquets having come up on the first alarm to support the advanced posts, patroles were immediately sent out; but they could discover nothing of the Enemy, except the noise of their Oars in going off in thier boats. The lofs of the Rebels could not be ascertained; but some of our men heard one of them say, "The adjutant is wounded."

I went over the ground this morning, and could plainly observe the tracks of three of their parties as they advanced and retreated, but could see no marks of wounded men.

Had the Rebels being pofsefsed of resolution equal to their cunning, and advanced to the doors of the house without firing, they must have destroyed most of the Guard, as the common precautions of having the whole of the men loaded, and one third of them constantly under arms throughout the night, had been neglected. The Rebels had thier pieces loaded with a ball and 3 Buckshot each.

The two men who were mortally wounded, died this day. So that the 54th lost two men, and the 22nd one. The man slightly wounded belongs to the 54th Regiment.

Sketch of the Ground
about the Subaltern's
Post — 10.th June 1777

Here the Rebels
partly landed.
9.th June 1777

Track of the Rebels to attack the post

Sandford's Orchard

Part of Common Fence Neck.

Part of The Townpond.

Sentries.

Redoubt.

Guard house

11th June   Fair, pleasant weather. Wind S. E.

It has been determined to throw up a slight work round the house in which the Subaltern's guard is posted near Common-fence neck. A very small Redoubt, capable of holding about 20 men, was constructed in front of it last Winter when the Hessians did the duty at that post; but the late attack was so sudden, that the guard had not time to throw themselves into it. Had it been made round the house, as I proposed to the Hessian Engineer last winter, it is probable the late misfortune would not have happened.

The Rebels, in the late attack, were certainly conducted by some persons who were perfectly well acquainted with the ground and the situation of the post.

12th June   Rain some part of last night, and most of this day. Wind S. E.

Another party of Rebels came on the Neck last night, and about 2 o'Clock this morning, having formed in small parties opposite most of the advanced Sentries of the Subaltern's post, commenced a fire upon them, but they were so well received by the Sentries and a part of the Guard which advanced immediately to their support, that they could make no impression; and after a good deal of firing they were driven off. No person was hurt on our side. Our men heard two of the Rebels cry out they were wounded. The situation and nature of the ground of the two necks, gives these fellows many advantages in these night attacks. They have a secure retreat by land or by water; and as there is no ascertaining their numbers by night, it would not be prudent to attempt advancing upon them with a small number of men; so that they have it in their power to insult our Sentries with impunity.

Came in The Cerberus from a Cruize.

Came in also The Flora from New York. She has brought a number of letters which came from Europe in the March Packet. It appears by the New York papers, that General Carleton's Army was within 7 miles of Ticonderoga the beginning of May, and had then met with no opposition.

Near 4000 men have arrived lately at New York from Europe.

13th June   Some rain. Wind N. E.

The Rebels came and fired at our advanced Sentries again last night; but they hardly ever shewed themselves. No hurt

done. There were some straggling parties of them on the Necks
at different times during this day, but they did not venture to
come within shot of the Sentries.

Several boats full of Rebel troops pafsed over from Mount
Hope to Howland's ferry.

A Rebel Frigate of 28 or 30 Guns, attended by a Brig, and
some smaller vefsels, came out of Providence River this morning, and anchored below the Narrows, about 5 miles on this side
of Providence. It is supposed they will attempt to go to Sea the
first fair wind.

14th June   Fine weather.   Wind W.
The Rebel vefsels remain at anchor below the Narrows.

Two Rebel officers came with a flag of truce to our advanced
Sentries on Howland's neck this morning. They had a letter
directed to Gen¹ Smith, the purport of which was, to desire he
would permit an old man to come on the Island. Gen¹ Smith
would not receive the letter, and ordered them to be again informed, that no flags of truce would be permitted to come near
our posts for the future. They went off seemingly much displeased with their reception, and said they did not treat our
flags of truce in that manner.

The Kingsfisher came in this Evening from New York.

15th June   Some rain the latter part of the day.   Wind S.
A Sloop of about 25 Tons came into the Seconnet pafsage
early this morning, and anchored under the Camp of the Hefsian
chafseurs below Fogland ferry. Two men immediately came
ashore from her. They say they came out of Stonington in Connecticut last night, with an intention of going into Newport, but
that they mistook the entrance. The Sloop is thier own property, and has about 50 bushels of Indian Corn, and Seven Casks
of bread on board. These men say that the Rebels will hardly
suffer any person to remain in the Country who will not inlist,
and that rather than take up arms against The King, they have
left their families and all they are worth, at the mercy of the
Rebels, and have made thier escape here in this small Sloop.
The Rebels find it very difficult to get men to fill up the Companies for their Quota of the Continental Army, or even to engage for the defence of the Province of Connecticut. They say
the Oliver Cromwell Privateer of 20 Guns, went out of New
London about 14 days ago.

16th June — Very fine morning. No wind 'till 12. Then S. E. Foggy in the afternoon, and heavy rain from 6 o'Clock.

By the laſt accounts from New York, part of the troops were then Embarking. Their deſtination was quite uncertain, but it was generally imagined they were going up the Delawar to attack Philadelphia on that side, while the reſt of the Army advanced towards it through Jersey.

17th June — Fine weather. Wind W.

A Prize taken by The Unicorn, was brought in today. She has 1200 barrels of flour on board.

Sir Peter Parker gave an entertainment on board the Chatham, to above 50 Ladies and Gentlemen.

18th June — Fair pleasant weather. Wind W.

A small Schooner came round Papasquash point laſt night about 9 o'Clock, and went into Briſtol bay. She was firſt discovered by the Galley, which gave the alarm, and it was repeated by the Lark and Diamond, as it was imagined she was a fire veſsel. About 9 this morning she paſsed through Briſtol ferry to Howland's, and had nine shot fired at her from our Redoubt, one of which ſtruck her, but the damage did not prevent her from paſsing on.

Our Galley went down to the Chatham this Evening.

19th June — Fine weather. Wind N. W.

Yeſterday Evening a Rebel Brig came down from Providence, and ſtood towards Papasquash point as if she intended to go into Briſtol bay; but about 7 o'Clock she tacked & appeared to be going back again. At 1 o'Clock this morning the Lark made a Signal that a veſsel was coming down, & soon after perceived her going round the point into the bay, and fired several Shot at her; but the diſtance was too great to do her any damage. She proved to be the abovementioned Brig; and about 2 this morning she came out of Briſtol bay, and having the advantage of Wind & Tide, she soon paſsed our battery. Seven shot were fired at her, one of which ſtruck her, but as it was dark the effect could not be perceived. She ſtood up the bay, and at day break anchored off Mount Hope. A Sloop came round Papasquash point with the Brig; but she did not chuse to attempt paſsing our battery, and therefore anchored in the bay, where she now lies. If our Galley had been at her Station, and followed the

Brig through the ferry, it is probable she would have taken her. The brig appeared to be the one of 14 Guns which came out of Taunton river some time ago, and went up to Providence.

The whole Rebel fleet may get out if they have only the spirit to risque a few shot from our Batteries as they paſs, for as our Frigates are now ſtationed they cannot prevent them, if they take the proper advantages of Winds & Tides.

The Kingsfisher resumed her Station in the Seconnet paſsage this morning.

The 22^d Regiment marched this morning from the Encampment on Windmill-hill, and encamped on Quaker hill, fronting the Seconnet, and with their left to the Meetinghouse. Two 6 p^{rs} are poſted with the 22^d. By this change the communication along the Eaſt side of the Island is better kept up, and the position of the troops rendered much more secure.

Two Officers horses which were grazing near the Encampment on Windmill hill, forced their way paſt the advanced Sentries at the bridge on Howland's Neck, and were taken by some Rebels from the other side who observed them.

The Niger Frigate arrived yeſterday from New York, with several transports under Convoy, having on board near 500 drafts and Recruits, and the Camp Equipage for the Regiments on this Island. When the Fleet left New York, the Army had moved into Jersey, and an attack on Washington's Army (consiſting of about 10,000 men, poſted in the hills behind Boundbrook and Quibbletown) was daily expected.

20th June.

A party of Rebels advanced laſt night towards our Sentries on the bridge at Howland's Neck, but as the Sentries and one of the Patroles fired a good many shot at them, they soon disappeared.

About 5 this morning the Rebel Sloop which lay in Briſtol bay got under way, and having a light fair wind at N. W. paſsed through the ferry. The Lark fired some shot at her at the diſtance of near two miles, all of which fell short. Eleven shot were fired at her from our Redoubt, one of which, a 24 p^r ſtruck her in the broadside, and caused great confusion on board; but she got through without any visible damage, & went round to Howland's ferry where she anchored. She appears to be a Privateer, and mounts about 10 Carriage guns besides Swivels, and was full of men. She is a very handsome Sloop, quite clean, and well rigged. She fired three or four shot at the

Redoubt as she pafsed. One half of a Doubleheaded 6 l^b Shot struck the Abbattis and was taken up.

The Brig which lay near Mount hope, was seen at anchor up Taunton River this morning. It is highly probable they will both go to Sea the firſt fair wind after the dark nights come on.

If the Galley had been up, and gone through the ferry after the Sloop, she must have galled her exceedingly with the 18 p^{rs} she carries in her bow. Our armed vefsels have very little to apprehend from the Rebel battery at Briſtol ferry. They muſt have seen that with our four Guns we have seldom done any material damage to the many Rebel vefsels which have pafsed; and the Rebels have but two Guns in their Battery, and not near so well served.

The Drafts and Recruits lately arrived for the British and Hefsian Regiments, disembarked this morning and joined their respective Corps.

21st June — Fine weather. Wind N. E.

A Rebel Brig has been sailing about the upper part of the Bay near Providence all day. The Frigate remains below the Narrows.

Our Galley is now Stationed near the Greyhound off Greenwich.

22nd June — Fine weather. Wind S. W.

A Sloop came down from Providence and about 2 oClock this afternoon pafsed round Papasquash point into Briſtol bay. The Lark fired 11 Shot at her, but without effect. The ship is at too great a diſtance from that point to be able by her fire to prevent vefsels from pafsing it.

Yeſterday and this day the Rebels have been busily employed in making a work on the hill above Howland's ferry where their guns have been placed all the Winter. It appears to be very extensive, and muſt coſt them a great deal of labour, as there is little or no soil on the hill.

23rd June — Rain, and thick fog moſt part of the day. Strong wind at S. E.

24th — A very warm day. Wind S. W.

The Sloop which lay in Briſtol bay, pafsed through the ferry laſt night under favor of the Fog, without being discovered. She was observed at anchor under Mount-Hope this morning.

25th June — Fine weather. Wind S.

Two shot were fired from our battery at Fogland at a boat which was rowing near the opposite shore; but without effect.

The Rebels have been very quiet for some days past, & have hardly appeared on either of the Necks.

26th — Fine weather. Wind S.

Some Rebels came and fired at the advanced Sentries last night, but having found them alert, and received their fire, they went off again.

We are extremely anxious to hear something of the operations of General Howe's Army in Jersey, and of Genl Carleton's to the Northward.

27th June   Foggy weather, but warm.   Wind S. E.

Came in a Schooner taken by the Unicorn, laden with Rum, Sugar, and some Pepper, from Boston to Egg-harbour.

28th — Great Thunder and Lightning, with heavy rain, most part of last night. Fair day, but very warm. Wind S.

The Rebels have erected a Flag staff in their New work above Howland's ferry: and this afternoon they hoisted the Rebel Colours on it; on which occasion they fired an 18 lb shot at our Guard near the bridge, which fell short.

29th June   Fine weather.   Wind S.

The Work which the Rebels have constructed on the hill above Howland's ferry appears to be irregular in its figure, but very extensive. From the situation, it must be strong.

30th June

Dull thick weather, inclining to rain.   No wind.

The Rebels fired two shot this morning from their New Fort, at some Recruits of the 54th Regiment who were firing at a mark near the Water side. The shot did not reach them altho fired at a very great Elevation.

Our Artillery officers are surprized at the distance which the Rebels throw their shot; and say that the quantity of Powder, and the Elevation required to throw them so far as they do, must damage the Gun Carriage, and endanger the bursting the Gun. By firing at such an Elevation they can never hope to do execution, except by mere chance, as the shot falls like a Shell, and buries itself immediately.

Two Negroes came over from Naraganset this day. They say the Country people are in the greatest confusion, and that many of those on the Coast, are removing farther into the interior, as they expect to be visited by The King's troops. That the paper money is so much depreciated, that hardly anything is to be got for it. That the Currency of one Province will not pass in another. That provisions are scarce and dear, and very little Corn to be had; — and that they find it so difficult to raise men for the Continental Army, that they inlist Negroes, for whom their owners receive a bounty of 180 Dollars, and half their pay; and the Negro gets the other half, and a promise of freedom at the end of three years.

1st July 1777   Fair weather. Wind S. E.

The Rebels are extremely cautious of late in passing Fogland ferry in craft or boats. As a proof of it, some fellows who came up from Seconnet point a few days ago in a boat, rather than run the risque of a few shot from our battery, landed in the Bay within the S. point, carried their boat on their Shoulders across the Isthmus, and then launched her, and proceeded up to Howland's.

2d July   Fine weather. Wind N.

A Soldier of the 43rd Regiment deserted last night from the advanced post at Commonfence Neck.

A flag of truce came down from Providence this Evening; but was not suffered to come any farther than The Lark.

3rd — Very fine weather. Wind N. E.

The flag of truce Sloop went back this morning. The people on board her say there has been a Skirmish in Jersey; but as they have mentioned no particulars, nor brought any Newspapers with them, we conclude the affair has ended to their disadvantage.

4th July   Fine weather. Wind S.

This being the first Anniversary of the declaration of the Independency of the Rebel Colonies, they ushered in the morning at Providence by firing 13 Cannon, (One for each Colony we suppose). At 12 o'Clock the three Rebel Frigates that lie at and near Providence fired 13 Guns each, and at one, 13 Guns were fired from their Fort at Howland's ferry. At Sunset the Rebel Frigates fired another round of 13 Guns each, one after the

other. As the Evening was very still and fine, the Eccho of the
Guns down the Bay had a very grand effect, the report of each
being repeated three or four times. Several Guns were fired
during the day, from other places in the adjacent Country. It
being usual with us, for Forts or Garrisons to fire at 12 o'Clock,
and the Ships at 1, on rejoicing days, we suppose they chose to
reverse it, for the sake of differing from our mode.

We are in great hopes thier independence has had a severe
blow before this. Some Women who came down in the last
Cartel say, that an expref s had arrived at Providence a few
days before they left that place, with an account of there having been an Action in Jersey; but no particulars had trans-
pired. If it had been favorable to them, we should have heard
enough of it.

5th July — A very warm day. The heat has been greater than
we have had hitherto. Wind S.

The Unicorn arrived this afternoon with a Privateer Sloop of
4 Guns, 8 Swivels and 40 men, which she captured off Nantucket; also with a Small Sloop from St Martin's to Boston,
laden with Rum, &c. The Unicorn is sheathed with Copper, and
outsails every thing she sees.

A Soldier of the 43rd was drowned this Evening. It is imagined he did it wilfully, as a paper was found in his Cloathes on
the shore, indicating such a design. He was seen part of the way
over towards the Rebel shore at Bristol ferry, and heard to call
for afsistance: The Rebels also called to him, but as they dared
not to put out a boat, he soon disappeared. He mentioned, in
the paper which was found, his having left a wife and child
desolate in England.

6th July.   Fine weather. Wind S.

A Soldier of the 43rd Regt shot himself last night in the rear of
the Camp. The discovery of a Connection he had with a married woman of the same Regiment, appears to have been the
cause of this rash action.

I cannot help observing here, that a Soldier of the 22d Regiment shot himself through the body, (of which he languished
about 12 days) and that another Soldier of the 43rd cut himself
with a Razor acrofs the wrists, since we have been encamped.
Several Soldiers also have deserted, some of them men of good
Characters who were not suspected of such an act. I am in-

clined to believe that many of these things proceed from our having remained so long in a State of inactivity. The Soldiers have nothing to do but to mount Guard once in three or four days. We attempt nothing against the Enemy by which their minds might be engaged; and as most of them have for the two last years been accustomed to a quick succefsion of interesting actions and circumstances which have engaged their thoughts and kept their bodies in activity, their present inactive state, while all the rest of the Army is in Motion, naturally leads some to gloomy reflections, and induces others to commit actions disgraceful to themselves, hurtful to the discipline of the Army, and destructive to the Cause of their Country. If we were to undertake little enterprizes against the Enemy, in which we could run no risque, it would employ the minds of the Soldiery, give them something to do and to talk of, fit them for the undertaking and execution of those of a more arduous and serious nature, and would at the same time teach the young Soldiers and give them confidence. Such enterprizes would also prevent the Enemy from undertaking anything against us, and would harrafs them greatly. A Contrary conduct invites them to make attempts, makes them insolent on finding they may be effected with impunity, and tends much to dispirit our own men.

7th July.   Very fine weather, and not too hot. Wind S.

A fine Sea breeze, which generally comes in about 10 o'Clock in the Morning, at this Season, and continues 'till Sunset, moderates the heat greatly, and makes this Island a delightful residence during the extreme heats of the Summer Months.

The Sea breeze seldom extends so far up the bay as Providence. We can frequently observe, when there is a fresh breeze from the Southward which agitates the Surface of the water all round this Island, that at some distance above Prudence Island the water is as smooth as if there was not a breath of air stirring. In fact the breeze dies away somewhat to the Northward of Prudence.

This Island used, before the War, to be much frequented by families from the West Indies, and the Carolinas, during the Summer months.

8th July.   Fine morning. Wind S. Cool in the afternoon.

By a person who was taken in the Sloop from St Martin's we learn, that The Beaver Sloop of War of 14 Guns, had taken The

Oliver-Cromwell, a Continental Frigate of 26 Guns and 225 men, after a smart Engagement off St Vincents, into which Island she was carried. The Rebel was at first cautious of attacking the Beaver, but was induced to follow her by Stratagem.

9th — Rain and thick fog most part of the day. Wind S. E.

10th July. Fair pleasant weather. Wind N. E.

A Soldier of the 54th Regt deserted last night from the advanced post at Commonfence Neck. As the Rebels have small parties on the Necks almost every night, and our deserters go immediately to the farthest point, it is very difficult to prevent them from getting off.

Two men came in this morning by way of Howland's ferry. They had been for some time confined in Taunton Jail, from whence they made their escape; and have been for 12 days past skulking in the woods and waiting for an opportunity to get on the Island, which they effected yesterday Evening by favor of the Fog.

11th July 1777

A little before 12 o'Clock last night, a party of Rebels landed behind Genl Smith's late quarters at Redwood's, about 5 miles N. of Newport, from whence they advanced very silently to General Prescott's quarters at Mr Overing's on the W. road. They surrounded the house about 10 minutes before 12, seized the Sentry, who had challenged twice, but who, not being loaded, could give no further alarm, and immediately forced open all the doors, they then went directly into the Chambers, where they laid hold of Genl Prescott, and Lieu^t Barrington, his aide-de-Camp, and in about 7 minutes quitted the house, taking the General, Lieu^t Barrington, and the Sentry with them, returned to their boats by the way they came, and immediately went off. Some of the party broke open Mr Overing's Chamber door, as also that of his Son, and endeavored to take them also, but after some struggling, and being in haste, they let them go. They took with them two small Silver Cups, a Great Coat, a Book, and some other trifles, and broke to pieces a large looking Glafs in the Parlour. They allowed the General to take his Clothes, except one Stocking, which could not be found in the hurry; but Lieu^t Barrington had nothing but his breeches and shirt on. The Rebels were in so great a hurry to

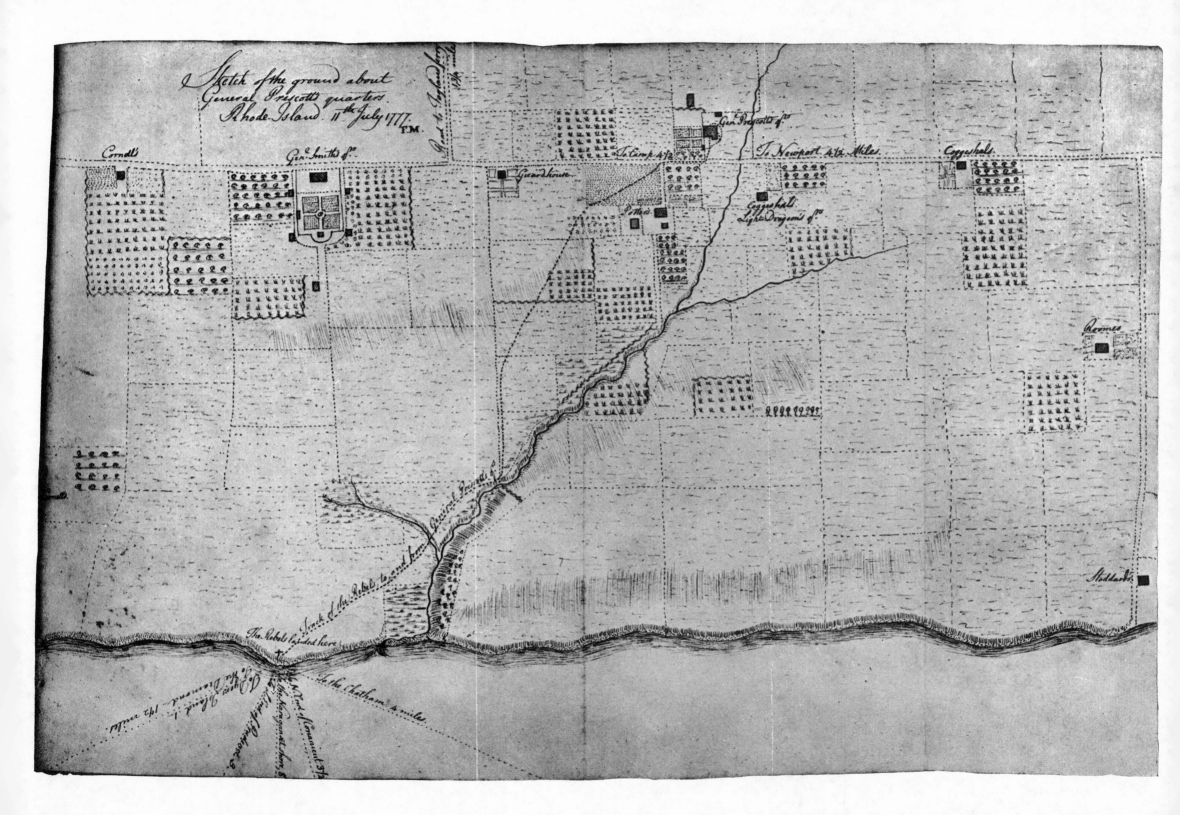

Sketch of the ground about
General Prescott's quarters
Rhode Island. 11th July 1777.
T.M.

Cornell's

Gen.l Smith's q.rs

Road to Oxford Ferry

Gen.l Prescott's q.rs

To Camp 4½

To Newport 4½ Miles.

Coggeshals

Guardhouse

Potter's

Coggeshall
Light Dragoon's q.rs

Reomes

General Prescott's q.rs

Stoddard's

Track of the Rebels to and from General Prescott's q.rs

The Rebels landed here

To the Chatham 4 miles

be gone, that they did not take some money which was in the General's room, nor a pair of pistols which hung up in Mr Barrington's.

A Dragoon who lay over the Kitchen, as soon as he found they had quitted the house, ran to the Guard house, which was about 300 yards from the General's quarters, but on being Challenged by the Sentry there, his fears made him imagine the Rebels had surprized and taken the Guard also, on which he ran back to Mr Overing's. Soon after a Negro fellow went and informed the Guard what had happened, who immediately came to the house, but as the night was very dark, and the Rebels had gone off with great silence, they could not discover which way they went, or which way to pursue. The Dragoon had by this time got his horse, and rode as fast as possible to the Camp at Fogland ferry, and there gave the first alarm. Parties were immediately sent out along shore to thier right, as it was imagined the Rebels had landed on the East side. The Dragoon then went to the Encampment of the 22^d Reg^t on Quaker hill, from whence Col^o Campbell sent parties acrofs the Island with orders to patrole down the W. Shore. About 2 oClock the alarm was given at the Camp at Windmill hill, from whence parties were also sent, and 2 Guns and a Rocket fired, as a Signal to the Ships up the Bay; but as there was no wind, they had no conception of the cause, and therefore did not send out any boats. Many parties were sent out in different directions, but to no effect, as the Rebels had gone off long before any of them reached the place where they took to thier boats. On going along the W. Shore, we found the place where they had landed, and as there was a heavy dew on the ground we could trace their track up to the house and back again. By appearances the party did not consist of more than 30 men. One Barton, a hatter of Providence was known among them by Mr Overing, and appeared to have the Command of the party. We imagine they came in two Whaleboats from the Naraganset shore, and that they returned the same way; which was very practicable, as the distance between the Chatham & The Diamond is near 5 miles; and that between the Renown and The Greyhound on the other side about the same, and no vefsel stationed between them. The place they landed at is directly oppofsite to the pafsage between the N. point of Cononicut, and the S. point of Prudence. The distance to the Naraganset shore is about 7 or 8 Miles.

Diſtances — R. Island

From the threshold of M[r] Overing's door to the place where the Rebels landed, following the track the Rebels came to the house, and went with General Prescott . . . . 1733 yards

From M[r] Overing's gate to the Guard house . . . . 466 yards
From the Guard house to Gen[l] Smith's gate . . . . 390 yards

Measured by Cap[t] F——.   Royal Artillery ——

General Prescott having a good deal of buſineſs to transact in Newport, and being desirous of being near the Camp at night, in case anything should happen, had fixed his quarters at M[r] Overing's, to which house he always came at night, and from whence he returned to town in the Morning. As he did not wish to encrease the duty of the troops, he had only a Guard of a Corporal and 7 men, at a house on the road about 300 yards from him, and which furnished a Sentry at his door. Four Light Dragoons were quartered at a house on the other side of the road, about 100 yards off. M[r] Overing's house is at leaſt 3/4 of a mile from the shore. In this situation and considering the ſtations of the several ships on the W. side of the Island, he thought himself secure from any insult: and altho it had been frequently suggeſted to him, that an attempt of this nature was practicable, it had not sufficient weight with him to induce him to move, or to take any further precautions.

The Rebels certainly run a great risk in making this attempt; as a shot fired by the Sentry would have given the Alarm, and a Single boat falling in with them, would in all probability have fruſtrated their design. They however executed it in a maſterly manner, and deserve credit for the attempt. It is certainly a moſt extraordinary circumſtance, that a General Commanding a body of 4000 men, encamped on an Island surrounded by a Squadron of Ships of War, should be carried off from his quarters in the night by a small party of the Enemy from without, & without a Shot being fired.

The Manner in which this enterprize was conducted, is a convincing proof that the Enemy receive from some of the Inhabitants of this Island, the moſt perfect intelligence of every circumſtance of which they wish to be informed. Some of those concerned in the execution of it, knew the ground perfectly well, particularly Barton who had been quartered at the house opposite for some time; and they muſt have been thoroughly well informed of the position of the Guards and Sentries, as they could not pofsibly have come a nearer, or a better way to the house.

It appears by the accounts published in the Rebel papers, that General Howe advanced lately to Somerset Court-house; about 7 miles beyond Brunswick, with a view of drawing the Rebel Army out of their ſtrong Camp; but that not finding his Scheme answer, he had retired from thence to Brunswick, and finally to Amboy, burning and deſtroying the Country between those places. They also say, that the latter end of June, he was embarking his Army, and on the point of quitting Jersey entirely. They supposed he intended to proceed up the North River, in order to endeavor to join, or favor the movements of General Carleton's Army. This retreat from Jersey seems to have given them great spirits.

12th July 1777.   Rain moſt part of laſt night, and 'till 3 this afternoon.   Thick weather.   Wind E.

The Command on this Island, & of the troops ſtationed here, devolves on Brigadier General Smith.

A flag of truce was sent up this day to Providence with a letter to Mr Cooke the Rebel Governor, and some things for the better accomodation of Genl Prescott and Lt Barrington, in their present situation.

The Rebel privateer which was brought in here laſt week was manned this day from the Chatham, and the Command of her given to Lieut Deane, 1st Lieut of that ship.   She sailed at 6 o'Clock this Evening for New York, with letters from Sir Peter Parker and General Smith to Lord, and Genl Howe, giving an account of the late unfortunate event.   Captain Welsh, Aide de-Camp to Genl Prescott, was the bearer of General Smith's letter.

General Howe's late movement from Brunswick towards Philadelphia, appears to have been made with a view to draw the Rebel Army from a very ſtrong position which it had taken in order to attempt saving that City, by which he might have had an opportunity of attacking them with advantage; but as Washington could not be induced to move either by that, or the appearance of a haſty retreat, which Genl Howe made back to Brunswick; it is probable the General thought it would only be waſting the Campaign to attempt any further operations in Jersey; and that he has it now in view to form a Junction or co-operate with our Northern army, or to fall upon the New England Provinces. If the former is the plan, and succeeds, he will probably leave a ſtrong force to guard New York, and the left bank of the North River, while with the Main body he enters New England, as those provinces for their demerits deſerve the moſt severe Chaſtisement. It is to be hoped, so severe an example will be made of them, as may induce the other Provinces to submit without further exertions.

When the situation of Philadelphia is considered; that it is an open town in a flat Country, and, if poſseſsed, would require a very considerable force to maintain it, which would weaken the further operations of the Army; that at this Season of the year the great heats render the climate an improper one to carry on Military operations in; that it would separate the Army too much, and not in the laſt contribute to the progreſs of General Carleton's Army, which certainly should be the great objeſt of the Campaign; it will not appear of much consequence that Genl Howe has given up that point. The principal advantage which might be expeſted from the poſseſsion of Philadelphia, is, that the Inhabitants of Penſylvania would then be induced to break off from the Rebel Confederacy, and aſsiſt in reſtoring Peace and their former happy Government; — but when it is considered that the majority of the people in that Province are Quakers, from whom no exertion of that nature is to be expeſted, the poſseſsion of that City does not appear to be an objeſt of importance. The chief ſtrength of the Rebels lying in the New England Provinces, if they are subdued, no material opposition will be made by the others; — and if there should, the fall of the year, and Winter are the beſt Seasons for carrying on War againſt them.

13th July — Rain moſt part of this day, with thick weather. Wind N. E. and cold.

About day break a Rebel Sloop came from Sea, and attempted to paſs our Battery at Fogland ferry. The 2nd Shot that was fired, ſtruck her; on which she immediately put about. Four shot more were fired at her before she got out of reach, one of which ſtruck her. She then anchored a short diſtance from the S. point of Fogland. About 8 o'Clock the Rebels brought down two pieces of Cannon into their battery there in order to proteſt her; and in the mean time they were busily employed in unloading her. Had The Kingsfisher discovered this Sloop when she came in, and sent her boats manned and armed after her, they would certainly have taken her, as she appears to have very few hands on board, and not armed.

If the two Medium 12 p^rs from the Artillery park had been brought down to the shore, they would have annoyed her greatly, or obliged her to have run lower down, where she could not be protected by their guns; but as the Rebels had two guns in their battery, it was not thought adviseable to run any risk for the sake of obliging her to move. I think however it might have been done without any danger; and if she weighed, the wind was so strong at N. E. she could not have got nearer their shore. If she run lower down she would have been taken by the Kingsfisher. She will be unloaded, and get off before morning.

Four small Sloops and a Schooner have lain all this day in the Stream at Howland's ferry; and it is probable they will endeavor to go out this night, if the wind continues fair.

The flag of truce returned this Evening from Providence River. The Rebels stopped her at their Frigate, which lies at the Narrows, and would not suffer Captain Barry (The town Major who went up with the letter) to go to Providence. The letter was addressed to Mr Cooke, the Rebel Governor, but as he was absent, Mr Stephen Hopkins, who signs himself President of the Council, answered it, from which answer, and a letter from Genl Prescott it appears, that he is on his parole, has lodgings in Providence, and is civilly treated. His Servant, and the things sent up, were conveyed to him. He is soon to be removed to Lebanon, in Connecticut. The Rebels told Captain Barry, that they attempted the enterprize, entirely with a view to have a person in their hands as an equivalent for General Lee.

The following account of the Capture of Genl Prescott, is taken from the Providence paper.

"*Providence, 12th July 1777*"

"Thursday Evening last, a party of 38 men of the troops "belonging to this State, under the Command of Lt Col^o Wil-"liam Barton of this town, accompanied by Major Adams of "the train, Captain Phillips, Lieu^ts Potter & Babcock, and "Ensigns Stanton & Wilcocks, went in five Boats from Warwick "Neck, with a view to take Major Genl Prescott, Commander "in Chief of the British and Hessian Troops on Rhode Island,

"whose quarters were then at a house about 4 miles from New-
"port. The Colonel and his party, after pafsing the Enemies
"ships and guard boats, landed about 12 at night, and with,
"*Infinite addrefs and Gallantry*, got to Prescott's quarters undis-
"covered. A Sentinel at the door hailed, but was immediately
"secured, and the party inftantly breaking open the doors and
"entering the house, took the General in bed. His Aide de
"Camp leaped from a window in his shirt, and attempted to
"make his escape, but was taken a few rods from the house.
"The party soon after returned to their boats with the prison-
"ers; and some time after they had put off the Enemy fired
"Rockets from their several pofts, as signals for an alarm; *but*
"*too late: the bird had fled*. The prisoners were safely landed
"about day break at Warwick-Neck. On receiving intelligence
"here, a Coach was immediately sent, and the General, with his
"aide-de-Camp, attended by Col° Barton and some other Offi-
"cers, arrived in town about 12 o'Clock. This bold and im-
"portant enterprize muft reflect the higheft honor on Col°
"Barton and his little party.
  "A Lieut Col° of Horse, with at leaft 70 Light Dragoons, took
"Major General Lee (betrayed by a Tory) five miles from his
"troops; A Lieut Col° of Foot, with only 38 Privates & 6 Offi-
"cers, has taken a Commander in Chief, when almoft encircled
"by an Army & Navy." *

It appears from some Rebel papers brought down, that our
Northern Army has taken Ticonderoga; but that the Rebels had
retired to a hill near the Fort, which they had fortified ftrongly,
and where they expected to be invefted. It appears also, that
Gen¹ Howe's Army had quitted Jersey entirely, had embarked
his whole Army, and when the laft accounts came away, was at
the Narrows, Staten Island. The Rebels supposed he intended
going up the North River.

14ᵗʰ July.   Fine weather.   Wind N. E.
The Rebel Sloop which came from Sea yefterday, went in the
night into a Creek to the Southward of Fogland. It is supposed
she has unloaded her Cargo, and is waiting for an opportunity
to go to Sea again. The Rebel vefsels which lay at Howland's
ferry yefterday, moved in the night; but it is uncertain where

* See Howe's letter to the British Ministry, Relative to the Capture of General
Lee.

they are gone to, as none of them were to be seen this morning, and they were not observed to have Paſsed Fogland ferry.

The Rebels had some small parties on the Necks laſt night, and there was some firing at the advanced poſts; but we had no person hurt. Some persons were also seen laſt night behind Gen¹ Smith's late quarters. Some of them came up near the house; — The Guards fired a few shots at, and pursued them, but they got off. I believe they were only some fellows who wanted to ſteal the poultry.

15ᵗʰ July.   Fine weather.   Strong S. Wind after 1 o'Clock.
A Cartel Sloop came in from Connecticut. The Rebels say that Ticonderoga was taken by Storm, and that they had 2,700 killed.

16ᵗʰ — Very fine pleasant weather.   Wind S.

17ᵗʰ July — Fine weather.   Wind S.
Two Soldiers (one of the 43ʳᵈ & the other of the 54ᵗʰ) deserted from the advanced poſt at the Bridge laſt night.
A veſsel arrived from New York this afternoon. She brings an account that General Pigot is coming here to take the Command.

18ᵗʰ — Very fine weather, and not hot.   Wind S.
A Soldier of the 54ᵗʰ deserted laſt night. The Rebels send over some people to the Necks almoſt every evening about Sunset. They do this principally to induce our men to desert, by shewing them how easy it is for them to get off.

19ᵗʰ July — A Warm day.   Wind S.
At 6 in the Evening a Rebel Galley came down from Providence towards Papasquash point, and fired three Cannon shot at The Lark. The ship got under way immediately and chaced her, but she run up towards Warren. When the Lark was returning near the Point, the Rebels began to fire at her from thence, which was briskly returned. She soon after anchored in her former Station. This Manoeuvre appears to have been entirely with a view to draw the ship near the point, that they might have a few shots at her. The Rebels have not had any Cannon on the point for some time paſt, so that the fire from thence was quite unexpected. One shot, an 18 pʳ ſtruck the ship near the Larboard Main Chains, but did no damage.

20th July.   Warm weather. Wind S.

Came in a vessel from New York, with dispatches to Sir Peter Parker. He is made a Rear Admiral of The Blue, and his Flag is hourly expected in The Swan Sloop of War, in which Major General Pigot is embarked, in order to take the Command of the troops in this Island.

The Rebels were so mean as to fire a Cannon shot this morning from their Battery at Bristol Ferry, at four Inhabitants who were Moving in a field near the Water side. The shot fell short of them.

21st July.   A very warm day, for this Island.   Wind S.

At 12 o'Clock arrived The Swan Sloop of War with Major General Pigot, who landed soon after, and was received by a Lieutenant and 30 Hessians with the proper honors.

Sir P. Parker having received his Flag, it was hoisted at one o'Clock, and saluted by all the Ships of his Squadron in the harbour.

The Niger Frigate came down the Sound yesterday with a fleet of 22 sail of Victuallers bound for England & Ireland; & parted with the Swan off the E. end of Long Island.

General de Heister, Commander in Chief of the Hessian troops in America, is gone home in The Niger, having been directed by The Landgrave to repair to Court in order to lay before him the exact State of the Hessian troops. 'Tis said The Landgrave is exceedingly displeased with the behavior of The Hessians in the affair at Trenton; and has ordered a strict examination to be made into the Conduct of every Officer concerned therein.

Those Regiments who lost thier Colours there, are not to have any others until they have distinguished themselves in some future Action.

The Command of The Hessian Troops in America devolves upon Lieu^t General Knyphausen.

22^d July — Rain all last night, and a thick fog. Wind S. E. Rain this day, and thick warm weather.

The Army under Genl Howe was embarked, and expected to sail from New York, on the 18th July; but the destination was kept so profound a Secret, that there was no forming any probable conjecture of the place they were intended for.

Lieu^t Genl Sir Henry Clinton, who arrived lately at New York from England, is appointed to remain at New York, and to have the Command of all the troops in the following posts, vizt New York Island, Paulus-hook, Kingsbridge, Long Island, Staten Island, and Rhode Island; — which in fact are all the places we posſeſs in these Colonies, from Georgia to New Hampshire, Inclusive.

We hope that Genl Howe's plan, whatever it is, will be crowned with all posſible succeſs.

23rd July — Rain laſt night. A very fine day. Wind S. W.

General Pigot came from town, and visited all the Poſts on the N. part of the Island.

A person who came lately from Boſton says, that the utmoſt diſtreſs and discontent prevails there. Provisions are very scarce and dear in the town, beef being 18d Sterling a pound, and other things in proportion. The Country people will not sell things for the paper money at the prices fixed by the Committees; nor will the Shopkeepers sell their goods at the Regulated prices; so that it is with difficulty they are prevented from coming to blows. The farmers publickly declare their wishes that The King's troops were there again; and talk of the plenty of hard money they had when they were there.

24th July — Fine weather. Wind S. W.

The Rebels have been working all day at their battery at Papasquash point, and in the Evening they fired three shot from thence at The Lark; but they all fell short.

The Swan Sloop sailed this Evening for New York, with 4 Transports, and a veſsel with Sir Henry Clinton's baggage.

A Deserter who came in two days ago from Providence, reports that the Rebel Frigate Warren, Captain Whipple, having her full Complement of Men, Guns, & Stores, on board, intends to come down the firſt fair wind, in order to proceed to Sea. She is to be accompanied by a Brig of 14 Guns, two Gallies, and a Fire ship. Three or four veſsels appear at anchor near her at present.

25th July — Fine weather. Wind S. S. E.

The Rebels fired 3 shot at the Lark, from Papasquash point, but without effect.

26th   Fine weather.   Rain towards night.   Wind S. W.

A number of Victuallers bound for Ireland, sailed this morning, but were obliged to put back when the breeze set in.

A boat with 7 men came acrofs the Seconnet pafsage yesterday opposite the encampment of the 22^d Reg^t to within 100 yards of our shore. As we have no Guards on that part of the Coaſt during the day, it was some time before they were observed; when some men were sent down, and one of the 6 prs got ready; but as soon as they perceived our people in motion, they went off.

27th July — Heavy rain laſt night.   Warm day.

The Ships for Ireland sailed again this Morning, but were obliged to put back, as the wind came in at S. W.

A boat, supposed to be the same which lately crofsed the Seconnet, was observed to come near the shore at the same place laſt night; but on being fired at by the Sentries, she went off. 'Tis imagined they want to carry off or land some person, or to observe what guards we keep there.

28th   Fog all day.   Close Sultry weather.   Wind S. E.

Two Soldiers of The Hefsian Regiment of Ditfourth, deserted laſt night from the Serjeants' Guard, at the point below Briſtol ferry Redoubt.

29th July — Heavy rain laſt night. A clear day and very warm. Wind N. in the afternoon.

The fleet sailed for Ireland.

Some boats appeared again laſt night near Blackpoint, but they went off on being fired at by the Sentries.

30th — Warm weather.   Wind N.

An armed Galley, Schooner rigged, came down from Providence this morning, and pafsed round Papasquash point into Briſtol bay, where she anchored, the wind not permitting her to go through the Ferry, which it is probable she intended. The Lark fired at her as she pafsed, but as she has anchored farther from the point within these two days, the shot did not reach. The Galley fired a Shot at the Lark.

31st July — Two Hefsian Soldiers deserted laſt night from the point guard.

A Flag of truce was sent up to Providence with some things for General Prescott, who is at present at Lebanon, with Mr Trumbull, The Rebel Governor of Connecticut.

The Galley which lay in Bristol bay, got under way about 10 this morning with the wind at S. W. As she was immediately perceived from the Redoubt, and was obliged to make several tacks before she could pass round their point of the Ferry, we had 21 Shot at her before she got quite clear. Two of them struck her, but no damage could be perceived. She fired a good many shot as she passed, of which 2. 18 prs struck the Redoubt, but did no hurt. She proceeded round the N. point of the Island, and about Sunset anchored at Howland's ferry. The Rebels fired some shot from their lower Battery at Bristol ferry, but without effect.

This Galley is the one they built on the keel of that which was burnt last winter. She appears to be a Stout vessel, and well rigged. She carries 2. 18 prs in her bow, 2, 9, or 12 prs in her Stern, and either 4, or 6. 4 prs in her waist, besides Swivels, &c. She has a Staffed netting all round, and there appeared about 40 men on board. She is Schooner rigged, and had topsails set when she went through. Also the American Colours, and a long pendant.

1ˢᵗ Augᵗ   Warm weather.   Wind S.

Came in a Cartel from New London. It appears by some papers which she has brought, that on the 6ᵗʰ July at daybreak the Rebel Army consisting of near 4000 men under the Command of a Mʳ Sinclair, abandoned Ticonderoga and Mount Independance, in the most precipitate manner, leaving their Cannon, Stores, Provisions, & Baggage behind. That they were immediately pursued by Genˡ Burgoyne's Army, which gained several advantages over them, and harrassed them exceedingly. That they were retiring as fast as possible to Fort Edward, at which place the British Army was daily expected; — and, that they were ill armed and badly provided. This retreat seems to have thrown the Country into the utmost confusion, especially as Genˡ Burgoyne, has a considerable body of Canadians and Indians with him. The Rebels censure their General exceedingly for making this precipitate retreat, and giving up that consequential post, without being attacked.

From this Success we may reasonably expect to hear of Genˡ Burgoyne's being at Albany shortly, especially as 'tis said that Sir John Johnson is coming down the Mohawk River with a body of Indians.

Mr Washington must now be in a state of great uncertainty with respect to the measures he should pursue. General Howe having embarked his Army, he dare not move until he can ascertain what his object is; nor can he venture to send any reinforcement to their Northern Army, lest he should weaken his own.

We have no certain accounts yet of Genl Howe's having sailed.

2^d Augt — Warm weather. No Wind. Thunder & Lightning in the Evening.

We find by the Rebel papers, that the Coast of Connecticut, and all this part of the Country was greatly alarmed on the 20th & 21st past, by the appearance of the fleet which came down the Sound under Convoy of the Niger & Swan. They concluded it was the Van of Genl Howe's Army, and that descent was to be made hereabouts. The alarm guns were fired, and Expresses sent through all the Country; in consequence of which, all the people they could scrape together were in motion towards the Coast. However, on the 22^d they were relieved from their fears on observing that the Ships stood out to Sea.

3rd Augt A very warm day. Wind S. E. Thermometer 83°. A heavy thunder shower in the afternoon.

At daybreak the Rebels opened a battery of two pieces of Cannon from the Naraganset Shore, upon The Renown, which lay in that passage. As The ship had orders to move in case of such an event, she went higher up, and anchored again out of Shot. One shot touched the head of her Foremast, and another went through her mizen topsail; but no other damage was done. The ship did not fire.

About the same time, the Rebels landed about 150 men from 18 Whaleboats on Connanicut Island, supposed with an intention to burn the magazine of Hay formed there. Five fellows, by advancing without arms, surprized and carried off a Hessian Sentry, but the Detachment stationed on the Island being soon alarmed, and advancing to the Waterside, the Rebels retired in such a hurry, that five or Six of them who could not reach the boats in time, were obliged to throw away their arms, and Swim to Dutch Island, which lies at some distance. No loss on either side except the above mentioned Hessian.

A Privateer sloop of 8 Guns, was sent in this day by The Unicorn, who took her yesterday near Martha Vineyard, on which Island she run another of the same force on shore, and burnt her. The Crews of both escaped.

4th Aug^t　　Rain last night. Thick Sultry weather. Wind N. E.

A Detachment consisting of 1 Capt 2 Sub^s and 40 men of each of the Flank Companies of the 54th Regiment, and 2 Captains, 4 Subs. and 120 men of the 22^d Regiment, the whole under the Command of Lieu^t Col^o Campbell of the 22^d embarked about half past 11 last night behind Genl Smith's late quarters, in order to make a descent on the Naraganset shore, spike up or destroy the Guns which fired at the Renown, and surprize a small encampment of the Enemy near them.

The Rebel Galley still lies at Howland's ferry.

A Considerable detachment has been stationed for some time past on Cononicut Island, where they have been employed in cutting and making hay for the use of the Army. It is computed that 1000 Tons may be made on that Island. The principal difficulty is to get people to cut, & make it, and then to bring it over to this Island, for we cannot afford to keep a sufficient force there to protect it from the attempts of the Rebels. A good deal has already been made and got in. 'Tis said that General Howe has ordered a Magazine of 2000 Tons of Hay to be formed on this Island. This quantity at 14 lb^s pr ration, would amount to 320,000 Rations. The forming so large a Magazine here, looks as if it was his intention to carry on his operations in the New England provinces in the fall of the year. If Magazines to that amount are formed here, the utmost care should be taken to secure them, not only against the attempts of the Rebels from without, but from those of the ill disposed Inhabitants of the Island.

5th Aug^t　　Thick weather, and some heavy rain. Wind N. E.

The Detachment which embarked the night of the 3rd Ins^t proceeded to the N. point of Cononicut Island, but finding when they had got that length, that they had embarked rather too late, and that the day would break before they could arrive at the place of thier destination, by which the object of the expedition would be defeated, Col^o Campbell landed the men on the N. part of that Island, and kept them concealed in some houses there until he received further instructions from the General and admiral, who determined to carry it into execution last night, and reinforced the Detachment with an officer and 30 men from the Haymakers, and directed the Galley to attend to cover the landing & re-embarkation. Accordingly the Detachment embarked about 1 o'Clock this Morning, and about 3 landed, without being discovered, near a place called The North ferry on the Naraganset shore, from whence they advanced to a house in which about 20 Rebels were posted. The Sentry Challenged, and snapped his piece, but it did not go off. Some of our people however firing very imprudently, gave the alarm, and most of those who were in the house made their escape. A Detachment was then sent to the place where the Cannon were said to be, but they could find only one 18 pr, which they spiked. There was at this time some firing between our men and some of the scattered Rebels, and as nothing more was to be done (the detachment which they expected to have found encamped, having gone off in the Whaleboats two days before) our people returned to the place of embarkation, where they destroyed 4 Whaleboats they found there, and brought off 4 prisoners who were taken at the first house. Four of the Light Infantry being at some distance from the Main body, found a Gun which they said was a 12 pr, but as they had not materials or time to render it unserviceable, it was left there. The whole Detachment re-embarked without molestation, after being four hours on shore, without the lofs of a man. When the troops had re-embarked, the Rebels brought down 2. 4 p^{rs} against the Galley which lay at some distance, and one shot striking her, killed one man. This was the whole of the lofs sustained on our part. That of the Enemy was about 8 killed & wounded, and 4 prisoners. The Detachment returned to their respective encampments about 5 this afternoon.

A Boat pafsed through Bristol ferry about 3 oClock; two shot were fired at her, one of which struck within a yard of her Stern. She afterwards went round Papasquash point towards Providence.

About 6 this Evening some boats full of Rebels were observed coming into the Bay between the Two necks. A party being detached from the Guard at Common-Fence, fired at them as they came near the orchard, on which they turned off and landed on Howland's neck, from whence they advanced to-

wards the bridge and fired at our Sentries. The Guard at Howland's, being quickly reinforced from Camp, advanced and
drove the Rebels back from the bridge, to which about 50 of our
men advanced. This being perceived from the other side, the
Rebel Galley came out from the wharf and stood towards the
bridge, upon which our people retired to the Guard house. Two
6 prs having been ordered down as soon as the Galley was perceived to be in motion, fired at her as soon as she came within
reach, which she returned; but three of the 18 prs on Windmill-
hill being brought to bear on her, and two brafs 12 prs being
brought from The Park to the Water side, they kept so brisk a
fire, that she soon tacked and stood back towards her former
Station, firing several shot as she went off. Some shots being
fired at the straggling fellows on the Neck, they presently disappeared. The Rebels fired four shot from an 18 p^r which they
have in the work on the hill above the ferry, and two from a 9
pr in their lower battery, but without effect, altho the 18 prs
came home. No person was hurt on our Side in this affair. The
Galley was struck once by an 18 lb shot, and three or four times
by the 12 p^{rs}. We therefore think she must have suffered some
lofs. It is imagined the Rebels began this affair with a view of
drawing our people on upon the Neck in order to gain some
trifling advantage over them; the wind being quite favorable
for the Galley to run out. But they did not expect to find Cannon brought down so soon, or to meet with such rough treatment.

The greatest alacrity was shewn by the troops in afsisting at
the battery on Windmill hill, and by The Royal artillery in
bringing down the Guns from the Park, which were served
with the utmost activity. They were in hopes the Galley would
have come nearer to our shore, and that they should have had
an opportunity of treating her in the same manner they did one
in the same place last winter.

This little affair will make the Rebels more cautious of approaching our advanced posts in future, as they now find how
soon we can support them with Cannon.

6th Augt Fine clear weather. Wind S.
The Rebel Galley certainly received some damage yesterday,
as they were seen to heave her down on both sides, this Morning
at Howland's ferry.

7th Aug^t   Fine weather. Wind S. Thick fog from 5 this afternoon.

The Cerberus came in yesterday from a Cruize in the Sound.

A Mr Logan, who was lately Comptroller of the Customs in the Province of New Jersey, came over this day from Howland's ferry, with his family and baggage, having obtained permifsion from the Rebels to come to this Island.

It appears by the Rebel papers, that The Fox Frigate, of 28 Guns, Captain   , was taken lately by two Rebel Frigates, vizt The Hancock of 32 Guns, Commodore Manley, and The Boston of 30 Guns, Capt McNeil, after an engagement of four hours. The Fox had only 105 hands on board, and had her Main yard shot away in the beginning of the Action, or she would not have been taken. The same papers say that The Fox has been retaken.

8th Aug^t   Warm day. Wind S. Thick fog all last night, and until Sunrise.

A Cartel Schooner arrived a few days ago from Boston with some Masters of vefsels and Seamen, who had been taken and carried in there. They say that the day they came out of Boston (2^d Augt) several large ships were seen standing towards the harbour, and that it was reported a large fleet had been seen in the Bay. They also say that the Inhabitants of Boston were in the utmost consternation, expecting a visit from Genl Howe's fleet and Army; in consequence of which they were removing their most valuable effects into the Country. Provisions were very dear at Boston, meat being commonly 1s/– Sterling pr l^b. One of the Masters afsured me he was asked four Dollars for a quarter of Lamb.

9th Aug^t   Hot weather. No wind 'till after 12 o'Clock; & then S. This has been the warmest day we have had this year.

Two Quaker Preachers, who have travelled through many parts of America this Summer, and have been for some weeks upon this Island, having obtained leave from Genl Pigot, went over to the Main this day, by way of Howland's ferry.

10th Aug^t   Great thunder & lightning, and some rain last night. Warm day. Wind N. E.

Two Letter of Marque Ships came in yesterday Evening, from England, but last from Halifax. They have brought a quantity of dry goods for Sale. These Ships confirm the account which we had lately received, that The Fox Frigate has been retaken by The Flora; and that The Hancock Rebel Frigate, has been taken by The Rainbow.

A Detachment of a Captain, 2 Sub^s and 100 men of the 22^d Regiment, marched this day and encamped near Tammany-hill near Newport, where they are to be employed in carrying on some works.

The Rebel Galley went up from Howland's ferry to Swansea the night of the 7th, and returned from thence last night. She certainly went to repair some damage which she received the Evening of the 5th Instant.

11th Augt Pleasant weather. Wind N. E.

We have received certain information that a Captain & two privates of the Rebels were wounded the Evening of the 5th Instant on Howland's Neck. Not a man of theirs has appeared on either of the Necks since that time.

Prices Current. Rhode Island. 12th Augt 1777

	s.	d.	
Beef — per l^b		8	Sterling
Mutton		7	
Lamb		7	
Veal		7, to 8	
Butter	2		
Geese, each	3	3	
Fowls	1	to 1. 6	
Ducks	2	3	
Eggs — pr Dozen	2	3	
Milk — Q^t		2	
Potatoes l^b		1	
Fish		2	
Salt fis^h pr Quintal		4	Dollars
Green Tea l^b		6	Do
Bohea	6^s/		
Suga^r Lum^p l^b	1	4	
Spermaceti Candles	2	3	l^b by the box
Madeira Wine	36^s/ pr^r Dozen		
Port	22^s/		
Sherry	21^s/		
Rum	6/6 Gallon		
Indian Corn	4/6 Bushel		
Hay	2^s/ Cw^t		

N. B.   25 pr Cen^t advance upon the Cost of all dry goods from New York.

12th — Warm weather. Thermr. 76°. Wind S. E.

13th Aug^t   Pleasant cool day. Wind N. E.
Came in The Flora from Halifax; and The Orpheus, Juno, and Amazon, from a Cruize. These Frigates have brought in several prizes with them, and have sent 14 or 15 to Halifax during their Cruize.

14th   Very warm day. Wind S. Great Lightning in the Evening towards Providence.
The Orpheus & Juno came up this Evening from Newport, as far as The admiral's Ship, whose Flag they saluted as they came up.

15th Aug^t   Warm weather. Wind W. A Great thunder Storm, with much lightning and heavy rain, from 6 this Evening 'till 9.
I have observed several times within this month, that the Southerly winds, which are those which prevail most, generally bring in a quantity of Fog and Vapour, and loosing their force about Providence and the head of the Bay, deposit them there about an hour before Sunset in very thick Clouds; these Clouds generally produce thunder & Lightning, and are driven down the Bay about night fall by a N. or N. W. wind. The ensuing morning is clear and hot, and without any wind, until about 10 o'Clock, when the Southerly breeze begins to come in. Easterly winds usually bring in rain & thick weather.
The high situation of this Island, and the fine Sea breeze which comes in before noon almost every day, during the Summer, renders it temperate and very healthy.
Providence, which is not more than 20 miles N. of this Island, is extremely hot and unhealthy, occasioned by its being surrounded by hills, and situated in a Sandy Soil.
When the Southerly wind has blown fresh here, I have frequently observed the upper part of the Bay without a Curl upon the Water.
The Inhabitants of this Island have a most promising appearance this year of a plentiful Crop of Indian Corn and Potatoes. These articles are their principal support. The Hay, Oats, Barley, and Rye, is all got in. Of the first, a great Crop. Very little Wheat is produced on the Island. Almost all their wheat flour is brought from New York, and Pennsylvania.

16th Aug^t   Fine cool day.   Wind N. E.

The Orpheus replaced the Diamond yesterday above Dyer's Island, and The Juno, the Lark off Papasquash point. The Amazon came up to Gold Island, from Newport yesterday; and this day she relieved The Greyhound near Hope Island. The Lark & Diamond went down today to Newport.

A Rebel Sloop came round Papasquash point this Evening, and anchored in Bristol bay. As The Juno is anchored 2 miles from the point, it is impossible for her to prevent the Enemy's vessels from passing.

The Rebel Frigate and other Armed vessels which lay at The Narrows at the head of The Bay, went up towards Providence about Eight days ago, where it is said they are laid up. They appear by this movement to have given up the attempt of going to Sea.

17th Aug^t — Fine weather.   Some small rain.   Wind N. E.

A fellow came into Newport harbour this day from Boston (as he says) in a large Schooner-rigged open boat, without any companion. He says he left Boston five days ago, & run away with the boat. His wife lives in Newport. He was not stopped, or questioned by any person 'till he came to one of the Wharfs. He has brought a Boston paper with him dated the 11th Augt; but as the whole of his Story does not correspond, he was put in confinement.

It appears by the abovementioned paper, that the Rebel Northern Army was at Stillwater, about 25 miles above Albany, on the 1st August; and that Genl Burgoyne was at Fort Edward. His Indians were continually harassing and Scalping the out-posts and Stragglers of the Enemy; who were in great consterna-tion, and in want of everything, having lost their Artillery, Tents, Baggage, Provisions, &^c at Ticonderoga and Skenes-borough. The people seem much discontented at Genl Sin-clair's having quitted a post of such consequence as Ticonde-roga. But in a letter from that officer to Congress, he justifies his conduct, and declares, that if he had remained in that post 24 hours longer, his whole Army would have been cut off, with-out a possibility of escaping. The desertion in the Rebel Army has been very great since that event, and many of the New England Militia have returned home. Everything seems in great confusion at Boston, as they are apprehensive of a visit from Genl Howe. The Inhabitants are removing their goods;

and even The Select-men, Committee-men, and Overseers, are obliged to take their tour [turn?] in mounting Guard at Fort hill. The poor people have afsembled in a riotous manner on account of the dearnefs of different articles, and the difficulty of pafsing the paper money. They have broke open several Stores, and distributed the goods.

Washington's Army remains about Morristown in Jersey, apparently uncertain which way to move until he can ascertain the object which Gen¹ Howe has in view.

18ᵗʰ Augᵗ   Thick weather, inclining to rain.   Wind S. E.

A Soldier of the 22ᵈ Regᵗ deserted last night. He threw off his Clothes, and waded through the Marsh above the Bridge at Howland's Neck.

19ᵗʰ   Fine cool weather.   Wind S. S. W.

20ᵗʰ Augᵗ   Fine weather. Thermr. 70°. Wind Variable in the morning.   S. W. in the afternoon.

The Diamond, Lark, and Flora, sailed on a Cruize.

At Sunset the Rebel Sloop which lay in Bristol bay, got under way with an intention of going through the ferry. She made several tacks in order to weather the point on which their battery stands, but the wind failing, and the Moon getting up by which she could be plainly seen from our battery, she thought it prudent to go back.

21ˢᵗ Augᵗ — Fine weather.   Wind S. S. E.

The Rebel Sloop went through Bristol ferry last night about 12 o'Clock. She rowed close along their Shore until she had weathered the point, when she hoisted sail, and had only two shot fired at her, as she was not discovered until her Sails were set.

A Soldier of The Landgrave's Regiment deserted last night from his post at the Serjeant's Guard at the point. Two other Sentries fired at him as soon as they perceived he was going off. As he cried out much, it is supposed he was wounded.

A Man with two boys, his Sons, Natives of Dartmouth, Massachusetts Bay, came in this morning from Howland's ferry, in a Canoe which they found on the opposite shore. This man says there are not more than 300 Rebel troops stationed from Howland's ferry to Seconnet point. The Rebels are busy in prefsing and drafting men to go to the Northward, since the lofs of Ticonderoga.

The Faulcon Sloop of War, came in this Evening from New York, with 6 Schooners and Sloops under her Convoy, laden with provisions.

22ᵈ Augᵗ   A very warm day.   Themr. 76°. Wind S.

Came in a Prize Sloop, from   , to Surinam, laden with lumber, taken by the Unicorn.

A Captain two Subˢ and 100 men from the 22ᵈ Regiment, marched this morning and encamped near the Windmills above the town of Newport, where they are to be employed in conſtructing a Redoubt, part of a chain of works intended to be thrown up for the defence of a position near the town, which it is proposed to take in case at any time it should be found necessary to abandon the Northern parts of the Island.

Mʳˢ Mackenzie and my family arrived laſt night from New York in the Adventure Schooner, Captain Parker. They were left at Halifax, Nova Scotia in June 1776, when the Army embarked there to go againſt New York, and wintered there. They came from Halifax a short time ago.

23ᵈ Augᵗ   Very warm day. Thermr. 82°. No wind.

It was reported at New York, when the Faulcon left it, that Genˡ Burgoyne had given the Rebels a considerable defeat near Albany, and advanced to that place. Also, that Genˡ Howe's Army had landed at the head of Chesapeak bay, and was advancing towards Philadelphia; near which place Mʳ Washington had taken poſt with the Rebel Army, amounting to about 12,000.

24ᵗʰ Augᵗ 1777   Fine cool day. Some thunder & lightning laſt night. Wind S.

A Detachment of one Field Officer, 2 Capts, 4 Subˢ and 100 men, ordered to be in readinefs to embark for Long Island to cut wood for the use of the troops on this Island.

25ᵗʰ   Cool pleasant day. Wind S. W. Rain in the afternoon.

The Rebels fired a Shot from their Fort above Howland's ferry, at some of our Soldiers who were gathering Apples in Sandford's Orchard.

26ᵗʰ Augᵗ   Rain all the latter part of this day. Wind N. E.

The Detachment ordered the 24ᵗʰ Insᵗ marched this day to Newport in order to Embark. Seven or Eight transports are going to Long Island with this Detachment, to be loaded with Wood for the use of the troops during the ensuing winter. A number of Small vefsels take this opportunity of going to Long Island for wood for the use of the Inhabitants.

27th Aug^t   Rain.   Wind N. E.

About 4 o'Clock this morning a Brig was discovered pafsing the Battery at Fogland ferry. She had almoft pafsed the battery before she was seen owing to a thick fog, and there was only time to fire two shot at her before she was again observed by it. A few minutes after the Guns were fired: The Kingsfisher Sloop, ftationed in the Seconnet, discovered a large ship very near her, under a prefsed sail. She immediately Slipped, got under way, and fired her bow chace at the Enemy, who immediately altered her course and run directly on Shore to the Northward of Seconnet point. The Kingsfisher followed and came to an anchor at a small diftance from her. She then fired a good many shot into the Rebel ship, which having obliged her people to take to their boats and row to the shore, the Kingsfisher sent her boats on board with an intention of bringing her off if pofsible; but as it was Ebb tide, and she had run on shore with great force, and all sails ftanding, it was found impracticable, and therefore orders were given to burn her, which was soon done effectually, and about 5 o'Clock she blew up. She proved to be a Rebel privateer, mounting 20. 6 prs on her Main Deck, and 2. 3 prs on her quarter deck; besides 16 Swivels, and a number of small arms. She was a new ship, well fitted, and clear for action. Our people found a light burning in the light room in the Magazine. She did not fire a shot; but after her people quitted her, a continual fire of Small arms was kept up from the Shore on the Kingsfisher's boats, without any effect. The brig which was in Company made her escape, as The Kingsfisher was fully employed in deftroying the Privateer.

Great praise is due to Captain Graeme and his ship's Company for their conduct and activity on this occasion. The want of spirit on the part of the Rebels was very conspicuous. It is probable she had not lefs than 150 or 200 men on board; and for a vefsel of that force to run ashore from a Sloop of War of 14 Guns and about 90 men, without firing a shot, was perfectly scandalous. She was Commanded by one Chase, and it is supposed came down from Taunton River.

28th Aug^t   Very fine weather. Wind N. E.

The Six small victuallers which arrived the 21st Ins^t having landed their Cargoes, sailed this morning for New York, under Convoy of the Greyhound.

The Wood Cutting Detachment embarked this Morning.

29th Augt Fine Weather. Wind N. E.

The wood fleet sailed this morning for Long Island, under The admiral Parker; Armed brig, Lt Deane, and the Grand Duke of Rufsia, a transport mounting 20 Guns. There are about 20 sail in all — 8 of them transports to bring wood for the troops, and the rest small vefsels sent by the Inhabitants.

Several men came in from the Naraganset side last night. They say the Rebels are in the utmost consternation on account of Genl Burgoyne's having advanced near Albany. It was however reported in the Country that there had been an action near Albany, in which 900 men were lost on the part of The King's troops, and Genl Burgoyne taken prisoner; and that the Rebel General Arnold was killed, and 12 men. As it [has] become a very difficult matter to get a Newspaper in the Country, it looks as if matters were not much in their favor.

30th Aug^t   Very fine weather, & not hot.   Strong wind at N. E.

The Rebel brig which escaped past the Kingsfisher the morning the Privateer was burnt, was brought into Newport this day, having been taken by the Chatham's Tender, a Schooner of 10. 4 prs and 50 men. She is laden with lumber for the West Indies.

A Rebel boat which had been loading hay from Hog Island, was taken this morning by the boats of the Juno. The men belonging to her escaped in a small boat.

31st Aug^t   Fine weather. Wind S. W.

A flag of truce came down from Providence this day. They afsert that Genl Burgoyne's army has met with a very severe Check near Albany, and that 700 of The King's troops were killed and taken; also many Officers; — but as they do not mention the name of any officer, or give any particulars, no great credit is given to their report.

1st Sept^r — Fine weather. Strong wind at S. W. A Thunder Storm in the afternoon.

A Soldier of the 22^d and one of the 54th deserted last night.

2ᵈ Septʳ   Very fine day. Wind N. E.

A Soldier of the 54ᵗʰ Regᵗ was shot laſt night by one of our advanced Sentries at Commonfence Neck. He and another Soldier of the same Regiment had by some means paſsed the Chain of advanced Sentries after it was dark, supposed with an intention to desert. The latter, about 10 at night, came near one of the Sentries, and being challenged & answering, "Friend," came forward and was secured. About half an hour after, the former was observed crawling upon his hands and knees towards the Sentries, & not answering when challenged, was fired at, and two balls lodged in his body, of which he died almoſt immediately. The man who was taken says he loſt his way in going from the Guard to the Camp, and denies having had any intention to desert. The man who was shot, was of a very bad Charaćter, and if he had no intention of deserting, of which however there is little doubt, deserved his fate, as he had no buſineſs in front of the advanced poſts at night, and should have answered when Challenged.

The Rebel Galley lies in the Stream at Howland'sferry.

A person came from Newport this morning, with a paſs from Genˡ Pigot, permitting him to go to the Main, but on going to the point, they refused to take him over, & he was obliged to return.

3ʳᵈ Septʳ — Very fine weather. Thermr. 65°. Wind N. E.

A Corporal of the 43ʳᵈ Regiment was unfortunately shot by accident in the Camp yeſterday Evening, by another Corporal of the same Regiment, his Comrade, & moſt intimate friend.

The Rebel Galley moved from Howland's ferry round the N. point of the Island this afternoon, and appeared as if she intended paſsing through Briſtol ferry; but the Juno having fired a Gun as a Signal for aſsembling the boats manned & armed, and having at the same time worked up a mile nearer to Papasquash point, she thought prudent to deſiſt, and run in behind Mount Hope.

A Man came in laſt night who reports, that the advantage obtained by the Rebels near Albany, was over a Detachment of 300 men only, which having been sent out by Genˡ Burgoyne to collećt Horses, Waggons, &c, for the use of the Army, was surrounded and attacked by near 4,000 of the Militia, and the whole, except about 80, killed, wounded & taken. The Rebels are said to have had about 100 men killed in the affair. Tis said that Gen¹ Burgoyne is at Albany; and that Gen¹ Howe had landed with his Army near Baltimore in Maryland, which Province & Virginia, had submitted. We impatiently expect authentic accounts of the proceedings of both Armies.

4ᵗʰ Septʳ   Fine weather. Wind W.

Two Soldiers of the 22ᵈ Regᵗ deserted laſt night; and as they were seen going towards Newport, there is no doubt there are some persons there who make it their buſineſs to intice the Soldiers to desert, and aſsiſt them in making their escape; which is no difficult matter as we have at present no Guards or Patroles from the right of the Encampment of The Chaſseurs at Point Pleasant, quite round to Eaſton's beach. The Kingsfisher indeed is ſtationed in that quarter, but boats may easily paſs her in the night without being discovered. Any Inhabitant convicted of such practices should be hanged immediately. The lenity shown so frequently to declared Rebels has been productive of numberleſs ill consequences.

The boats of The Juno having been sent early this morning to water on the North part of Prudence Island, were attacked there by above 100 Rebels who came from the Neighbouring points, and who killed two men, wounded another, & took a Midshipman & 8 men prisoners. The Signal for the boats of the ships, manned & armed, was made about 7 o'Clock, soon after which a considerable number of Seamen & Marines were landed there, but the Rebels having observed their approach, retired before they could come up with them.

The Detachment of the 22ᵈ Regiment employed on the works near Newport, was relieved this day by the like number of The Landgrave's Regiment.

5ᵗʰ Septʳ   Fine weather. Wind S. W.

One of the Seamen killed by the Rebels yeſterday on Prudence Island, was mangled in a moſt shocking manner, having several shot through him, particularly three through his head; — He was also Stabbed in several places with a Bayonet. The Crews of the Ships vow vengeance againſt them for this act of barbarity.

A Rebel sloop which lay at the N. part of Hog Island, loading hay from thence, had 4 Shot fired at her from our Redoubt at Briſtol ferry. The Shot ſtruck very near her, but the diſtance being considered as too great, we then desiſted. The Rebels fired one Shot from their lower battery at our Redoubt, but it went over without effect.

6th Sept^r   Very hot day. Wind S.

Two Seamen belonging to the Kingsfisher, who slept on shore in a tent opposite the ship, were carried off last night: supposed by some Rebels from the opposite shore. The tent was torn to pieces.

It has lately been discovered that some persons from the Eastern shore, have made a practice of coming over during the night in a boat, which they sunk near the beach to prevent her being discovered; that they have then gone into Newport, where they have purchaced Rum and Salt, and the following night returned to the shore, weighed their boat, and crossed the Seconnet again. There is no doubt these persons have come for the purpose of gaining intelligence, which is not difficult to be obtained, as the majority of the Inhabitants are friends. This practice was not attended with much danger, as we have neither Guards or patroles from the Southward of Black point, round the S. E shore of the Island to Easton's beach, an extent of near 7 miles.

7th Sept^r   Fine weather. Strong wind at N. E.

The two letter of Marque ships which arrived lately from Liverpoole and Halifax, sailed this Morning for New York. They intend proceeding from thence to join The fleet and Army under Lord, and General Howe.

8th — Fine cool day. Strong wind at N. from 12 last night 'till one this day.

A Brig from New York came in this afternoon. The Syren, Frigate, with several Storeships & Victuallers from thence, are off the harbour.

9th Sept^r — Pleasant weather. Wind S. W.

The Syren and her Convoy came in. The Syren has brought letters which came from England by the July Packet.

It appears by the accounts from New York that the Fleet under Lord Howe anchored off Swan Island, near Baltimore in Maryland, the 21st Augt and that the Army was then preparing to land.

The Rebels made an attack on Staten Island the 22^d Augt with about 2,000 chosen troops under Mr Sullivan, and had at first some success against the Provincial troops stationed near the place of landing; but the 52^d Reg^t and the 3rd Battalion of Waldeck having come up and attacked them briskly, they were obliged to retire with precipitation, leaving behind them about 120 killed, & 340 prisoners. Their boats were Cannonaded as they went off, by which they muſt have suffered considerably. The loſs on our side was 5 killed, 7 wounded, and about 80 prisoners.

The Rebels appeared the same day with about 600 men in front of the Redoubts at Kingsbridge; but on Genl Tryon's advancing with some troops, they retired. Some prisoners were taken by him.

The same day likewise they landed about 700 men under the Command of Brig^r Genl Parsons, at Satucket on Long Island, and Summoned Lt Col^o Hewlett, who Commanded the Provincial troops in that poſt to Surrender; but as he did not think proper to do so, Mr Parsons retired without making any attack, owing, as he said, to the extreme heat of the weather.

The letters which paſsed on this Occasion are somewhat curious.*

The Rebel papers say that a considerable detachment of Genl Burgoyne's Army was cut off the 16th Augt at a place called Bennington. We have no accounts, of that affair, except from them.

10th Sept^r — Very heavy rain laſt night, and 'till 11 this day. Wind E.

We know very little from any authority which can be depended on, of the situation or Strength of Genl Burgoyne's

---

* "Brigadier Genl Parsons, Commanding Officer of the troops of the United American Army, now investing the Enemy's post at Satucket, to prevent the effusion of human blood, requires the immediate surrender of the post. The Officers & Soldiers, and those who are under their proteƈtion, shall be entitled to their baggage, and treated with that humanity which prisoners are entitled to. Your answer is desired in ten minutes. I am fully sensible of your condition, and as my whole strength and artillery will soon be here, if your refusal should oblige to the effusion of human blood, you must charge it to your own obstinacy. —

Colonel Hewlett's Compliments to Genl Parsons, and requests half an hour to consult his Officers on the subjeƈt of his Summons.

General Parsons's Compliments to Col^o Hewlett & grants him ten minutes only for consideration. Longer time will not be granted.

Colonel Hewlett presents his Compliments to Genl Parsons, and is determined to defend his post while he has a man left.

General Parsons's Compliments to Colonel Hewlett, and should have been happy to have done himself the pleasure of paying him a longer visit, but the extreme heat of the weather prevents him."

Army. By what we can gather from different accounts, he has about 7,000 men with him; and a Corps under Col⁰ St Leger and Sir John Johnston is endeavouring to penetrate by way of Fort Stanwix, down the Mohawk river, and to join him at Albany; which appears to be the point to which all the Northern troops tend. The many posts the General will be obliged to occupy in order to preserve his communication with Canada, must necessarily weaken his army and give the Enemy many advantages. I think he will meet with more difficulty in penetrating to Albany than is generally imagined; and if he should meet with any considerable check which might retard his advancing to that place, until the end of this month, his situation must then become extremely critical; as he must then either determine to retire to Ticonderoga, or make one push with all the force he can collect to gain Albany and open a Communication with some part of the Army in these Provinces. As to his advancing into Connecticut, or towards Boston, it is a measure attended with so many difficulties, that I think it is impracticable; for altho the Militia of that Country may with some difficulty be induced to march to the Northward to oppose him, yet the moment he enters their respective districts, they will assemble with alacrity to retard or oppose his progress; and in a Country so full of Inhabitants and so Rebellious as New England, numerous bodies of people will be found opposed to him. No diversion can be made in his favor from hence, as the troops here are not sufficiently numerous to afford a Detachment of any consequence. The troops at New York and its Environs under the Command of Gen¹ Clinton, have enough to do to defend the posts assigned them, until the dispersion of one of the Rebel Armies enables him to undertake something; so that no material operation in General Burgoyne's favor can be undertaken from thence at present. Our hopes therefore are fixed on Gen¹ Howe, and if something decisive is not speedily done by him, it is difficult to say how this Campaign will end. Should he give Washington's Army a total defeat, (of which I am afraid Washington will never give him another opportunity) the affairs of the Rebels will be in a bad way, as a defection of some of the Provinces would be the immediate consequence; and then our whole force might be turned against the Rebel Northern Army and the New England Provinces; which, as the most Rebellious, should be chastised most severely.

The distance at which the Army under Gen¹ Howe is, affords little prospect of his operating in favor of that under Gen¹ Burgoyne, unlefs his having drawn Washington's Army to Philadelphia, may be said to have done so already. Some persons are of opinion that if Gen¹ Howe had commenced his operations in Connecticut or New England, the progrefs of Gen¹ Burgoyne's Army would have been more rapid.

11ᵗʰ Septʳ   Fine weather. Wind S.

The Rebel Galley came down from Swansea to Howland's ferry yesterday Evening. She had a great number of men on board.

The Rebels have had a good many men at work for some days paſt at their Fort above Howland's ferry. They appear to be repairing and Strengthening it. We can see but one Gun (an 18 pr) there.

The Ration of forage has this day been fixed at the undermentioned proportions for the troops on this Island.

	lbˢ of Hay	lbˢ Oats	lbˢ of Oatmeal
For The Light Dragoon horses	15	6	2
For Artillery, Waggon, & Draft,		lbˢ Peas	
horses	14	3	3
For Officers horses	10	3	3

12ᵗʰ Septʳ   Fine weather. Wind N.

Forty men began to work this afternoon in conſtructing a small redoubt near Howland's bridge, in which the guard is to be placed as soon as it is finished. The Rebels fired two shot from Howland's fort at the working party as they were coming off. The shot went over them without effect.

We saw about 200 men under arms to day near Howland's ferry. They appeared to have been at exercise. Many of them were without Coats. Barton, who Commanded the party that took General Prescott, Commands at Howland's.

13ᵗʰ Septʳ — Fine weather. Wind N. and cold in the morning.

As The works intended to be made for the defence of the North part of the Island, require a good many workmen to complete them, and the duty of the Soldiers is rather severe, General Pigot sent a Summons this day to the Inhabitants of the township of Portsmouth to afsemble on the 15ᵗʰ Inſtant at Windmill hill in order to afsiſt in carrying them on. They are required to work three days in the week.

14th   Fair pleasant weather. Wind S. W.

A Redoubt for 80 men and two pieces of Cannon, was traced out this day on Barrington's-hill, close on the left of the Artillery Park.

15th Sept^r — Fine weather. Wind S. W.

Came in a Schooner, laden with lumber, from Stonington to St Eustatia, taken by the Cerberus. Several other prizes with the same kind of Cargoes, have been sent in here of late. Those materials will be found very serviceable in the construction of Barracks and Guard houses for the Troops.

In consequence of the General's summons to the Inhabitants of the township of Portsmouth, to assemble in order to be employed to work on the Redoubts, 17 only appeared this morning at the place appointed. The Majority of the Inhabitants being Quakers, they informed the General that it was contrary to their principles to assist, in any manner in matters of War, and that therefore they could not appear. They even refuse to be employed in constructing Barracks for the accomodation of the troops.

The accounts published by the Rebels of the affair at Bennington the 16th August, makes Genl Burgoyne's loss to be very considerable. Above 700 men killed & prisoners. They also report that the Corps under the Command of Col^o St Leger, has been obliged to raise the siege of Fort Stanwix, and retire. In one of their papers the Rebels give a Copy of the Instructions given by Genl Burgoyne, to Lieu^t Col^o Baum, who commanded the detachment defeated by them at Bennington; by which it appears that the objects of that Expedition were, to try the affections of the Country, to mount a Regiment of Dragoons, to obtain large supplies of Cattle, Horses, and Carriages, and to disconcert the Enemy. To effect the last, he was to give out that his Corps was the advanced guard of the Army, which was to penetrate through Connecticut towards Boston, and that they were to be joined at Springfield by a body of troops from Rhode Island.

Although this was well calculated to alarm the Country, it had not the desired effect. The people who defeated Col^o Baum were almost entirely Militia of the adjacent Country. Colonel Baum appears to have committed a great fault in venturing so far into the Country without support, and without having been thoroughly informed of the Enemy's force in that neighbour-hood.

If the defeat of Colonel Baum's detachment has been as con-siderable as the Rebels give out, and Col° St Leger has been obliged to raise the Siege of Fort Stanwix, General Burgoyne's difficulties in penetrating to Albany will be exceedingly en-creased, as his force is not only weakened, but his flanks are uncovered.

16th Sept^r — Very fine weather. Wind N. E. The mornings and Evenings begin now to grow cool.

Fifty men began to work on the Redoubt on the left of the Park of artillery. The Inhabitants, and 12 Soldiers, are em-ployed on that near Howland's bridge.

17th Septr Thick cloudy weather; Inclining to rain. Wind N.

A working party of a Captain, Subaltern, and 60 British, marched to Newport this morning to relieve the detachment of Hessians, and to be employed on the works there.

Information has been received that the Rebels are collecting a great number of boats at Providence, preparatory to their making an attack upon this Island.

If Genl Burgoyne's Army should not be able to penetrate to Albany; and Genl Howe should find it impracticable to bring Mr Washington's Army to action, and be detained to operate in Pennsylvania during the remainder of the Campaign, it is highly probable the Rebels will make some attempt to recover this Island. Many advantages would follow the possession of this Island. They would render the harbour useless to our ships, and by that means, in a great measure, command the Navigation of the Sound, and be enabled to receive supplies. They would also deprive the Army of a large supply of forage, which is collecting here to a considerable amount.

We are at present very busy in fortifying different posts on the Island; and there are already more works planned and traced out, than can possibly be finished by the end of December. Those intended are a Redoubt for 30 men and 2 Cannon oppo-site Howland's bridge. A fortified Barrack on Windmill hill for 200 men. . A Redoubt on Barrington's hill for 80 men and 2 Cannon. A Redoubt at Fogland ferry for the like numbers. A Redoubt on Quaker-hill, and a Barrack there for 200 men. A Redoubt and Barrack for 60 men on Turkey hill. But the principal work is the enclosing the town of Newport, from Easton's beach, round by the three Windmills, to the North Battery, an extent of 3,000 yards, in which are to be four or five Redoubts, connected by a line with Redans. The Chief Engineer has also proposed erecting a Redoubt between that opposite Howland's bridge, and Common-fence. Two between Windmill hill & Bristol Redoubt, and one between Windmill hill and Common-fence. The Redoubt near Howland's bridge; that on Barrington's hill; also one near Easton's beach, and one at the three Windmills, near Newport, are now carrying on.

All these works are planned on a supposition that Gen[l] Howe may have occasion for part of the troops now here, and that 2,000 men only will be left for the defence of the Island during the Winter. If that should be the case, it is said the troops are to be disposed of in the following manner;

1000 for the defence of Newport, & Cononicut Island
 200 at Windmill hill
  80 at Barrington's hill
  60 at Turkey hill
 200 at Quaker hill
  60 at Fogland ferry
 200 at Lopez's house on the East side ⎫
 200 at Roome's house, on the West side ⎭ about 4 miles from Newport
————
2000

If all the intended Redoubts are completed, and are to be occupied and have guards in them, one great objection against this disposition is that 600 men are too few for the North part of the Island, and by being so much dispersed we should run the risk of being beaten in detail. There are other objections also. The troops advanced would be much harrafsed, would be very ill accomodated, & from their dispersed state, ill attended to. In laying down a plan for the defence of this Island, I conceive the security of the N. part to be the principal Object; and as from the peculiar situation of Commonfence, and Howland's, Neck; particularly the former, the Enemy have it in their power to land any number of men on those parts of the Island without our knowledge, or the pofsibility of preventing them, it is from thence we should expect any attack of consequence. Many difficulties attend their making any serious attack by water; such as the afsembling any considerable number of boats without our being acquainted therewith, and taking measures to destroy them; the want of vessels of force to cover a landing; the breadth of the water on all sides; and above all the uncertainty of being able to retreat in case of ill success.

To secure the North part therefore, it would seem adviseable to strengthen the Redoubts at Bristol, Common-fence, & Howland's bridge, so that they could not be taken by assault. 50 men and 4, 18 or 24 p^{rs} would be sufficient for Bristol Redoubt. 2 of these Guns should fire on the passage, and the other two command the ground from the mouth of the town pond, to the road at Commonfence. 30 men and 2. 12 p^{rs} in Commonfence Redoubt, and 30 men & 2. 18 p^{rs} in Howland's bridge Redoubt. The two guns in this last Redoubt, would command a great part of Common fence Neck, and the Bay between the two Necks, all Howland's Neck, and great part of the bay round Gold Island. These Redoubts should have a good Abbatis round them, and their parapets fraized, which would secure them against surprize, and enable the people in them to defend them a great while against a very considerable force. In order to support the advanced posts, and to render the force at the N. end of the Island respectable, Barracks for a Regiment, or 400 men, should be built at Windmill hill and Barrington's hill; so that a sufficient body of men would always be at hand in case of an attack. The 18 p^{rs} on the Battery at Windmill hill, command all the ground between them & the above mentioned Redoubts. A Regiment should be quartered on the E. road, from Fogland ferry to Quaker hill. A Small redoubt at each of those places would secure their quarters sufficiently. Another Regiment should be quartered on the W. road, from Roome's to Turkey hill inclusive. I do not think any Redoubt necessary within their quarters, as that side of the Island would be sufficiently guarded by the Ships of War. These three Regiments would be sufficient to furnish all the duties out upon the Island; and the other two would be able to do the duty of the town, & furnish a Detachment to Cononicut. A Frigate in the Seconnet passage would deter the Enemy from making any attempt of consequence on the S. E. part of the Island.

The Rebels would have many difficulties to surmount before they could succeed in an attack on this Island. If they make it by way of Commonfence & Howland's Neck, they must land a body of at least two or 3,000 men, during the course of the night, with the requisite Artillery, Horses, &c. &c; the three advanced

Redoubts muſt be attacked, and two at leaſt, of them, carried, before they could advance further. If they were properly defended this would take up some time, and enable the troops in the adjacent poſts and quarters to aſsemble to support them, or at leaſt to take poſt on Quaker hill and the other heights in that line, which is the moſt advantageous poſt in the Island; and our troops muſt be forced from that poſt, before the Rebels could be said to have done anything. If during this time the wind was favorable for one of our Frigates to push through Briſtol ferry, and another to come up the Seconnet, so as that the former might command the ground on Commonfence, and the latter annoy the Enemy's left flank, I am convinced they would desiſt from their attack and make a precipitate retreat. The Rebels would not think of making any considerable attempt by means of boats, as from the breadth of the Seconnet, and our having a Ship of war there, their retreat, in case of ill success, would be extremely precarious. They would hardly attempt it from Briſtol, as the guns in Briſtol-ferry Redoubt command the passage between Hog-Island & Briſtol; those of the Frigate that between Hog Island & Rhode Island: and those in the Artillery Redoubt, the shore opposite Hog-Island. The guns on the battery at·Windmill hill, might also be brought to bear on that quarter. If they landed any where between Windmill hill and Quaker hill, they would be between two fires; which would also be the case if they landed in any place Southward of Quaker-hill. Upon the whole, I am of opinion, that with such a disposition of our force, the Rebels would fail in any attack of consequence. They may indeed land a few men, attack some of our guards, and give us an Alert: but I am confident they will never succeed in any attempt to make themselves maſters of the Island. The General should use every means in his power to obtain information of any intended attack, and as they muſt, previous to such an enterprize, collect boats, provisions, and Stores in places adjacent, we should endeavor to deſtroy them if within our reach.

If the Rebels have any intention of making a serious attack on this Island, it is probable they will previously endeavor to poſseſs themselves of Cononicut and Prudence, which would facilitate their attempt. We should use every means in our power to keep poſseſsion of Cononicut, to prevent the Rebels from fortifying themselves there, and erecting batteries to obstruck the entrance to the harbour, by which we should be much distressed, and our supplies and subsistence rendered extremely precarious, as the Island affords no other harbour, or good landing place but Newport. Batteries on the Dumplins, apart of Cononicut which forms the entrance of the harbour, would greatly annoy any vessels coming in. The possession of Prudence would not be of much consequence, as the communication of the Rebels who might take post there, with the neighbouring shores, would be extremely precarious while we had the Command of the Bay by means of our ships.

18th Sept^r — Heavy rain all last night, and high wind at N. N. E. Rain all this day, with the wind at N. E.

Two Soldiers of the 54th Reg^t deserted this day. As it is almost certain they did not go off by either of the Necks, there is little doubt but they are assisted by some ill-affected Inhabitants in getting off from the S. E. part of the Island.

The officers on this Island have been forbidden, in orders, from purchasing Oats, or any other forage for private use, as it will hinder the Commissary from completing the Magazines. They are told they must remain satisfied with the proportions of forage allowed them by Government.

The Detachment of Hessians employed on the works near Newport, were relieved yesterday by a Detachment of British.

19th Sept^r   Rain most part of last night, and high wind at N. E. Thick weather 'till 4 this afternoon, when it cleared up with a N. Wind. Very fine Evening.

A Rebel boat full of men, passing through Bristol ferry this afternoon, was fired at from our battery: One shot struck within two feet of her, covered her with water, and alarmed those in her so much, that they pulled directly in for their shore; and all quitted her, except three, who soon after rowed her up toward Swansea.

20th Sept^r   Very fine day. Wind N.

A Soldier of the Hessian Regiment of Ditfourth, attempting to desert early this morning by way of Commonfence Neck, was discovered by some of the British Sentries, who fired at him, shot him through the wrist, and took him. Another Soldier, his companion got off.

A Redoubt for 100 men, and 2 pieces of Cannon was traced out this day on the height behind the present battery at Fogland ferry, and 60 men began to work on it.

A great number of Cannon were fired this day towards Providence. Some think it was a Salute or rejoicing. It is more probable it was a proof of guns, which are cast at a foundary in that Neighbourhood.

21st Sept^r — Fine weather. Wind S. W. Thunder, Lightning, and some Rain about 7 in the Evening, from the Westward.

A Sentry of the 54th Reg^t had his hand so much shattered by the accidental going off of his firelock, that it must be cut off.

A Printed paper, containing the Rebel account of the defeat of the Corps detached from Genl Burgoyne's Army, near Bennington the 16th Augt last, was found this morning about 100 yards in front of our advanced Sentries on Commonfence Neck. On the back of it the following words were written in a very good hand. —

"A present of a piece of agreeable intelligence to people con-
"fined and coop't up on Rhode-Island, particularly to the de-
"luded Hefsians, who are invited by their own brethren who
"have deserted from Slavery, and are now enjoying the inesti-
"mable sweets of freedom, and living on fat, fresh Congrefs
"Beef in Plenty. —

"To The Rebel Officers on
"Rhode-Island."

22d Sept^r — Rain most part of last night. Clear, Cold Morning. Wind W. N. W. Strong N. W. wind from 12 oClock. Some rain in the Evening.

This being the Anniversary of The King's Coronation, the ships of War stationed in the different parts of the Bay, & in the harbour, fired 21 Guns each at 1 o'Clock.

Came in the Wood fleet from Long-Island.

A man came in from the Naraganset shore yesterday, who says he saw in one of the Rebel papers, a letter from Mr Washington to Congrefs, informing them, that Genl Howe, by the superior fire of his Artillery, had obliged him to retire from Ironhill, or Yearn-hill; but that Genl Howe must have lost at least as many men as He did. His letter is dated from Wilmington, and the affair is said to have happened the 27th August.

The same man says that the Rebel Northern Army is at Half-moon, 11 miles from Albany.

23rd Sept^r   Frequent heavy Showers.   Wind N. N. E.

The Detachment that was on board the Wood fleet, disembarked and joined their respective Corps in Camp.

The fleet has brought about 450 Cords of Wood for the use of the troops. Some of the Inhabitants who brought wood in their own vessels, for sale, ask the exorbitant price of 10 Dollars pr Cord for it. A Cord of wood measures 8 feet long, 4 feet high, and 4 feet wide. Consequently it contains 128 Cubic feet.

Two Soldiers of the 43rd Regiment deserted yesterday. They did not go off from the advanced posts, which puts it past a doubt that they are afsisted in their escape by the Inhabitants. I am almost certain they are furnished by the Inhabitants with the means of going off from the S. E. part of the Island, which is seldom visited by any of our parties or patroles, and is very little frequented. It is a matter of consequence, and should be attended to, as above 25 British Soldiers have deserted from the three Battalions since the 1st of June last. The first Inhabitant convicted before a General Court Martial of having persuaded or afsisted a Soldier to desert, should be punished with the utmost rigor of Martial law. The first example would probably put a stop to the practice.

The Rebels have had small parties upon Common fence Neck frequently of late, but they appear to be only gathering some fruit in Hicks's orchard, and cutting some Marsh-hay near it. Two fellows crept up this morning towards our advanced Sentries, fired at them (without effect) and then took to their heels. They were pursued by some of our men, but got clear off.

It appears by a New York paper of the 11th Ins^t that Genl Howe had routed a Corps of 5,000 Rebels, and had taken a considerable Magazine, and many Cannon.

24th Sept^r   Fine weather.   Wind N.

The Rebel Galley came out of Quaket pond this Evening to Howland's ferry. She was driven in there the 22^d by the violence of the wind.

A Garden has been for some time formed, and Cultivated under the direction of Doctor Nooth, for the benefit of the Sick of the troops, and considerable quantities of vegetables have been issued from thence. Two bushels of Potatoes, 2 bushels of

Turnips, 50 Cabbages, and 50 Onions, are now delivered weekly for the use of the Sick of each Regiment.

25th Sept^r   Fair pleasant weather.   Wind N. W.

The Cerberus came in yesterday from a Cruize in the Sound. She has brought in with her, Lieu^t Deane, and the Crew of the Admiral Parker Armed Schooner, which, in coming from Shelter-Island with the wood fleet, on the 22^d Instant, gave Chace to a Rebel Privateer off Stonington, and unfortunately run upon a reef of Rocks, where she stuck fast; and as it was found impossible to get her off, the boats of the Cerberus assisted in taking everything of value out of her, and then set her on fire; during which they were fired at by the Privateer and a Battery on shore, but without suffering any loss.

26th Sept^r   Rain all last night from the N. E.   Clear day. Strong wind at N. W. from 8 this morning.

A Soldier of the 54th Reg^t one of those who absented themselves on the 18th inst, was apprehended by some of the Inhabitants of the S. E. part of the Island, and lodged in the Provost. He was observed Skulking about that part of the Island, waiting an opportunity to get off.

27th   Fair weather.   Wind N.

The Rebels fired two shot from their battery at Bristol ferry at some Carpenters who were repairing a house near the Windmill, but they did not reach.   One shot was fired at their battery from our Redoubt.

28th Se^p — Fair pleasant weather, but cold.   Wind N. E.

The Rebel Galley went up from Howland's ferry this afternoon behind Mount Hope.

A good many boats have been observed for some days past, moving about at, and near Howland's ferry.   Several have gone into a Small Creek opposite Quaker hill, where it is imagined they have collected a number.

29th Se^p —   Cold weather.   Wind N. E.

Eight men came into the harbour this afternoon in a Sloop from the Eastward.   The Sloop is loaded with wood and some other articles; and they say they seized and run away with her, in order to avoid being drafted to serve in the Rebel Army.   The General and Admiral have given them the entire property of the Sloop and her Cargo, as a reward.

These men report that an exprefs had arrived from the Weft-ward, with an account that the Rebel Army had been defeated by General Howe and had loft 7,000 men. The remains of the Rebel Army were driven within five miles of Philadelphia.

The Rebels to the Eastward have been employed lately in drafting a considerable number of men, in order, as they give out, to make an attack on this Island; but it is supposed they are intended to be marched to the Northward to reinforce that Army.

30th Septr Very fine warm weather.   Wind N. W.

A large Schooner came down laft night to Howland's ferry. It is probable she intends going to sea the firft favorable opportunity.

1st Oct^r — Fine weather.   Wind N.

The Rebels appear to have more boats than usual at Howland's ferry.

The Cerberus sailed for New York.

A flag of truce came down from Providence this Evening. It appears by the Rebel papers which she brought, that Genl Howe attacked Washington's Army the 11th Septr at the Brandywine Creek, 12 miles above its junction with the Delaware; that he had driven them as far as Germantown, 12 miles from Philadelphia, and that they had loft near 1000 men and 10 pieces of Cannon. To palliate this lofs they say that Genl Howe has loft between 3, & 4,000 men. From all their accounts we are pretty certain that they have been well beaten. We are anxious to receive General Howe's account of this action.

2^d Octr Fine pleasant weather.   Wind S. S. W.

The Rebel Galley came down this Morning from behind Mount Hope to Howland's ferry; and went back there again in the afternoon.

Two boats endeavoring to go down the Seconnet pafsage, through Fogland ferry, were fired at by our battery. One of them put back, and the men drew her over the Neck. The other pafsed without any damage.

3rd — Very fine weather.   Wind S. W.

The Chatham, went down from near Gold Island, to Newport.

The Rebels have something in agitation at Howland's ferry. They have a considerable number of boats, and more men aſsembled there than usual.

They had about 50 men at work to day, completing the Fort on the hill.

4ᵗʰ Octʳ — Fine weather.   Wind S. W.

The Greyhound Frigate came in yesterday Evening from New York in two days. She brings an account of the defeat of the Rebel Army on the 11ᵗʰ Septʳ near Chad's-ford on the Brandy-wine Creek; and that the loſs of the Rebels was about 4,000 and 12 pieces of Cannon. The loſs on our side between 4, and 500 men. No particulars had been received at New York when the Greyhound left it.

The Lady Parker Armed Schooner arrived from New York this morning. The accounts by her are, that Washington's Army has been almoſt totally defeated; and that General Howe is in poſseſsion of Philadelphia, and is pursuing the remains of the Rebel Army, who are retiring towards the Northern parts of Jersey. Tis said the Rebels burnt all their shipping before they quitted Philadelphia. It was reported at New York, that there had been a Second Action.

Large working parties continue to be employed here daily in completing such works as are thought of moſt consequence.

5ᵗʰ Octʳ — Very fine pleasant weather.   Wind S. W.

A fleet from England under Convoy of the Experiment and Briſtol of 50 Guns each, arrived at New York the 25ᵗʰ September. They had on board Generals Robertson & Wilson, and many other Officers, with about 2500 Troops. — also the Clothing, Camp-Equipage, &c. &c., for the Army.

General Clinton was preparing to move from New York with a Corps of about 5000 men, up Hudson's River, with an intention, as it was supposed to effect a Junction with Genˡ Burgoyne's Army.

6ᵗʰ Octʳ   Fair pleasant day.   Wind S. W.

Came in The Syren Frigate, Captain Furneaux, from a Cruize.

The Rebels fired a Shot from their lower Battery at Briſtol ferry at some men of ours who were pulling down one of the old houses below the Redoubt. —

7th — A fine day. Wind N. W.

A large Rebel Frigate came down from Providence this morning, and anchored at the Narrows, 5 or 6 miles below that town.

8th Octr Fine weather. Wind N.

A Report was made to Genl Smith about 9 o'Clock last night from Fogland ferry, that a very considerable number of boats had been seen towards the close of the Evening on the Rebel Shore, a little way below the S. point of Fogland. This matter was first mentioned by a young lad who lives at Mr Bowler's house, and at that time it was too dark to ascertain whether what he said had any foundation or not. In consequence of this report strong patroles were ordered to go out along that Coast all night, and the troops were ordered to be in readiness to get under arms on the firing of two Cannon, which was to be the signal of the Enemy's intention to land. The night however passed without any appearance of the Enemy or their boats.

At day break I was at the Camp of the Chasseurs, directly opposite where it was said the boats had been seen, and on looking at the place with a good glass, I immediately perceived that what had been taken for boats was nothing more than about 150 small Cocks of Marsh hay, which had been put up there in a field by some of the Country people in the afternoon, and were disposed in rows, near the beach. It is probable the Setting Sun had lengthened the Shawdows of these Cocks into the shape of Whaleboats, and that they were actually taken for such by the lad who made the report. The cause of this alarm was truly ridiculous.

The Rebel Galley is now at Howland's ferry.

Several Small Craft and boats have been plying about Mount hope bay, Taunton River, and Howland's ferry all day.

9th Oct^r — Fine Morning. Wind S. E. At 12 o'Clock it began to blow hard and to rain. The wind & rain encreased to a great degree before night.

The Rebels fired three shot from their battery at Bristol ferry yesterday morning; One of which went over a house on this side of the Windmill. The others fell in a field on the left of the road. It is quite uncertain what they fired at, as there were no people near the place. Perhaps it was to try the utmost range of their shot. They have now 2. 18 p^{rs} in their lower battery, but none above.

As there are many indications of the Rebels having something in agitation, directions have been given for putting the Arms of the troops in the most perfect order, and completing every man with 60 rounds and 3 flints.

The Hessian Sentries at Bristol ferry having imagined they heard boats rowing through there last night, a false alarm was given to The Hessian Regiments, who got under arms. It was soon found that the alarm was without foundation.

10th Octr   Very Strong gale of wind all last night, which shifted from the S. W. to the N. E., and was attended with heavy rain.

Many tents were blown down in the Encampments, particularly in the Hessian Regiments, as they have not had any new tents this year. They therefore suffered severely by the Storm. The Camp Equipage and Clothing is daily expected from New York, where it arrived in the last fleet from England.

The Morning clear and cold. Wind N. W. Slight frost early this morning; the first observed this Season.

Two Soldiers of the 54th, and one of the 43rd Regt deserted last night. A Negro fellow who lived at a house near the advanced post at Commonfence, absconded last night also. It is imagined he went off with the Soldiers, and that he has been instrumental in the desertion of some of those who have gone off lately.

The Rebels fired 2 Cannon shot from their Battery at Bristol ferry at some Hessian Soldiers who were employed in pulling down one of the old houses below the Redoubt; but without effect. We gave them a shot in return.

11th Octr — Slight frost this morning. A fine day. Wind N. W.

A Detachment of one Field Officer, 2 Captains, 4 Subalterns, & 120 men from the British and Hessians, has been ordered to be in readiness to embark for Shelter Island, to cut wood.

12th — Thick, cloudy weather, and some rain. Wind E. S. E.

About 3 o'Clock this morning the guard in the battery at Fogland ferry heard some boats rowing down the Seconnet, and altho they could hear the men in them speak, they could not discover them. A Shot was fired towards the place where they were heard, in order to give notice to the Kingsfisher to look out.

There was no appearance of them this morning.

13th — Fine weather. Wind W.

14th Oct^r   Very fine day. Wind N.

Came in a Sloop, with Flour and Tobacco, taken by The Lady Parker, Armed Schooner.

A great many people have been seen to day at Howland's ferry; many of them on horseback.

A flag of truce sloop having been sent up to Providence the 6th Instant, and no account whatever having been received of her since that day, a boat was sent this day to Bristol, with letters to Mr Cooke, the Rebel Governor, and Genl Spencer who Commands in the adjacent district, requesting to know what is become of her.

15th Oct^r — Fine weather. Wind S. W.

The Syren Frigate came in to the harbour yesterday from the Sound.

Great numbers of people seen all day about Howland's ferry, and many Sloops and small craft are continually coming there from the adjacent rivers. A Schooner which lay for some days a little above the ferry, is now in Quaket gut, and they appear to be loading her with something in Casks. Many Carts covered with Red painted Cloth, like the Hessian Ammunition Carts, have been seen about Howland's ferry lately.

The Rebels have four or five pieces of Cannon mounted in their Fort above the ferry.

It appears by the answers to the letters sent to Bristol, that the flag of truce Sloop which was lately sent up to Providence is detained there and the officer and men made prisoners, in consequence of the Officer's having been detected in taking a sketch of the River, with the Soundings, &c. &c. The Rebels are in possession of the Sketch. It is probable this affair will make some noise, and occasion a good deal of trouble. The imprudent conduct of a young Officer is frequently productive of great difficulties to those who Command.

The uncommon movements among the Rebels, and the numbers of people who have been seen of late about Howland's ferry, strongly indicate some enterprize, and make it prudent for us to be on our guard.

16th Oct^r — Very fine weather. Wind N. E.

A great many small arms were fired at Howland's ferry in the course of the day. Numbers of people appear in that quarter.

A Captain and 100 men of the 54th Reg^t marched to the heights above Newport, and relieved the like numbers of Dit-fourth's Regiment employed on the works there.

The Detachment for Wood Cutting, consisting of 120 men under the Command of Lieu^t Col^o Bruce of the 54th Reg^t marched to Newport this morning and embarked on board the transports ordered on that service.

The 43rd Regiment, and the Flank Companies of the 54th, marched this afternoon, and at 5 o'Clock embarked on board transports at Codrington's Cove. These troops are under the Command of Lieu^t Col^o Marsh of the 43rd, and are to sail this night on an Expedition to the Eastward. The transports with the wood cutting party are to go with them, and they are to be convoyed by the Syren and Kingsfisher. It is generally supposed that Bedford, a town about 25 miles to the Eastward, where the Rebels have some Privateers and a number of other vessels is the object.

17th Oct^r — Fair morning, but windy, & likely to rain. Wind N. E.

Everything perfectly quiet last night. This Morning a considerable number of men were observed about Howland's ferry. In the course of the day a great many small arms were fired on the opposite shore. The almost continual irregular firing of small arms for the last two days, where such numbers of people are assembled, are strong indications of their making some attack soon.

A Jew named Isaac Goodman came over last night from the Bristol side, and was brought to Genl Pigot's quarters about one oClock this morning, where he gave the following account — That he left Providence yesterday morning in the Packet for Warren, and came from thence in a Canoe with a man who was going to Bristol; — that after they had got round Papasquash point and had got near Hog Island, he told the man he would give him his watch if he would put him ashore on Rhode Island; which he accordingly did near Arnold's point, and went off without being discovered by our Sentries, as it was dark. He says the Rebels have collected a very formidable force, and intend to attack us very soon. Nine or 10,000 men are now assembled in the vicinity of Howland's ferry for that purpose. That during the Summer a great number of flat boats have been built at & near Providence, and that within a short time, near

300 boats of different descriptions, but most of them flat boats and Scows, have been brought from Providence to Warren, from whence they have been carried over Warren Neck into Kikemuit river, beyond Mount Hope. That most of them are now in Quaket pond (or Wanton's Cove) near Howland's ferry. That they intend making three attacks — One at Howland's ferry, another at Fogland's ferry, and the third at Easton's beach. That two fire ships came down from Providence yesterday Morning, and are now anchored near their Frigate, which is The Providence, Capt Whipple; and that they are to come down the first fair wind, supported by the Frigate, and endeavor to burn our Frigates, while theirs gets out, and the attack is made on the Island. That they have near 40 pieces of Cannon at Howland's, which are to be brought over in Scows. That this Expedition has been concerted for some months, during which time they have been making preparations for it. That 3000 of the troops are Militia of Connecticut, who crossed lately from Warwick to Warren, and from thence by Kikemuit River to Howlands. That they keep a strong guard every night in the Redoubt at the point of Howland's neck. That our last deserters told them we had not above 2000 men on the Island, and that they might easily force us. That they have exact intelligence of everything doing on the Island, and that some Rebels were lately at the house of a person who conveys information to them. He added that the troops they have assembled are all Militia, except about 70 Continental troops and some Artillery, and that they are engaged until the end of October. That many of them were induced to come upon this expedition by the hopes of the plunder of Newport, which was promised them. General Spencer has the Chief Command. He mentions several other particulars with great accuracy and confidence; and declares they give out that we are to be attacked very soon.

In consequence of the abovementioned information, General Pigot thought proper to postpone the attempt against Bedford, and ordered the troops destined for that service to disembark, which they did at one o'Clock this day, and marched to their respective Encampments. The Wood cutting party was also disembarked and joined their Corps.

Bedford was the object of the Detachment under the Command of Lieu^t Colonel Marsh. The Rebels having several Privateers there, and also some West India ships which had been taken by them, our troops were to have taken or destroyed them, and spiked up the Cannon upon a Battery at the entrance of the Port. The force for this service was 400 of the 43rd, 100 of the Flank Companies of the 54th, 120 of the Wood party; 2 Frigates, and the Kingsfisher.

It certainly was a very fortunate circumstance that the Jew came in at the time he did, and that the wind was not quite favorable for the fleet to sail at the time appointed; otherwise it would have gone out with 600 troops; and the Rebels perceiving it, would probably have chosen that time for making the attack. And as the Kingsfisher was to have gone from her Station, the part of the Island where one of the attacks was to be made, would have been left exposed.

There was some great neglect in not sending the Jew to Head-quarters as soon as he came to the first post. He says he landed before 8 o'Clock in the Evening, and yet he did not arrive a Genl Pigot's quarters till one in the morning. The delay might have proved of the utmost consequence; and this instance is a convincing proof of the necessity of sending Deserters, Spies, or persons bringing intelligence, as soon as possible from the ad-vanced posts to Headquarters. The night before the Battle of Minden, the Prince of Anhalt Bernburg, who Commanded the outlying Picquets, detained for two hours at the post where he was stationed, two Deserters who brought information of the march of the French Army to attack the Allies; which delay had nearly been the cause of the Allied Army being surprized.

It appears by some Newspapers brought in by the Jew, that there has been another action to the Northward, near a place called Stillwater. They say Genl Burgoyne has retreated in con-sequence of this Action, and that he has lost a considerable num-ber of men. That Genl Fraser is killed, and 3 Lt Colonels, 6 Captains, 10 Subalterns and 300 men taken prisoners. That their loss is only 30 killed and about 100 wounded, and that Arnold and Lincoln are among the latter. The Rebel papers likewise mention their having taken near 300 men on Lake George, as also all Genl Burgoyne's Batteaux, with a consider-able quantity of Cannon, Stores, &c. &c., and all the Forts & Posts in that quarter, except Ticonderoga & Mount Indepen-dence, which had been summoned to surrender. The Rebels acknowledge that Genl Clinton has gone up Hudson's River, with a large force, and taken Fort Montgomery and Fort Clin-ton, at the entrance of The Highlands, by Storm.

If the Rebels have got into the Rear of Gen¹ Burgoyne's Army, as they afsert they have, it is impofsible he can return to Canada; and therefore the only ſtep he can take, is by one bold movement to endeavor to join Gen¹ Clinton, who, we have reason to suppose has gone up towards Albany with a considerable force in order to facilitate such a movement and form a Junction with him.

The Rebel accounts mention that a 40 Gun Ship has been deſtroyed, and another much damaged in attempting to go up the Delaware to Philadelphia; and that Washington is on the E. side of the Schylkill, and Gen¹ Howe on the Weſt.

18ᵗʰ Octʳ — Thick weather, and ſtrong wind at N. E. with rain.

A Flat boat or Batteaux, marked No. 73, with Six muffled Oars in her, and capable of carrying about 20 Troops, was blown over laſt night to Fogland ferry, and taken up by some men of the Flank Companies.

Great numbers of Rebels appeared to day about Howland's ferry and towards Fogland. They are particularly busy at Quaket Gut, and several Carts and vefsels laden with barrels, appear to be unloading there. No great number of boats can be seen in any part; but they certainly have a considerable number in the Neighbourhood, and have some enterprize of consequence in agitation. There was a good deal of firing yeſterday and this day at Howland's. The firing appears to be at a Mark.

19ᵗʰ Octʳ — Fine weather. Wind S. W.

About 12 oClock laſt night, about 200 Rebels came forward on Howland's neck, and fired at two Hefsian Sentries poſted at the bridge. The Sentries, and a patrole of Six men who happened to come up at that time, fired a good many shot at them, and then retired, at which time an 18 pʳ being fired from Windmill hill at the Rebels, they retired without firing another shot. Not lefs than 500 Musquet shot were fired at our people without effect. Our Sentries resumed their poſt at the bridge soon after, and all was quiet during the remainder of the night.

The firing was so brisk for the time it laſted, which was about 12 minutes, that it was concluded the Rebels meant a serious attack upon that poſt, and the troops were ordered to get under arms, which they did with great expedition. But on finding there was no reason to apprehend an attack, they returned to their tents.

This morning two bayonets and some hats were found near the place from whence the Rebels fired.

Everything was quiet during the day.

Our Galley having undergone some alterations lately at Newport in order to make her sail better, was ordered round this day to the Seconnet paſsage, but in turning out of the harbour she was found to be so totally out of trim, that it was judged unsafe for her to proceed, and she returned into the harbour.

20th Oct^r — Fine weather.   Wind S. W.

About 9 o'Clock laſt night the Sentries of the 22^d Regiment, discovered several of the Enemy's boats going down the Seconnet towards Fogland ferry, and immediately fired to give the alarm. Many boats were perceived soon after from the battery at Fogland, and were fired at from thence. The alarm being quickly communicated, the troops got under arms immediately at the several encampments. The Enemy's boats continued paſsing Fogland to the Southward 'till 2 o'Clock this morning, and whenever they could be perceived were fired at. As it was imagined they intended to land somewhere below the Kingsfisher, and to make an attempt upon the town, The 22^d Regiment marched from Quaker hill to Fogland, and proceeded thence, by an order from Genl Pigot to the Windmill near the General hospital. The 54th replaced the 22^d at Quaker hill. At 11 o'Clock at night the Rebel Galley came out from Howland's, and endeavored to work down towards Fogland, but the wind being unfavorable she was obliged to give it up, and in returning she fired three Shot at our shore without effect, and then anchored between Quaket Gut and the point of Howland's neck.

The troops remained under arms all night at the different poſts in expectation of an attack from the Enemy, as the movement of their boats indicated such an attempt, but there was no further appearance of them, nor did The Kingsfisher observe any boat to paſs her during the night. Above 70 boats, as well as could be judged paſsed Fogland. A great many shot were fired at them; and the people on duty at that battery say that two of them were certainly deſtroyed. Altho the Moon shone clear it was not easy to discover them, as they paſsed one by one, and kept close under their shore. At daylight very few could be seen; so that they muſt have taken them into the Creek behind the South point of Fogland.

A Serjeant and a Private of the 17th Dragoons who were patroling laſt night towards Sachaweſt beach, were surrounded and carried off by a party of about 20 Rebels who had landed thereabouts. One Taggart, and his Son, who lived near the place, went off with the Rebels; and it is supposed were concerned with them in surprizing the Dragoons.

The Rebel Galley changed her position this morning, and went a little above Howland's ferry. In going off, she fired an 18 p^r at the Bridge Redoubt, which ſtruck within 30 yards of it.

The 54th Reg^t returned after Sunrise to their Camp at Windmill hill. The 22nd having been ordered to encamp near the General hospital, they sent for their tents & baggage this Morning; and in the afternoon the 54th marched, with two 6 p^{rs} and take up their position on Quaker hill.

In order to ſtrengthen the poſt at Howland's bridge, an Abbattis of large apple trees from the Neighbouring Orchards was thrown acroſs the Neck about 200 yards on this side of the bridge, which will prevent the Enemy from advancing in that part with Cannon, or any considerable number of Troops without firſt removing them, which will take up some time, and muſt be done under our fire.

The troops are ordered to lie dreſsed till further orders, and ready to take their arms on the shorteſt notice.

,21st Octr Fine weather.   Wind N. W.

About 12 o'Clock laſt night a party of Rebels came forward, & fired at our Sentries at Howland's bridge, but retired again as soon as a Cannon shot was fired at them. An Officer's Bayonet was found on the beach beyond the bridge this morning. No person was hurt on our side, nor could we be certain that the Rebels suffered any loſs.

The Unicorn Frigate came in yeſterday from New York with some Victuallers under her Convoy. The accounts by her are, that there has been another action in Pensylvania on the 3rd Inſtant, in which the Rebels left 3000 men on the field, and were totally dispersed, with the loſs of all their Cannon, baggage, &c; and that Washington is wounded, and has not above 500 men with him. The particulars of the action had not been published at New York.

It appears that General Clinton, who had gone up Hudson's River with about 3000 men, had on the 6th Inſtant ſtormed & taken Forts Montgomery and Clinton; and had also taken Fort

Conſtitution. The poſſeſsion of these poſts opens to him a free
paſsage to Albany; to which place it was supposed he was proceeding, as it had been reported that Gen¹ Burgoyne's advanced guard had penetrated to Albany after defeating the
Rebels at Stillwater.

A great many disaffected persons have been taken up in Newport within these few days, and sent on board the Prisonship.
It was high time to confine them, as they have spoken their
sentiments very freely of late, and no doubt would do all the
mischief in their power, if they had their liberty, in case of an
attack.

We have had some convincing proofs of late of the bad con-
ſtruction of Howland's bridge Redoubt. The 9 pʳ placed in the
right Embrazure could not be brought to bear on the ground
from which the Rebels fired the night of the 18ᵗʰ Inſtant; and
the following night it could not be brought to bear on the boats,
nor is there room to work it, and yet the Embrazures are so
placed, that if the work is attacked in front the flanks are so
enfiladed that the troops ſtationed there could not long ſtand on
that part. Its principal ſtrength consiſts in a good Abbattis,
which, however, has undergone considerable additions and alterations since the Engineer reported it to be complete.

22ᵈ Octʳ — Fine weather, but rather cold. Strong wind at N. E.

The Syren & Unicorn got round into the Seconnet paſsage
today, and anchored to the Southward of the Kingsfisher. As
that part of the Island is sufficiently guarded by this movement,
the 22ᵈ Regᵗ marched and encamped near Elam's house on the
right of the Chaſseurs. A Battery for two Guns was ordered to
be made on the shore to the right of the Chaſseurs, in order to
Command that part of the adjacent beach Which is favorable
for landing on. As soon as the party began to work, the Rebels
fired at them from their battery on the South point of Fogland.
One shot took place and killed a Heſsian. The same shot went
So near the head of a Soldier of the Light Infantry as to Strike
him down senseleſs; so that he was obliged to be carried to the
hospital.

We began this morning to throw an Abbattis acroſs Commonfence Neck, from the head of the town pond to the Creek which
runs to Howland's bridge.

The Cattle and Corn of Taggart who went off with the Rebels
the night of the 19ᵗʰ were seized by order of the General. The

Cattle were distributed to the troops; the Corn sent to the Magazine; and the house given up to the Hefsians; who first plundered it, and then pulled it down to the ground.

23ʳᵈ Octʳ   Cold raw weather.   Wind N. E.

About 9 o'Clock last night 5 boats of the Enemy came near the Officer's guard at the house near Howland's bridge, and fired at the men on duty there; the Guard returned the fire briskly, and obliged them to Sheer off. They soon after rowed towards the bridge and the men having landed a little beyond it, fired at our Sentries. Two shot being fired at them from the Redoubt, they retired, and did not appear again during the night. A Bayonet and several Cartridges were found on the beach near the bridge this morning.

The Rebels began to Cannonade the Encampment of the 22ᵈ Regᵗ this morning from the S. point of Fogland, and as the shot came home, it was prudent for them to move, in consequence of which they encamped near Lopez's house. No hurt was done, although three Shot came into the Camp. The Rebels also fired some shot at the New Battery, and at the Encampment of the Chafseurs, but without effect.

The New Battery on the shore to the right of the Chafseurs, appears to me to be placed very injudiciously. The intention of the battery is to Scour that part of the adjacent beach which is favorable for landing on, but this end would be as effectually obtained if the work was higher up on the hill, and it would have the additional advantage of not being Commanded by the Enemys battery, which it now is. We are told the Guns which are to be in it, are to be placed En Barbette; if so, they will certainly be dismantled by the Enemy. Our System of Field fortification is certainly a new one. We erect Batteries with Embrazures on heights where it is impofsible for the Enemy to bring a Gun against them; and we construct them En Barbette in situations under the Enemy's fire!!!

A boat from one of the Ships of War went over to the Eastern shore last night, and brought off from a house near the Windmill, two men; one of whom says he was drafted to serve on the Expedition against Rhode Island. They say that the Rebels have near 200 boats in the Mill-Creek behind the S. point of Fogland; that they have near 10,000 men afsembled in the Neighbourhood, and intend making their principal attack near lower Black point. That most of the troops have been drafted for the present service, and their time expires on the laſt day of this Month, at which time, if nothing is done, they will disperse. They add, that some of them are much difsatisfied, and that many have gone home already.

The General having some reason to Suppose the Rebels will attempt something this night, ordered the working part of 100 men of the 54th Regiment, to march from Newport to ſtrengthen the poſts near Black point.

About 70 of the moſt disaffeſted Inhabitants of Newport, were taken up yeſterday and this day, and sent on board the Prison ship.

The Abbattis acrofs Commonfence Neck, was finished this day. It affords considerable ſtrength to that part, and will be a great obſtacle to the Rebels if they make an attack in that quarter.

A Soldier of the 54th Reg[t] who was poſted on the outside of Sandford's Orchard while the Oxen were drawing away the trees to form the Abbattis, deserted in sight of all our Sentries, and made immediately for the point, where he fired two Shot as a signal to the Galley to take him off, which was affeſted before our people could prevent him.

24th Oct[r]   Thick weather all day, and some rain. Wind E.

About 7 o'Clock laſt night the Rebels made a large fire on Papasquash point, which was answered by 3 Rockets from Briſtol, and the Rockets by a fire at Howland's. They however remained quiet during the night, except firing a shot from their battery on the S. point of Fogland at some of our boats which were on the look out near their shore.

The Battery on the right of the Chafseurs was finished this Evening, and 2. 12 p[rs] brought into it. It has been found necefsary to conſtruſt it with Embrazures. The Rebels fired two shot at the workmen, and one at the Camp of the 22[d] but without effeſt.

Two 12 p[rs] were placed in the artillery Redoubt this day. We cut an Embrazure in the rear face of Briſtol Redoubt this afternoon, in order to place a 12 pr there to fire on Commonfence Neck. The Rebels seeing our men at work, fired three Shot at them from their side, but did no damage.

About 4 this afternoon, some person of diſtinſtion among the Rebels put off from Briſtol in a boat, and was saluted with 13 Guns; and on going round Papasquash point he was saluted with the like number from thence. The boat proceeded towards Providence.

Some Rebels having advanced on Commonfence Neck towards the Captain's Guard this afternoon, two shot were fired at them from the 3 pr, on which they retired.

Many of the Loyal Inhabitants of Newport having signified to the General some days ago, their desire to afsociate, and take arms for the defence and security of the town, and the General having accepted and approved of their offer, about 180 of them who have signed the articles of association, were this day formed into three Companies under the Command of Col° Wanton.

25th Octr 1777   Thick rainy weather moſt part of laſt night, and this day. Wind E. S. E.

About 12 laſt night a party of near 100 Rebels came forward, and commenced a brisk fire upon our Sentries at Howland's bridge & Commonfence Neck. Our Sentries withdrew after returning their fire; and the Rebels having advanced pretty near, they were saluted with the Guns at the bridge Redoubt, & Commonfence; and also the 12 pr at Briſtol Redoubt, on which they retired. A New Whaleboat, marked N° 28, was found on the beach beyond Howland's bridge this morning, and brought in by some of our men, in spight of a party of Rebels who endeavored to prevent them.

A 12 pr was brought from Briſtol Redoubt this morning, & placed in that at Howland's bridge, where it will be of much service.

26th Octr — Thick weather, and some rain. Wind S. E.

Laſt night was extremely dark and ſtill, and a very favorable one for the Rebels to have made their attack; but they remained perfeɕtly quiet. We now begin to think they will not make any general attack on the Island, and that in a few days they will begin to disperse and return to their respeɕtive homes. The late news from Pensylvania will make them extremely cautious of attacking us. Indeed the attempt to conquer this Island situated as we at present are, is an enterprize attended with numerous and great difficulties, and such a one as would hardly be undertaken by the ableſt General at the head of the beſt troops.

The Rebels have made a new Battery a little to the Northward of the S. point of Fogland. This afternoon they brought a 12 pr on a travelling Carriage into it, and fired several shot at the Camp of the Flank Companies, some of which came home, but did no damage. They threw two shot a good way over our Battery at Fogland ferry. A 24 pʳ with a Charge of 9 lbˢ of powder was fired at them, but as the shot fell short, another was fired with 11 lbˢ of powder, and the Gun elevated till the breech rested on the transam of the Carriage; but that shot fell short above 300 yards. The ground on our side is about level with theirs. Their throwing their Shot so much farther than we can, (which I have generally observed to be the case) is only to be accounted for by supposing their powder to be much better than ours.

Our Galley came round into the Seconnet this Evening from Newport. We have now there the Unicorn, Syren, & Kingsfisher; the Galley and an Armed Schooner.

It is to be observed that in the Month of October 1777, The Rebels had a greater number of Troops actually serving, than at any other period during the War.
For instance —

		Men
	At The Action of Germantown, the 4ᵗʰ Octʳ 1777, Washington's force was computed at	14000
13ᵗʰ Octʳ	At Saratoga, at the time of The Convention, Gates had about	16000
	About The 14ᵗʰ Octʳ 1777, Spencer had collected for an attack on Rhode Island — about	11,000
	Total	41,000

Exclusive of The troops stationed at all their other posts, in the different provinces.

27ᵗʰ Octʳ — Rain most part of the day, with a strong wind at N. E. Everything quiet. A Soldier of the 22ᵈ Regᵗ deserted.

The Abbattis on Commonfence Neck was extended toDay along the edge of the most practicable part of the Morafs towards Howland's bridge. It is now extremely difficult to advance that way with troops, and impofsible to bring forward Carriages without removing some part of it, which must be done under fire of the Redoubts.

A body of about 400 Rebels, with their arms and knapsacks were seen yesterday evening marching up the Boston road from Howland's ferry.

The force now on this Island is disposed as follows —

The Hefsian Regiments of Ditfourth & Landgrave, Encamped on the left of Windmill hill.

The 43rd Reg^t on the hill behind Windmill hill redoubt.

The 54th on Quaker hill, fronting the Seconnet.

The Flank Companies — At Fogland ferry.

The Chafseurs. At point Pleasant, about a mile S. of Fogland.

The 22^d — At Lopez's house.

The Hefsian Regiments of Hyne & Bunau, on the height above Eaſton's beach. The Detachment of a Capt & 100 men of the 54th employed on the works near Newport, are encamped at the 3 Windmills at the entrance of the town.

The Park of Artillery is on Barrington's hill, near the Artillery Red^t.

The poſts at night are,	C	S	S	C	D	P.
Provision guard on the Weſt Shore, opposite						
The Juno				1		6
Artillery Redoubt		1	1	1	1	24
Behind Anthony's house, near Briſtol ferry						
Windmill		1	3	4	1	50

From which are detached,
To the shore on the left 1 Serj^t & 12,
To Do. on the right 1 ......12.

At Briſtol ferry Redoubt	1	1	3	3	1	56

	S	C	P
From which are detached			
To the house next the Windmill	1		8
To the ferry house	1		12
To the house at the point, near the Pond..................	1		12
To Wm Anthony's house, near Com^{n}fence		1	6

At Commonfence Redoubt	1	2	2	2	1	54
At Howland's bridge Redoubt		1	1	1	1	30
At Howland's ferry house		1	1	1	1	30
At Upper Black point		1	1	1	1	30
At Ewing's house		1	1	1	1	30
In front of 54th Regiment		1	1	1	1	30

All the above are furnished by the 2 British and 2 Hefsian Reg^{ts}.

At Fogland ferry Redoubt	1	1	3	1	30
From the Flank Companies, detaching small poſts to the Right and Left.					
At Point pleasant. From the Chafseurs	1	1	3	1	30
From the 22^d Regiment	2	2	4	2	60

Communicating with the Chaſseurs on their left, and extending as far as the Lower Black point, opposite the Kingsfisher.

From thence round to Eaſton's beach, there are no Guards or Picquets, the Ships of War in the Seconnet having undertaken to guard that part of the Coaſt.

	S	S	C	D	P
At the Redoubt above Eaſton's beach	I	I	I	I	30
At the Junction of the roads, by the 3 Windmills	I	I	I	I	30

These poſts, as well as all the Guards in Newport, and a Detachment of a Captain and 60 men at Cononicut Island, are furnished by the troops near town.

By this disposition of our poſts, there is a Chain of Sentries from the Provision store on the left of the Camp near Windmill hill, quite round, by the shore, to the lower Black point, a space of near 8 miles. Patroles go conſtantly during the night from one poſt to the other, by which a communication is kept up, and the earlieſt notice given of the movements or approach of the Enemy.

There are no guards on the W. side of the Island, from the Provision Store guard to The North Battery in Newport, except a Guard of a Serj^t and 12 men at Redwoods house, near Genl Smith's Winter quarters, which guard sends patroles down to the shore behind the house. A patrole of the aſsociated Inhabitants goes from the town as far as Codrington's Cove.

The disposition of the Artillery is as follows —

With the two Heſsian Battalions at Windmill hill ..	4. 3 p^{rs} braſs	
With The 43rd Regiment	2. 6	D^o
With the 54th	2. 6	D^o
With the 22^d	2. 6	D^o

Remaining at The Park. 2 Medium 12 prs; 1–3 pr; 1–5½ Inch Howitzer.
With the 2 Heſsian Battalions near Newport — 6. 3 p^{rs} Braſs.

In the Redoubts & Batteries at the N. part of the Island.

Artillery Redoubt	2. 12 p^{rs}		
Windmill Hill Redoubt	4. 18 ...		
Briſtol ferry Redoubt	1– 24	1– 18 p^r	1– 12 p^r
Commonfence Do.	1– 3 braſs		
Howland's bridge Do.	1– 12 p^r 1– 9 p^r		
Fogland ferry Do.	4– 24–		
Point pleasant Battery	2– 12–		

There are a number of heavy Guns in the Forts and Batteries at and near Newport.

The Naval force is disposed of as follows —

The Chatham - - -	In the harbour opposite the town.
The Renown - - - -	⎰ In the West, or Naraganset passage, between ⎱ Cononicut and the Naraganset shore
The Amazon - - - -	Above Hope Island; W. of Prudence.
The Orpheus - - - -	⎰ About a mile above Dyer's Island, between ⎱ Prudence and Rhode Island.
The Juno - - - - - -	⎰ In the same Channel, & nearly equidistant from ⎱ Prudence, Papasquash point, Hog-Island, and ⎱ Rhode Island.
The Kingsfisher -	About a Mile below Black point, Seconnet passage.
The Unicorn ⎱ The Syren ⎰ - -	Between the Kingsfisher, & Sachawest point.
The Alarm Galley & ⎱ Lady Parker, ⎱ Armed Schooner ⎰	Ahead of the Kingsfisher, & near Blackpoint.

As The whole force of the Rebels appears to be collected on the Eastern shore, we have turned our attention almost entirely that way; but I think we should not neglect the defence of the W. side so much as we have done. The placing the Orpheus in the passage between Cononicut & Prudence, would prevent the Enemy from making any attempt from that quarter, and would render the W. side much more secure. She would answer any Naval purpose full as well there as in her present station; for any wind which brings an Enemy down to attack the Juno, prevents the Orpheus from going to her assistance; and if the Juno should be obliged to quit her station, she might as well run down to the Orpheus in the proposed station, as to that in which she now lies. The proposed station would also enable the Orpheus to go to the assistance of the Amazon, or the Renown; or to proceed to the town.

If during an attack at Howland's or any part of the E. side of the Island, the Rebels were to land but 50 men on the W. side, which they might easily do by coming from Warwick point down the W. side of Prudence, the alarm they would occasion, and the uncertainty, until daylight of their numbers and situation, would cause considerable diversion, & might be attended with ill consequences to us.

28th Octr — Rain most part of last night, and all this day. Strong wind at N. E., and very cold.

This weather is extremely unfavorable for the Rebels, if they mean to make an attack on us.

Came in The Cabot, Armed brig from Halifax, in her way to join Lord Howe. She was directed to call in here with a letter from General Maſsey, intimating that he had received information from Boſton, that a large force was collecting to attack us.

A man who says he was a Marine on board The Fox Frigate, when she was taken, and has been confined on board The Rebel Galley, above three weeks, made his escape from her, and came over to us laſt night. He positively aſserts that the Rebels intended to land below Fogland ferry the night of the 19th, but that finding we had discovered their boats in motion, and the wind rather againſt them, they put it off. He says one man was killed, and another had his arms shot off in one of their boats as they paſsed our battery. That many of their boats have since returned to Quaket pond, where they now have about 200 of all descriptions. That they were in their boats again the night of the 26th, and intended to land near Howland's bridge; but the wind rising a little, with some rain, the attack was given over. That they have about 9,000 men aſsembled for the attack of the Island, and have a good many Cannon. That the time for which the greateſt part of thier men are engaged expires the laſt day of this Month; and that he heard some of the Officers of the Galley say, orders had been given not to send any more provisions to Howland's ferry. He says the Galley mounts 2. 18 prs 2. 9 prs 4– 6 prs 2. 4 prs, and 10 Swivels, and that there are but 22 persons on board her, all of whom except one, call themselves Officers.

29th Octr — Strong gale of wind and heavy rain all laſt night, from the N. E. High wind all this day, and much rain.

A Barrack for 200 men is to be built immediately on Windmill hill.

30th Octr   Laſt night was perfectly ſtill and altho there was some rain, it was a favorable night for the Rebels to make their long intended attack.

A Deserter came in this morning in a small boat from Howland's ferry. The information he gives is, that we were certainly to have been attacked the night of the 19th. That 11,000 men were actually aſsembled that night for the purpose, and that three separate attacks were to have been made; one by Howlands ferry of 3,000 men; another below Fogland, for which 7,000 men were prepared; and the third of 1,000 men, who were to come from Seconnet point, and land as near the town as posssible. That the attack at Howland's was to commence three hours before the others, in order to draw our attention and force that way. That their artillery, consisting of Eighteen 3 and 4 prs (4 of which were brass) were embarked in Scows with the Artillery Companies, and were to have been towed over with the different attacks. That the people assembled with the greatest readiness, and had the most Sanguine hopes of success, as our deserters had all along informed them that we had not above 2,500 men on the Island. That the attempt was laid aside for that night in consequence of our having discovered their boats in motion, and the wind being rather too high and unfavorable. That they were assembled again the night of the 23rd, and were to have made one grand attack at Howland's Neck, (all the boats having been previously brought back to Quaket pond) but Genl Spencer finding he could not muster above 4,000 men, and a deserter who went over to them that day having informed him that our strength was much greater than they imagined, and that we were well prepared for an attack at Howland's, thought that number insufficient, and therefore gave over the design and dismissed them. That some of them were again assembled the night of the 25th, but as great numbers of the Militia had by that time left the Army and gone to their respective homes, they found their strength quite unequal to the Enterprize, and they were again dismissed. He says they have now given up the intention of making any attack upon us, and that part of the troops returned home four days ago. The Boston Artillery, consisting of two Companies, with four Brass 4 prs, marched yesterday. Others are going this day, and that only 1,000 men are to remain to guard the Coast from Howland's ferry to Seconnet point. He says, that during the time they have been assembled they have suffered greatly from the weather, and want of many articles: numbers of them having been under the necessity of lying out under the Walls and hedges, as the houses and barns were not capable of containing them. That they are in general badly clothed, every article of that nature being extremely scarce and dear. Shoes cost 6 Dollars a pair. Worsted Stockings 4 Dollars, and other articles in proportion. They have not had any Rum given them since they have been assembled. Some people who had Rum there sold it at 3s/ a Gill. This man further says, they were informed that the whole of Gen¹ Burgoyne's Army was taken prisoners, and were not to serve during the War; and that they were to march from Saratoga, the place where they surrendered, to Boston, where they were to remain until Ships arrived to carry them to England.

Soon after day light this morning, we saw a number of boats full of men put off from Howland's ferry. They rowed round the N. point of the Island, crossed Mount Hope bay, and went towards Kikemuit River. In the course of the day above 60 boats of different sizes, and several small Sloops, all full of men, went up that way. Many covered Carts were also seen going up the Boston road, each of them escorted by 8 or 10 men. It is now evident that the Rebels have given up their intention of attacking this Island, and that their troops are dispersing and returning to their respective homes.

Another deserter came in about 2 o'Clock this day. The men in the boat he belonged to, landed on Commonfence Neck to gather Apples; and as his Mother lives in Newport, he made use of the opportunity of coming away from them. He confirms the account of the deserter who came in this Morning, and says the Rebels are all upon their return home, having given up all thoughts of attacking us at present.

31ˢᵗ Octʳ   Frost last night.   Fair clear day.   Wind N.

Some Soldiers being employed this morning in felling trees near Howland's bridge, in order to form an Abbattis along the shore, the Rebels fired four Cannon shot at them from their lower battery at Howland's ferry, but without any effect.

The flag of truce Sloop which has been detained by the Rebels for some time at Providence, came down last night. There is no doubt the real cause of her detention was, to prevent our receiving information of the attack which was then in agitation. The imprudent conduct of the Officer who commanded her, certainly afforded them a pretext for detaining her, as he had been observed taking sketches of the upper part of the Bay, and the situation of their ships. The Sloop in her way down saw many of the Rebel troops going up towards Providence.

In one of the Newspapers brought down by the Sloop, the Rebels have published the articles of a Convention between Gen¹ Burgoyne, and Gen¹ Gates, by which it is agreed that The King's Army shall lay down their Arms, and be allowed a free paſsage to Great Britain, upon condition of not serving in North America during the present contest; and that they shall be conducted to Boſton, and remain there until transports arrive to carry them home. This matter is mentioned as an undoubted fact. If it is true, it is a moſt unfortunate buſineſs, & will be attended by numerous bad consequences.

The Rebel papers say that General Howe's Army is nearly in the same situation which Gen[l] Burgoyne's lately was. But we truſt this is without any foundation whatever.

1st Nov[r] — Slight froſt. Fine weather. Wind S. W.

The Cabot sailed yeſterday to join Lord Howe.

General Pigot, being apprehensive that, if the accounts of the surrender of Gen[l] Burgoyne's Army are true, the Rebels may again be able to collect a force for the attack of this Island, has ordered the different works to be finished with all expedition. In consequence of which 100 men of the 22[d] Reg[t] marched and encamped near the town, to work thereon. Trees are felling and laying along the moſt practicable landing places on the Eaſtern shore of the Island.

The Park of Artillery broke up Camp this day, and such Guns and Stores as will not be wanted at this end of the Island, were removed to Newport.

Two ships of War are for the future to be ſtationed in the Seconnet paſsage.

2[d] Nov[r] — Very fine weather. Wind S.

The 22[d] Reg[t] marched this morning and encamped at the 3 Windmills near Newport. They are to be employed on the works near the town.

3rd Fine weather. Wind S. W.

Came in The Lark and Flora frigates from a Cruize. The Syren and The Galley came round from the Seconnet to Newport.

The whole of the 22[d] Regiment is now employed on the lines and works near the town. One face of the principal Redoubt near the 3 Windmills having fallen down, a large party is now employed in repairing it.

4th Nov[r] — Fine day. Wind S. W.

A Soldier of the 43rd Reg[t] deserted laſt night from his poſt at Commonfence, and got clear off.

Came in The Diamond frigate from a Cruize: — also an Armed ship from New York with four Victuallers under her Convoy.

Five boats came in from Block Island with live Stock for sale.

5th — Pleasant weather. Wind W.

Several Rebel Sloops, having a number of boats in tow, went from Howland's ferry, towards Kikemuit river. The boats were empty.

A Detachment consisting of one Field officer, 2 Captains, four Subalterns, 6 Serjeants, 6 Corporals, 4 Drummers, and 100 men, from the British and Hessians, embarked this day at Newport, on board the Fleet which is going to Shelter Island for Wood. Mayor Eyre of the 54th Commands.

6th Nov^r   Rain all last night and this day. Wind N. E. About 6 in the Evening it cleared up, with a strong wind at N.

The wood fleet sailed last night under Convoy of the Syren.

7th Nov^r   Clear Cold weather. Wind N. W. High wind all last night.

About 4 o'Clock yesterday morning the Syren Frigate, a transport ship, and a Schooner, belonging to the Wood fleet, by some unfortunate mistake or mismanagement, ran ashore upon Point Judith, where the Syren immediately bulged. Every effort was made by Captain Furneaux to get the ship off, but the Rebels having very soon brought down three pieces of Cannon against her, and the ship unfortunately keeling towards the shore when the tide left her, he was under the necessity of surrendering himself and his people prisoners to the Enemy. The Lark and Flora went out of the harbour at 4 in the afternoon in order to afford assistance, but they came too late. A Sloop which went out soon after the first Signals of distress were made, arrived in time to save the people of the transport; and it is probable that had the two Frigates gone out at the same time, they might have saved the Crew of the Syren. The vessels now remain on shore, without any hopes of getting them off. The rest of the Fleet escaped the danger, and proceeded to Shelter Island.

8th Nov^r — Fair day. Wind S. W.

The weather being moderate, it is probable the Rebels will make every effort in their power to get what they can out of

The Syren. The Ships are seen on shore at Point Judith, with their Masts standing.

About 12 this day above 20 boats, many of them large, and all full of men, went from Howland's, crofsed the bay, and went towards Kikemuit River. There appeared to be about 300 men in them. They had been observed under arms about 8 o'Clock this morning opposite Quaker hill, and were seen to march from thence to the place where they embarked.

9th Nov[r]   Rain moſt part of laſt night and this day. Wind N. N. E. and cold.

The late accounts from New York mention that Gen[l] Clinton had returned to New York from the Expedition up the River, and was preparing to sail with a considerable Corps for the Delaware.

The account of the Surrender of Gen[l] Burgoyne's Army, is confirmed by Lord Petersham, one of Gen[l] Burgoyne's Aides-de Camp, who was arrived at New York on his way to England, with the particulars of that unfortunate affair.

Tis said that Gates had detached 11 Battalions to reinforce Washington's Army.

The laſt accounts from Gen[l] Howe are, that he was at Germantown near Philadelphia. The Ships of War had not then forced the pafsage of the Delaware.

Washington certainly attacked Gen[l] Howe's Army at Germantown on the 4th October, but was beat back with great lofs. Gen[l] Howe's principal objeƈt appears now to be, to open a Communication with the shipping in the Delaware, by reducing the Forts and works which command the navigation of that River, & by that means facilitate the reception of provisions and supplies for his Army. The Rebels having ſtrengthened the defences of the River, it will be impofsible for Gen[l] Howe to have the neighbourhood of Philadelphia until those places are reduced and this service effeƈted, and should it take up any considerable time, it will enable Washington, especially since the Surrender of Gen[l] Burgoyne's Army, to receive great reinforcements from Gates, and pofsibly make head again. If Washington can colleƈt his whole force before the reduƈtion of the Forts which command the Delaware, Gen[l] Howe will find some difficulty in receiving his supplies, as they muſt until then, come from The Chesapeak. If Lord Howe should fail in forcing the Delaware, Gen[l] Howe may perhaps find it expedient to burn

Philadelphia, pafs the Delaware, and march through Jersey towards Staten Island.

10th Novr 1777   Rain moſt part of the day.   Wind N. E.

The several quarters for the troops on this Island, during the ensuing winter, were appointed. Six Battalions are to be ſtationed in Newport, and one in the several Barracks and poſts at the N. part of the Island, to do the duty there. This Battalion is to be relieved Monthly.

11th — Very cold day. Strong wind at N. W. Some Snow in the morning, and hard froſt at night.

It being found impoſsible to get The Syren off, she was sat on fire laſt night by our people.

12th Nov^r — Cold day, with much rain, and Strong wind at W.

The Barracks at Windmill-hill go on so slowly for want of materials, that there is a prospeact of the troops remaining in Camp for three weeks to come. The troops suffer a good deal from the severity of the weather :nd the badnefs of the tents, particularly the Hefsians, whose tents are almoſt torn to pieces, this being the second Campaign they have been in use. The Hefsians are also in great want of their clothing, as they have not had any new since they came to America.

13th Nov^r   Cold day, and ſtrong wind at N. W.

A flag of truce came down this Evening from Providence, with letters from Captain Furneaux of The Syren, and proposals from Mr Cooke, the Rebel Governor of the Province, for an exchange of the Seamen of The Syren for an equal number of Rebel Seamen now confined on board the Prison ship in this harbour.

14th   Sharp froſt, and cold wind at N. W.

A court of Enquiry has been ordered by the Rebels to examine into the cause of the failure of the Expedition againſt Rhode Island under Genl Spencer; who is much censured for not having attempted to land.

15th Nov^r   Sharp froſt. Strong wind at N. W., and very cold.

Everything quiet, and hardly a Rebel to be seen on the opposite shores. The troops continue to work at fitting up the Barracks in Newport, and at the advanced poſts.

16th   Frost, and cold wind at N. W.

A Deserter came in this morning with his Arms. He says the Rebels have only one Regiment, consisting of about 800 men, doing duty along the Eastern shore.

The Diamond and Flora Frigates, came up today to relieve the Orpheus and Juno.

The Lark Frigate, having got the Small pox on board, has hauled inside of Goat Island, and put her people on shore there. The Ship is ordered to be cleansed and purified.

17th Nov^r   Frost. Wind S. W. Snow from 12 till 4.

18th   High wind all last night at W. and severe frost. Frost this day, and strong wind at N. W. A good deal of Snow lies on the Main, but none on this Island.

The Orpheus and Juno, went down to Newport.

19th Nov^r — Hard frost last night. Cold day. Wind N. W.

The Inhabitants here say we shall have a very severe winter; and the reason they give for this opinion is, that they have found by experience that when much rain falls in October and November, the ground being wet when the frost sets in, the winds are much colder than when there has been a dry autumn. It is indeed a general observation that the more Ice the wind passes over, the colder it is.

The Galley came down to Howland's ferry this Morning from behind Mount Hope.

'Tis said that General Spencer, late Commander in Chief of the Expedition against this Island, has been broke by the sentence of a Court Martial, for not attacking us; — and that Col° Barton, (who took Gen¹ Prescott) is appointed to the Command in our Neighbourhood, and is preparing to pay us a visit.

20th Nov^r   Hard frost. Wind N. W.

Seven boats belonging to the Rebels went down this Morning from Howland's ferry to Fogland. There were only a few men in each of them.

21st   Fine soft day. Thaw. Wind S.

Four men deserted from the Rebel Galley last night, & came in a small boat to our guard near Howland's bridge. Two of them are Negroes; the other two are British Seamen, one of them belonging to the Juno and was taken lately on Prudence Island. The other belongs to the Unicorn.

A flag of truce came down from Providence this afternoon, with 60 Seamen belonging to the Syren, to be exchanged.

22ᵈ Novʳ   A good deal of rain last night. Wind S. W. A fine clear day, with the wind at N. W.

A Soldier of the 43ʳᵈ Regᵗ deserted last night from the Guard at Commonfence Redoubt.

About 4 this afternoon 12 Rebel boats went down from Howland's to Fogland. There were only a few men in them. This movement of boats towards Fogland, looks as if the Rebels intended something in that quarter. But it is more probable these boats are some of those which were said to have been brought round from Bedford the 19ᵗʰ October, and are now going back there.

The men who came over yesterday say there is only a Colonel Shelburne's Regiment, consisting of about 800 men, doing duty on the Eastern side. They also say the Rebels have three Privateers ready for Sea up Taunton River, and that they intend to attempt going to Sea the first favorable night.

23ʳᵈ Novʳ   Fine weather. Wind N.

Accounts have been received of the arrival of General Burgoyne's Army at Cambridge near Boston, and that they are quartered in the Barracks in that neighbourhood which the Rebels built during the Blockade of Boston.

24ᵗʰ   A Cold day, & Some rain. Wind S. E.

Several victuallers and other vessels which went out of the harbour yesterday under Convoy of the Juno, for New York, were obliged to put back this morning.

25ᵗʰ   Thick weather, and some very heavy rain this morning. About 12 it cleared up. Wind W.

26ᵗʰ Novʳ — Clear fine weather. Wind N. W.

An Abbattis was made this morning from the shore at the Mouth of the town pond, for 300 yards to the right, along the edge of the pond, which in that part is passable at low water.

The Rebels fired a shot from their battery at Bristol ferry at some of our men who were cutting down trees below the Redoubt. The Shot having struck against a rock, broke into several pieces, which fell among the men, but did no damage.

Two men, with a woman, and two young children came in laſt night in a small boat from the Eaſtern shore. They landed near the pond on Commonfence neck. Their boat was deeply laden with provisions, and some of their moſt valuable effects. They say they have fled from the persecution of the Rebels who have filled the Jails of the Country with those who have shewn the leaſt attachment to the King's Government. They say that Colonel Barton is daily expected from Congreſs, after which he is to raise men for another expedition againſt this Island. General Spencer is in confinement on account of his ill conduct in the late Expedition. It is currently reported in the Country that there has been another action near Philadelphia, in which Washington was defeated and taken prisoner.

27th Novr Clear Cold day.   Wind W.
The fleet for New York sailed this morning under Convoy of The Juno.
Our Galley came round from Newport into the Seconnet paſsage, where she is to be ſtationed.

Detail of Duty.   N. End of Rhode Island.   27th Novr 1777

		C	S	S	C	D	P
British	Commonfence Redoubt..........	I	I	I	I	I	24
	Reinforced at night by		I	I	I	I	24
	Howland's bridge Redoubt.......		I	I	I	I	24
	Ewing's house. (A Picquet)		I	I	I	I	21
	Quaker-hill. (A Picquet)		I	I	I	I	21
	Redwood's house			I	I		12
	General Smith's			I	I		12
	Magazine				I		3
	Windmill hill...................						3
		I	5	7	8	5	144
Heſsians	Briſtol ferry Redoubt	I	I	3	3	2	56
	Near Anthony's house (a Picquet)		I	2	2	I	50
	Howland's ferry house		I	I	I	I	30
	Provision Store			I	I		12
		I	3	7	7	4	148
Total		2	8	14	15	9	292

28th   Fine weather.   Wind W.

The Galley came up the Seconnet, and anchored opposite Quaker hill, about half a mile from our shore.

A Rebel Brig came down yesterday from Warwick, and anchored about a mile and half ahead of The Amazon. As soon as it was dark, Captain Jacobs sent his boats up, and took pofsession of her without any resistance. She is an empty vefsel, and had but a few hands on board. There is little doubt but the intention of the people in her, was to endeavor to get out to Sea in the night; but as soon as they were boarded they declared they had made their escape from the Rebels in her, and intended to deliver themselves up. She was sent down to Newport this morning.

29th Nov^r   Heavy rain, and very strong wind from the N. E. part of last night, and most part of this morning. The latter part of the day very thick, cloudy and cold.

30th   Thick weather.   Wind N. E.

A Rebel privateer of 16 Guns (formerly a British ship called The Blaize Castle) came down the River last night. She pafsed near the Amazon, who immediately on perceiving her, made the proper signals, to the ships below her, but nothing being done by them, and the Privateer having the advantage of a fair wind and a dark night, she got clear out to Sea. She came down between this Island and Cononicut, and must have pafsed very near to the Admiral's ship. Tis said two Merchant ships went out at the same time. The Naval people here, whose businefs it is to prevent any of the Enemy's ships escaping, deserve severe censure for this neglect of duty.

A flag of truce came down from Providence this day. In her came a Mr Polworth, Aide-de-Camp to Mr Heath the Rebel General Commanding at Boston, with letters from Genl Burgoyne who is at Cambridge, desiring that a quantity of Shirts, Shoes, Stockings, Cloth for breeches and leggings, with other necefsaries, may be immediately bought, and sent to Boston for the use of the troops now prisoners with him.

1st Dec^r — Fine weather.   Wind S. W.

The 54th Regiment, and the Hefsian Chafseurs broke up Camp and marched into the quarters allotted for them in Newport.

It having been determined that one Battalion shall take the duty of the advanced posts upon the Island, for one Month during the winter, while the others are quartered in Town; The Hefsian Regiment of Ditfourth, which is to remain on duty for this Month, took the several advanced posts and Guards this morning. A Detachment of that Regiment, consisting of 1 Capt 3 Sub^s 3 Serjt^s 3 Corpl^s 2 Dr^s & 60 Privates marched this morning to Fogland ferry Redoubt, where they are to be posted. The Barracks for the Regiment on duty, are finished.

Number of Troops on duty at The North end of Rhode Island for the Month of December 1777

	Officers	Men
Regiment of Ditfourth	17	537
Royal Artillery	2	52
British Seamen	1	12
Total	20	601

Barracks for the abovementioned Troops

Names of Barracks & where situated	Rooms for officers	Births for men	Each at	Men	Total men	Numbers now actually in Each	
						Officers	Men
Windmill hill	8	{ 64 / 24	2 / 3	120 / 72 }	192	8	254
Windmill hill Redoubt	1	18	2	36	36	1	45
Artillery Redoubt	4	40	2	80	80	3	102
House near Bristol ferry	1	38	2	76	76	2	60
Fogland ferry..............	4	68	2	136	136	4	88
Artillery Barrack, near ..... the Artillery Redoubt	2	{ 18 / 2	2 / 3	36 / 6 }	42	2	52
Total	20	268			562	20	601

Detail of Out Posts and Guards furnished daily by the Regiment on duty at The North End of Rhode, & the Detachment of Artillery and Seamen. 2nd. Decr 1777

	Names of the Posts and Guards	Captains	Subalterns	Serjeants	Corporals	Drummers	Privates	Artillery men	Seamen	Sentries	
										By day	By night
Out Posts	Commonfence Redoubt	I	I	2	2	2	40	5	.	5	12
	Bristol ferry Redoubt		I	I	I	I	24	4	.	4	7
	Howland's bridge Redoubt .		I	I	I	I	30	3	.	5	9
	Lower Redoubt, at Fogland		I	I	.	20	1	3		2	7
	Windmill hill Redoubt			I	I	.	20	1	.	3	7
	Artillery Redoubt			I	I	.	12	1	.	2	4
	House near Bristol ferry ...				I	.	6	.	.	I	2
	Artillery Barrack							4	.	I	I
	Total	I	4	7	8	4	152	19	3	23	49

Disposition of The Artillery. North end of Rhode Island. 2nd Decr 1777

Where placed	24 p^rs	18 p^rs	12 p^rs	9 p^rs	6 p^rs	3 p^rs	Total
Bristol ferry Redoubt	I	I	I	.	.	.	3
Commonfence Redoubt						I	I
Howland's bridge Redoubt			I	I	.	.	2
Windmill hill Redoubt		4	.	.	2	.	6
Artillery Redoubt			2	.	.	.	2
Fogland ferry, lower Redoubt	4	.	.	.	.	.	4
Total	5	5	4	I	2	I	18

N. B. The 2. 3 p^rs of Ditfourth's Regiment are placed on the Battery with the 4. 18 p^rs on Windmill hill.

2^d Dec^r   Frost, and some showers of Snow.   Wind N. W.

The 43rd, and The Landgrave's Regiment, and the Flank Companies of the 54th, marched at 9 oClock this morning into the Barracks prepared for them in Newport. The Regiment of Ditfourth marched at the same time into the Barracks at the N. end of the Island.

Came in The Senegal Sloop of War from The Delaware. She was bound to New York with dispatches, but was obliged in consequence of bad weather to put in here. We learn by her, that Gen¹ Howe's Army has been for some time in quarters at Philadelphia, and that by way of giving greater security to their position there, they have thrown up a Chain of Redoubts from the Delaware to the Schylkill. Mud Island in the Delaware which had been fortified by the Rebels, and Redbank on the Jersey side, which places prevented our shipping from going up to Philadelphia, had been reduced; and the Cheveaux de frize which they had placed acrofs some part of the Channel had been removed, some time in November, so that the navigation of that River is now open, and there is a free Communication with the town. The baggage & Camp Equipage of the troops was juft arrived in the Delaware when the Senegal left it. The troops had no Camp Equipage and very little baggage with them until the navigation of the River was opened. The September Packet from England had arrived in the Delaware before the Senegal sailed. The letters for this Island may be daily expected in the Briftol of 50 Guns, which is coming here to carry Sir Peter Parker to Jamaica, to which Station he is appointed.

3ʳᵈ Decʳ   Cold weather and hard frost. Wind N. W.
    Came in a Schooner from Barbadoes, with Rum & Sugar.
    The 22ᵈ Regiment, and the Hefsian Regiments of Huyne & Bunau, marched into their Barracks in Newport this morning. The troops are now all in their winter quarters.
    Laft night was the firft I have lain in Newport since the troops landed on this Island; having been conftantly on duty at the North end.

4ᵗʰ Decʳ — Cold wind at N. W.
    The Duty of this Garrison is ordered to be done by Battalion; British and Hefsian alternately. The Flank Companies & Chasseurs are not to do any Garrison duty; but are to be in conftant readinefs to move on the shorteft notice. All the troops are ordered to have their Arms & Accoutrements so disposed of in their Barracks that they can take them immediately, by night or day.

Detail of The Guards — Newport, Rhode Island — 4ᵗʰ Decʳ 1777

Guards	C	S	S	C	D	P
Main Guard	I	I	2	2	I	42
Hay Magazine		I	I	I	I	24
Easton's Redoubt		I	I	I	I	20
South end		I	I	I	I	27
Long wharf		I	I	I	I	18
Hay Magazine on the hill			I	I	.	12
North Battery				I	.	6
1ˢᵗ Provision Store				I	.	6
2ⁿᵈ Provision Store				I	.	6
General Pigot's				I	.	6
Orderlies			2	.	.	I
Total	I	5	9	11	5	168
Each Regiment to have a Picquet consisting of Ready to turn out on the shortest notice.	I	I	2	2	I	50

The Guards mount at 10 oClock

5ᵗʰ Decʳ — Strong wind at N. W. and very cold.

Came in five empty transports, part of a fleet of 25 Sail which are under Convoy of The Raisonable 64 Guns, from the Delaware.

The Raisonable and 10 more are in sight, but will not be able to get in on account of the violence of the wind. These ships are ordered here to take on board the Troops of Genˡ Burgoyne's Army, now at Boston, which it is expected will embark at this port or Providence for Europe.

6ᵗʰ Decʳ   Cold day. Wind W. and moderate.

The Raisonable and the rest of the fleet are endeavoring to get in, but will hardly be able to reach the harbour this night, as the gale yesterday drove them a considerable distance off.

The Detachment of Hessians which had been stationed on Cononicut Island during the Summer, was withdrawn this day.

An officer and 30 men from each Corps in Garrison, began yesterday to work on the lines, in order to finish them as soon as possible. There is still a great deal to do before they are perfected.

7th Dec^r — Thaw laſt night and this day. Wind S. Very pleasant weather.

Eight more of the transports got in laſt night. The Raisonable and the remainder of the Fleet came in about 12 this day. The whole is now in, amounting to about 27 sail. They left the Delaware the 2^d Inſt.

Came in the Juno Frigate, Capt Dalrymple, from Sandy hook. She had extreme bad weather from the time she left this port, 'till she arrived off Sandy hook, and Captain Dalrymple is apprehensive that several of the veſsels which sailed from hence under his Convoy are blown off the Coaſt or loſt.

8th Dec^r — Thick weather. Thaw. Wind S. Thick fog in the afternoon.

About 4 this Evening came in the Wood fleet from Shelter Island, under Convoy of the Unicorn. The veſsels have brought about 300 Cords of wood for the use of the troops, and about 400 for the Inhabitants.

A considerable quantity of Poultry, Pigs, Corn, Potatoes, Butter, and other articles, has also been brought for sale.

A Small Sloop was driven on shore early this Morning on Coggeshal's ledge, Brenton's neck. Three men came from her in a small boat to a house near, and said they had intended to come into Newport. On being desired to go there for aſsiſtance they declined it, and quitted the house. Information of this having been sent to The General, he sent a Serjeant and 4 men to secure them, but before they could reach the place, the fellows had got the veſsel off, and put to Sea.

9th Dec^r   Froſt.   Cold wind at N.

The General being apprehensive that the Rebels will endeavor to eſtablish themselves upon Cononicut, and in the end erect batteries there to obſtruct the entrance of the harbour, (which might easily be done from that part called The Dumplins) has ordered a Detachment to take poſt there again, and A Detachment consiſting of 1 Capt 1 Subⁿ 2 Serjt^s 2 Corpl^s 1 D^r and 50 men from the three British Battalions, with a 3 p^r and two Artillery men, went over there this morning. The Detachment is at present poſted in the Redoubt which was made there laſt Summer near the watering place. Captain D'Aubant, the Commanding Engineer having been over to Cononicut to examine and fix upon the moſt proper situation for the Detachment, pro-

poses to erect another Redoubt on the height which Commands
a beach which forms the only communication between that part
called Beaver-tail, and the rest of the Island, and which will prevent the Enemy from having access to The Dumplins, which is
the only part on which they could erect batteries to have any
effect upon the shipping.

The Senegal Sloop of War sailed from hence for New York.
The Detachment at Cononicut is to be relieved weekly.

10th Decr   Frost   Fine weather.   Wind N.

Five men came in last night from the Main, by way of Howland's ferry. Four of them were prisoners of war, and made
their escape from Worcester Jail. The other is a Countryman
who acted as their guide. Ensign Clarke of the 43rd Regt who
was taken prisoner on Commonfence neck last winter, broke out
of Jail with them, but being unable to go through the fatigue of
marching through woods and unfrequented ways in the night,
(having lately recovered from a violent fever) they were obliged
to leave him behind the second day. He has since been taken up
and lodged in Providence Jail, where it is probable he will meet
with rough usage, as this is the third attempt he has made to get
out of their hands.

11th Decr — Frosty weather.   Wind W.

A Detachment of a Capt and 50 men from this Garrison, went
over this morning to Cononicut, to be employed in cutting wood
for the use of the troops. A transport is ordered to attend them,
and is to be stationed near the ferry. The detachment is to lie on
board her every night, and when they land in the morning are
to take their arms with them.

12th Decr — Very fine day.   Wind S.   Thaw in the afternoon.

The Faulcon Sloop of War came in this afternoon from New
York with letters. In her passage down the Sound she took a
Rebel Sloop in which she found a Mr Webb, a Rebel Colonel,
with 6 other officers and 53 Soldiers, part of a Detachment that
was going on some plundering expedition from Connecticut to
Long Island.

13th — Thaw.   Thick weather and some rain.   Wind W.

Came in the Somerset 64 Guns, Nonsuch 64, and Strombolo
fire ship from the Delaware; and The Buffaloe Navy Store ship,
from New York.

East Ferry

Dutch Island

Barrack

Narraganset Passage

Part of Conanicut Island

14th Dec^r — Slight frost last night and this day. Fine weather. Wind W.

A flag of truce came down from Providence with letters to General Pigot.

It is confidently afserted by some persons who came down in the flag of truce, that 7 sail of vefsels went out to Sea the night of the 29th Novr last, and that 15 vefsels have got out within this fortnight. The Navy have certainly been very remifs in this part of their duty. We have hitherto done our part in defending the Island and frustrating the attempts of the Enemy. The Gentlemen of the Navy, when talking of the surprize of Genl Prescott, said they had nothing to do with the defence of the Island, their businefs being to prevent the Enemy's ships from getting out.

Although the transports for the reception of Genl Burgoyne's troops have been ordered to this port, upon a supposition that in consequence of an application which had been made for the purpose, they would have been permitted to march from Boston, and embark here, it now appears that Genl Heath and the Council of the Mafsachusetts bay will not consent to their marching through the Country to embark here or at Providence. They say they have no power to alter the place of embarkation mentioned in the Convention of Saratoga, without consent of Congrefs, which has not yet been signified to them; but that they have written to Congrefs on the subject.

I think it very improbable the Rebels will consent to those troops coming this way to embark, because the longer they keep them in the neighbourhood of Boston, the greater the advantage, as every article with which they are furnished must be paid for in Cash, or bills of Exchange; and there is no doubt they will make them pay at the present exorbitant prices in paper Currency for every thing with which they are furnished. This influx of Cash or good bills is a most desireable circumstance for the people in the neighbourhood of Boston, and they will not easily part with such good customers. Should Congrefs oblige the troops to embark at Boston, they will be detained there till the end of February at least, for at this season as [of?] the year the pafsage from hence to Boston, especially with light ships, is extremely precarious, & hardly to be undertaken but in cases of the most prefsing necefsity, the strength & constancy of the N. & W. winds rendering it extremely difficult for vefsels to reach that harbour. Should the ships after leaving this port meet with the usual strong N. W. winds, they may be blown away to The West Indies.

15th Dec^r — Fine weather. Wind W.

The Swan Sloop of War, Capt Ascough, came in yesterday Evening from the Sound. Captain Ascough was wounded a few days ago by a party of lurking Rebels, who fired on him in his boat, as he was going on board his ship which then lay off Huntington, Long Island.

Came in also The Tortoise and Grampus Store ships, with about 30 Sail of Victuallers, transports, &c., from New York. These ships have brought the Clothing and Camp Equipage of the Hefsian Regiments: the clothing of the 22^d, & 43rd Regiments: about 40 British and 20 Hefsian Recruits, and some Officers belonging to the Corps on this Island.

16th Dec^r — Raw, cold morning. Snow from 4 in the afternoon. Wind N. W.

The Faulcon Sloop of War sailed this morning for New York.

17th — Snow most part of last night. About 6 Inches has fallen since it commenced. Fair day. Thaw. Wind S.

The Guard houses in the Redoubts in the lines round the town being now fit to receive the troops, a Detachment consisting of 1 Sub^n 1 Serj^t 1 Corp^l 1 Drum^r and 31 men the Picquet of each Reg^t has been ordered to take post in them this Evening. The Picquet of each Corps is to take post in the Redoubt nearest to its quarters, vizt Landgrave's Regiment — Easton's Redoubt.

22nd Reg^t	Redoubt No. 1
43rd	No. 2
54th	Barrier Redoubt
Bunau's Reg^t	Redoubt No. 3
Huyne's.	Dyer's Gate.

These picquets are to march from their respective parades at half [after] 4 in the Evening, and remain until 8 in the Morning, when they are to return, leaving 1 Serj^t 1 Corp^l & 12 men for the day duty.

The Swan Sloop of War sailed this Morning for her Station in the Sound.

18th Dec^r — Thaw, and Rain most part of the day. Wind N. E.

A Detachment of a Sub^n and 50 men from the British &

Hefsians went over to Cononicut this day, to be employed in completing the Redoubt which is erecting there.

19th — Thick, moist weather.   Wind W.

The Swan Sloop put back this morning, the wind being unfavorable for going up the Sound.

20th Dec^r — Frost last night, and this day.   Wind N. W.

This harbour is now fuller of Shipping than it has been at any time since our first arrival; there being near 100 sail of Vefsels, besides Seven two Decked Ships, (vizt Chatham 50 Guns, Somerset 64, Raisonable 64, Nonsuch 64, & the Buffaloe, Grampus & Tortoise, formerly line of Battle ships but now employed as Store Ships) and Several Frigates and the Strombolo Fire ship.

21st — Frost.   Fine weather.   Wind N. W.

It has been reported to the General, that more Rebel troops have been seen about Howland's and Fogland ferry within these few days, than usual.   But there are no certain accounts of more men being afsembled there than common.   If there are, it is probably occasioned by the arrival of so large a fleet here, which having made them apprehensive of a visit from us, has caused them to bring down some more troops for the defence of the Coast.

22^d Dec^r — Thaw last night and this day.   Soft, open weather. Wind S. W.

Came in The Bristol, 50 Guns, Capt Cornwallis, in three days from The Delaware.   She saluted the admiral as she came in, who returned it.

23rd — Severe frost.   Wind N. W.   This has been the coldest day we have had this Season.

The accounts brought by The Bristol are, that The Army is in quarters in Philadelphia, and, having thrown up a Chain of ten Redoubts, which are connected by a line, from the Delaware to the Schylkill, are under no apprehension of any disturbance from the Rebels during the winter.   The main body of the Rebel Army is about 40 miles from Philadelphia, with their advanced posts at Germantown.   Genl Howe made a movement with the Army the beginning of this Month from Philadelphia, as far as a place called White Marsh, with a view of bringing the Rebel army to action; but as he found them strongly posted, and it was not thought prudent to attack them in the position they had taken, the Army returned to Philadelphia, after having obtained some advantage over one of their detached Corps. A large detachment of our army had been on an Expedition over the Schylkill, from whence they returned with a considerable quantity of Cattle, Forage and Wood.

Lord Cornwallis is gone home in the Brilliant Frigate.

24th Decr   Frost.   Wind N.

A flag of truce Sloop came down from Providence. In her came Captain Money of the 9th Regt afsistant QuMr General of Genl Burgoyne's Army, who was taken prisoner some time before the Convention of Saratoga. He obtained leave to go to New York to get exchanged, which having effected, he was permitted to pafs through Connecticut to Providence, and came from thence here in expectation of getting a pafsage to Europe with the Convention troops.

It appears by a Providence paper of the 20th Instant, that the Rebels are exceedingly alarmed at the arrival of so large a fleet as is now in this harbour; and have ordered all the Inhabitants of the State to be in readinefs to march with their Arms, Ammunition and Provisions to Providence, upon the first alarm, which is to be given by lighting Beacons and discharges of Cannon. Tis said many of the Inhabitants have removed their effects from thence.

25th Decr — Hard frost.   Wind N. W.

About 12 o'Clock last night two Rebel vefsels attempted to go to Sea by Fogland ferry, the night being very dark and the wind fair. They were soon discovered by our Galley stationed near our battery and were fired at. One of them, a brig, in standing too close to their shore, run ashore on the N. point of Fogland; — the other got clear, notwithstanding she was chaced by The Kingsfisher. But as the Kingsfisher is a remarkly bad Sailer, and the Rebel vefsels are generally light and clean when they attempt to go out, it is not surprizing she escaped. The Kingsfisher returned to her Station this morning, the Rebel vefsel having got safe into Bedford.

Sir Peter Parker applied to The General this Morning for a Detachment of the Hefsians stationed near Fogland, to burn the vefsel on shore, but as there are no boats on that side, nothing could be done until something comes round from Newport. The Galley should have made the attempt early this morning.

26th Decr   Frost. Wind N. W.

The Rebel brig remains on shore at Fogland. An attempt was made this day by the Galley to burn her, but as the Rebels had brought two pieces of Cannon down, and fired on the Galley, she was obliged to draw off. The Galley & our battery fired several shot at the brig, and hulled her four or five times. Our Galley being ill fitted out weakly manned, and a bad Sailer, it was not though safe to venture so near the shore as she should have done to have effected the service intended. From the un-accountable delays which have happened, it is probable the Rebels will get the vefsel off before we can destroy her. If a Single boat had attempted it yesterday morning early, it might have been effected with ease.

27th Decr   Rain last night and this morning, which froze as it fell, and encrusted every thing with Ice. Wind N. E.

Some boats have been sent round into the Seconnet, for the purpose of burning the Rebel brig which remains on shore. A great number of Shot were fired at her from the battery, which has damaged her so much, that she cannot be got off.

28th Decr   Some Snow last night and this day. Wind N. and a hard frost. Every thing covered with Ice.

Two Masters of vefsels who came down in the last Cartel, & who were lately at Boston, say, that the Inhabitants of that town are in great dread of a visit from our Fleet.

The Barracks on Cobble-hill near Boston, in which part of the British prisoners were lodged, were burnt down lately; and the Rebels suppose it was done on purpose by our troops.

A Puncheon of Sour Kraut has been ordered to be delivered weekly to each Corps. The troops are very fond of it.

29th — Heavy rain part of last night, and this day. Hard frost, and very strong cold wind at W. The Rain becomes congealed as soon as it touches anything, so that everything exposed to it is encrusted with Ice. Walking is very dangerous, and the roads are almost impafsable for horses and Carriages.

This has been by much the coldest day we have had this year.

30th Decr — Hard frost. Very cold day. Wind W.

The Rebel brig was set on fire last night by a party of the Troops, under cover of the Galley. They met with no opposition, and she was entirely destroyed by 9 oClock this morning. She had been so much damaged by the shot we fired at her, that it was impossible to get her off.

The Wood party, and the working party returned this day from Cononicut. The Redoubt which was erected there last Summer, has been repaired and Strengthened, and a Barrack for two Officers and 50 men built in it. A Detachment of that strength is now Stationed in it. No other Redoubt has been erected on Cononicut.

31st Dec.r — Very hard frost. Wind S. W. Everthing continues encrusted with Ice. The Streets are so very slippery that walking is very dangerous unless Creepers are used.

The Detachments of the 22d Regiment, which is to relieve the Regiment of Ditfourth on duty at the N. end of the Island, marched from town this morning to relieve the Detachments now on duty of that Regiment. The 22d Regiment, and the Hessian Chasseurs are to take the duty out on the Island for the ensuing Month.

At 2 oClock came in The Venus and Apollo Frigates from New York, which place they left yesterday Morning. Came in at the same time The Rose 20 Guns, with 13 Sail of Victuallers & other vessels under her Convoy from New York.

A fellow came in last night by way of Howland's ferry. He pretends he came from Swansea, and for the purpose of obtaining a passport from The Admiral and The General, for a Sloop now lying there, to go to Sea. He was sent to The Admiral. But his pretence is so extraordinary, that there is little doubt he came as a Spy; and as such he should be immediately confined.

To George Wightman Esqr.

Sir —

You are hereby authorized and empowered to raise for his Majesty's service, a Regiment of able bodied men, to be composed of 30 Serjeants, 30 Corporals, Ten Drummers, and 500 Privates, divided into 10 Companies: each company consisting of 1 Captain, 1 Lieut, 1 Ensign, 3 Serjeants, 3 Corporals, one Drummer and 50 Privates, who will engage to carry arms under my orders, or the orders of the Commander in Chief of His Majesty's forces, for the time being, for two years, or if required during the continuance of the present Rebellion in North

America: to receive the same pay, and be under the same discipline as His Majesty's Regular troops.

The Officers are to be approved of by me, and as their appointments by Commifsion, will depend on their succefs in Recruiting, they are to be instructed to raise the following numbers to entitle them thereto (vizt) a Captain, 30 men: a Lieu^t 15 men: an Ensign, 12 men; and it is to be made known to them, that their pay will not commence until half the above number is raised, and brought to the Rendezvous of the Recruits at Rhode Island.

In like manner when one half the Corps is raised, mustered, and approved of by a reviewing officer, a Major will be commissioned: and your Commifsion as Lieu^t Colonel will be made out on 400 men being raised. In the mean time you will receive pay as Captain until 250 men are raised: as Major until 400 are raised; and as Lieu^t Colonel from that period.

Forty Shillings currency will be allowed as bounty for each man inlisted and approved.

All officers civil and military, and others His Majesty's liege Subjects, are hereby required to be aiding and afsisting unto you and all concerned in the Execution of the above service. For which this shall be to you and them a sufficient Warrant and Authority.

> Given under my hand and Seal at
> headquarters, New York, 21st March
> 1777

By His Excellency's Command   W. Howe   Seal
    Robert Mackenzie

IV

NEWPORT. RHODE ISLAND

IV

NEWPORT. RHODE ISLAND

1st Jany 1778
Clear weather, and very hard frost. Wind W.

The 22^d Regiment marched this morning at 8 o'Clock to Windmill hill, and a Captain, One Subaltern and 70 of the Hessian Chasseurs to Fogland Ferry, to relieve the Regiment of Ditfourth on duty at those places. At 4 oClock in the afternoon that Regiment marched into town.

The Juno Frigate sailed this morning on a Cruize.

2^d — Thaw. The morning fine, with the wind at S. The afternoon thick, with small rain.

At 11 this morning came in the Brune Frigate with about 30 sail of vessels under her Convoy from the Delaware. At the same time Came in The Eagle of 64 Guns, having the Flag of Lord Howe on board, in three days from the Delaware. Lord Howe was saluted by Sir Peter Parker, with 15 Guns, which was returned with 13. As soon as The Eagle dropt anchor his Lordship was saluted with 17 Guns from The North Battery, which was returned with 11 only.

3rd Jan^y   Some heavy rain last night. Fine day. Wind S. The Streets almost clear of Ice.

Lord Howe came on shore this Morning, but returned on board to Dinner. He does not intend to take any quarters in town.

4th   Fine clear frosty day. Wind W.

A Master of a vessel who came lately from Boston says it is generally understood there that Congress are willing to permit Genl Burgoyne's Army to come to this place by way of Providence, in order to embark for England; but that the people of the Country will not admit of it, and insist on their embarking at Boston.

5th   Snow part of last night and 'till 2 this day. About 6 Inches of Snow fell in all. Wind E.

6th Jan^y   Clear frosty weather. Wind W. Slight thaw in the middle of the day.

Parties have been ordered out from each Regiment to clear away the Snow from that part of the line allotted to each.

A Flag of truce Brig went up to Providence this morning having on board a considerable quantity of Clothing and necefsaries for Genl Burgoyne's Army, which are to be conveyed from thence by land to Boston. These things are under the charge of Lieu^t Piper, afsistant Q^r Mr General, but as the Country people are in the utmost want of almost every article he has with him, it is highly probable he will be plundered of part of them before he reaches Boston, notwithstanding he is furnished with all the necefsary pafsports. It is expected that when the vefsel returns we shall know for certain whether the Rebels will permit the troops to march through the Country and embark at this port.

Came in The Juno Frigate from a Cruize.

A Ball and Supper was given to the Ladies of this place, by 44 Officers and Gentlemen of the town: to which Lord Howe was invited.

7th Jan^y   Fine weather. Thaw. Wind N. E.

Five Frigates sailed this day, vizt Apollo, Venus, Juno, Rose, and

8th   Rain all last night. Thick weather all day. Wind E.

By the accounts which have been received from Philadelphia it appears that Sir William Howe marched out from thence on the 4th Decr with the greatest part of the Army, as far as Chesnut-hill, with a view to bring Washington to an Action; but as he was found too strongly entrenched to be attacked, and was too cautious to risk anything, the Army returned again. A Skirmish happened near a place called White-Marsh, in which the Rebels lost about 300 men.

9th Jan^y   Slight frost last night. Very fine day. Wind W.

The Dispatch Sloop of War came in yesterday Evening from New York. She mentions the arrival of the October & November mails there from England; but has brought no letters for this Island.

A Flag of truce came down last night from Providence. She had brought letters from Genl Burgoyne, by which it appears that Congrefs will not permit the troops to march through the

Country in order to embark at this port, but insist upon the terms of the Convention of Saratoga being strictly complied with.

A person is come here from Gen[l] Burgoyne to endeavor to procure £130,000 in Specie, to defray the expences already incurred by the troops under his Command, as the Rebels insist upon being paid in ready money for everything, before the troops are suffered to embark. They talk at Boston of having the Convention ratified by The King & Parliament, and that hostages shall be given for the due execution of it, before they will allow of the departure of the troops. There is no doubt they will make use of every pretext and every art in their power, to keep the troops there, as the money they spend among them is of great benefit to the Country.

10th Jan[y]   Fine soft weather.   Wind S.

Two Soldiers of the 22[d] Regiment deserted last night from the advanced posts, and made their escape notwithstanding they were pursued as soon as they were missed. As the Rebels always have boats ready to take off deserters, it is extremely difficult to apprehend them.

11th   Snow from 12 to 3 this day, when it turned to a heavy rain which continued 'till night. Wind E. About 2 Inches of Snow fell.

12th Jan[y]   Thaw.   Mild weather.   Wind N.

About 9 o'Clock last night the Signal for an Enemy was made by the advanced ships up the Bay, which was soon after ansered by Lord Howe in The Eagle; who at the same time made a Signal for the Unicorn to Slip. She soon got out to the harbour's mouth; and about 12 oClock a good deal of firing was heard to the Westward. Nothing appears this Morning but a Frigate coming in. Tis now said that two of the Rebel Frigates went down the Naraganset passage, past the Renown last night.

A Rebel Sloop came through Bristol ferry last night, and was not discovered until she came abreast of the Diamond stationed near Dyer's Island, who immediately sent a boat on board and took her. It appears she came from Swansea, and was bound to Hispaniola with a Cargo of Fish, Onions, Apples, &c., and had five men on board.

Sailed the Neptune Armed Schooner for New York.

13ᵗʰ Janʸ   Slight frost last night.   Soft day.   Wind S.

The Unicorn returned into Port. She saw nothing the night of the 11ᵗʰ, but a small Schooner at which she fired a good many Cannon shot, and at length drove her ashore within point Judith, but in a situation where she durst not follow her. It is imagined she must have suffered considerably by the fire of the Ship.

An addrefs was presented this day by the Principal Inhabitants of Newport, to Lord Howe, on his arrival in this Port.

14ᵗʰ   Soft weather.   Wind S. W.

Arrived The Maidstone Frigate from New York, with the letters which came from England for this Island by the October and November Mails.

15ᵗʰ Janʸ   Hard frost.   Strong wind at W.

Sir Peter Parker sailed this morning in the Bristol, 50 Guns, for Jamaica, having been appointed to the Command on that Station: He saluted Lord Howe on going out, which was returned.

Sailed at the same time The Solebay Frigate for the Delaware with dispatches for Sir William Howe. There is some reason to suppose that the Delaware is frozen up by this time; but the Solebay is directed to get up the River if pofsible. Two Navy Victuallers sailed under Convoy of the Solebay, supposed to be intended for the supply of The Ships of War in the Chesapeak.

16ᵗʰ   Hard frost.   Wind W.

17ᵗʰ   Snow this morning from 11 'till 3, when it turned to rain which continued all day.   Strong wind at S.

18ᵗʰ Janʸ   Heavy rain most part of last night, with a strong wind at S.   Clear day.

About 10 o'Clock last night a Rebel Sloop came ashore on the S. W. point of Brenton's neck. She luckily struck on a narrow piece of Sandy Beach, and was but little damaged. She is about 60 Tons burthen, from Surinam to New London, laden with 60 Hogsheads of Molafses, 2000 weight of Coffee, some sail cloth, and a few dry goods; and has 8 hands on board. She sailed 30 days ago in company with 3 other vefsels for the same port. A party of Light Infantry was sent down early this morning who secured the people and took pofsefsion of her.

Came in The Sphynx from New York, with three small trading vefsels under her Convoy.

19th Jany Frost — Clear fine weather. Wind N.

A Soldier of the 22^d Regiment deserted from the advanced posts last night.

This being the day appointed for the Celebration of the Queen's birthday, at 1 oClock a Royal Salute was fired by each of the Ships of War in the harbour, and at the different Stations in the Bay. Generals Pigot, Smith and Losberg, with their respective Suites & the public Officers, dined with Lord Howe on board the Eagle; and at night Lord Howe gave an Elegant Ball and Supper in Newport, at which were present about 60 Ladies and 150 Gentlemen.

Lord Howe signified to General Pigot when he was on board The Eagle, that the Sloop which was driven on shore the night of the 17th Instant on Brenton's neck, was entirely his (Genl Pigot's) property, as Lord of the Manor. Tis supposed she will prove worth £800, or £1,000.

20th Jany Slight frost this morning. Wind E. At 12 it snowed a little, which soon after turned to rain. The frost quite gone before night.

Came in The Swift Sloop of War, with a prize.

21st — Mild weather. Wind S.

Came in The Cabot, Armed brig from Halifax.

22^d Jany Fine weather. Frost. Wind N. W.

I rode to the N. end of the Island, and visited all the advanced posts. Everything quiet there. Very few of the Rebels appear on the other side.

A Flag of truce Sloop which had permifsion from the General to go to Howland's by way of Bristol ferry, was fired at in the Evening yesterday by our battery at Bristol Redoubt, as no Notice had been sent from Headquarters to the Officer Commanding there, that such a vefsel had leave to pafs.

Fortunately no damage was done. She sent a boat on shore immediately after the first shot was fired, to explain the matter.

23rd — Hard frost, and very cold. Wind N. W.

24th Jan^y — Very hard frost, and cold wind at N. W. This has been the Coldest day we have had this season.

Firing for the troops on this Island is so scarce and difficult to be had, that only two thirds of the Regulated allowance has been ifsued since we have been in quarters. This Scarcity has in some measure been occasioned by the interruption in sending to Long Island at the time of the late threatened attack, and by an accident which a large ship laden with Coals from New York met with in the Sound, and which obliged her to put back. Very little has arrived since.

The greatest part of the wood upon this Island has already been used. A small quantity is procured from Cononicut, but nothing equal to the consumption of the Garrison, which amounts to about 300 Cords p^r week. Some wood is now brought by the proprietors from the Center part of this Island, and sold for 9 Dollars p^r Cord.

The Fleet which went from hence to Shelter Island in November last to bring wood for the Troops, returned with not more than 400 Cords, after having been out five weeks, so that it was not worth the trouble, risk, and expence of sending there again for that article. Indeed Sir Peter Parker said he could not spare a Frigate for Convoy, & after Lord Howe's arrival the weather proved too Severe.

25th Jany Snow part of last, and greatest part of this day. About 3 Inches of Snow fell. Wind E.

The Brig which went up the 6th Instant to Providence with Clothing and necessaries for Genl Burgoyne's army, returned last night. She has lain the greatest part of the time at Patuxent. Lieu^t Piper, after many difficulties, went forward with the things he had in charge, to Cambridge, near Boston.

26th Hard frost. Wind N. W. and very cold.

27th Jany Hard frost. Wind W.

The frost has not been so severe at any time this winter as to freeze up any part of the Rivers, Creeks, or passages round this Island. The Inhabitants say that about five years ago the Ice was fixed so strongly between this Island and Bristol and Howland's ferries, that people passed over with horses and carriages. It is an observation made by the Inhabitants of this town, that whenever the Pond to the Northward of The Long wharf is frozen over, the River Delaware is, and the Navigation to Philadelphia impracticable. As the abovementioned Pond has not been frozen over yet, it is probable the Delaware is open, and that the Solebay may get up to Philadelphia.

28th Southerly wind this Morning, and consequently a change of weather. Thaw all day.

29th Jan^y   Rain most part of last night, and 'till 1 this day. The rain was very heavy for the last three hours. Wind S. The frost quite gone. A fine clear afternoon.

Notwithstanding the frequent changes in the weather, the healthiness of this Island is beyond a doubt. As a proof of it, the three Hessian Regiments of Ditfourth, Huyne & Bunau, amounting to very near 1800 effective men, have not more than 70 Sick men on the lists, of all descriptions. The Landgrave's Regiment, indeed, out of 560 men, have about 60 Sick. The extraordinary sickness in this Regiment is differently accounted for. It commenced in April last, and continued during the whole Campaign. Their Officers say it was owing to the severe duty the Regiment had during the last winter, for as the Regiment was quartered nearest to Newport, and furnished their proportion for the Guards and working parties at the North end of the Island, their men were greatly harrassed by marching 8 or 10 miles to do duty, in all weathers, and bad roads. This may have contributed to it, especially when it is observed, that as the Captains are obliged to furnish their men with Shoes for a certain allowance, it is probable they were not so well provided with them as those Regiments that wore out fewer. In my opinion the principal cause was their having lost their Regimental Surgeon early in the Spring; and it is well known the Company's Surgeons have very little Physical knowledge, and are totally ignorant of Medicine and the proper method of treating Dysenteries and intermittent fevers, which the Soldiers are subject to at that Season, and in the begining of a Campaign. Some neglect perhaps in the interior Oeconomy of the Regiment, may have contributed to it, as much as anything; as I have frequently observed that those Regiments that are most deficient in attention to interior Oeconomy and management, have fewest men fit for duty.

The Sick of the British Regiments have in general been more numerous than the Hessians. During the last Campaign we never had less than 100, and sometimes 180 Sick, out of 1700 men.

There was a good deal of Sickness among the Inhabitants last Summer, but I think it should be attributed more to their want of the usual quantity of fresh provisions, than to any insalubrity in the air of the Island.

30th Jany Fine weather. Wind S.

Came in The Ariel, 20 Guns from England. She has had a pafsage of 11 weeks, and her Captain died on the voyage. She saluted Lord Howe on coming in, but the salute was not returned. Lord Howe gave orders when he firſt arrived at Staten Island, that there should be no saluting for the future, except between Flag Ships, as it occasioned during a time of War, many accidents and inconveniences, and an unnecefsary expence of powder.

The Ariel has brought out dispatches for Ld Howe, said to contain directions to send out several frigates to look out for 10 or 12 Rebel vefsels which sailed from France with valuable Cargoes, in Company with a French Frigate, which was to Convoy them to a certain latitude, from whence they were to make the beſt of their way to their respective deſtinations.

31st Jany 1778 — Slight froſt laſt night. Rain from this morning, which continued, and very heavy, till night. Wind E.

The Detachments of The Landgrave's Regiment for the relief of those of the 22^d, on duty at the advanced poſts, marched from Newport this morning at 8 o'Clock.

The 22^d Reg^t having been ordered to send a party to Commonfence Neck to cut down the Orchards and trees growing there, the party went out very early yeſterday morning. The Rebels having discovered them as soon as it was light, they began to Cannonade them from the Battery on the hill above Howland's ferry; but finding the diſtance rather too great, they brought down a 9 p^r to the shore opposite the party, and fired at them from it, but without any effect. The party continued to work, and cut down above 200 trees, after which they returned without any lofs. The Rebels fired 18 Shot.

A man came in from Swansea laſt night.

1st Feb^y   Much rain laſt night. Fine day. Wind S. W.

The Roads are now extremely bad, and much broken up by yeſterday's rain.

The Landgrave's Reg^t marched at 8 this morning to relieve the 22^d at Windmill hill; which Reg^t came into town about 4 in the afternoon. The 2^d Company of Hefsian Chafseurs marched at the same time and relieved the 1st Company at Fogland ferry.

The Flag of truce Sloop that went to Howland's ferry the 21st January, returned yeſterday.

2ᵈ Febʸ — Fine weather. Slight froſt. Wind S. W.

Three men came in from the Naraganset side laſt night. They say there is a draft to be made soon of 15,000 Men from the New England Provinces, part of which is to be sent to Washington's Army.

Lieuᵗ Piper returned this day from Boſton where he delivered the articles he was charged with from hence for the use of General Burgoyne's Army. Captain Dowling of the 20ᵗʰ, and Captain Farmer of the 21ˢᵗ Regiment came back with him. They are going to England.

3ʳᵈ — Fine open weather. Wind S. E.

The transports intended for the reception of the troops under Genˡ Burgoyne in the neighbourhood of Boſton, received orders this day to prepare for Sea.

4ᵗʰ Febʸ — Mild weather. Wind W.

A Soldier of The Landgrave's Regiment deserted yeſterday from the advanced poſt at Commonfence.

Sailed The Sphynx with several veſsels under her Convoy, for New York.

As there is now no Oats remaining in the Magazines or in the Island, the Ration of Hay for the Dragoon horses is ordered to consiſt of 20 lbs, and for the other horses of 15 lbˢ till further orders.

5ᵗʰ — Mild weather. Wind S. W.

The Raisonable of 64 Guns, and the Renown of 50, went out of the harbour this morning, supposed for Halifax.

Arrived a Brig from New York with Merchandize.

6ᵗʰ Febʸ Fine mild weather. Wind E.

Lord Howe has made but few changes in the disposition of the Ships in the Bay since his arrival. The Somerset lies in the Naraganset paſsage, in place of the Renown. The Nonsuch lies above Gould Island, between Cononicut and Prudence. The Lark off Greenwich; the   above Dyer's Island; The Flora above Papasquash; and The Mermaid in the Seconnet. The laſt ship relieved the Kingsfisher, which came in to the harbour to clean & refit. A Frigate always lies at Single anchor in the Channel, a little to the Northward of The Dumplins, ready to slip after any veſsel upon the Signal being made. The Galley is ſtationed under our Battery at Fogland.

7th Feb^y   Snow from 6 o'Clock yesterday Evening 'till 11 this day. Strong gale of wind all last night at N. E. The violence of the Wind was such that many of the ships in the harbour dragged their anchors, particularly the Amazon Frigate Captain Jacobs, which being in danger of driving on shore on Brenton's neck, it was found necefsary to cut away her Masts to save the ship. Some trifling damage was done to some of the other vessels in the harbour.

The Snow drifted much. About 10 Inches of Snow fell in all. This has been a very cold day.

8th   Hard frost — Inclining to Snow.   Wind E —

9th Feb^y   High wind at E. N. E. all last night with Snow, which continued to fall 'till 10 this morning. Hard frost with wind at N. E. all day. The Snow drifted much. About 10 Inches fell.

10th   A fine day. Wind N. in the morning. Thick cloudy afternoon. The Snow drifted to the height of 12 feet in some places yesterday. Many parts of the new Lines are covered by it.

The Signal was made this morning by Lord Howe for the Chatham, with the Buffaloe, Tortoise, and Harcourt, for England, to get under way; but as the wind came in from the Southward about 10 o'Clock they were prevented from sailing.

The Regiments here have been ordered to examine their tents, and to have as many of them repaired as will admit of it.

11th Fe^b — Heavy rain all last night and this day. Thick weather. Wind N. E. Much of the Snow gone.

The transports for Boston have been ready for Sea for some days, but the damage done to The Amazon by the late Gale, and the bad weather since, has prevented the fleet from going out. The Amazon was to have gone with the transports. The Juno and Cerberus are now ordered for that service.

The transports are victualled for 8 weeks, and they are to go, over the Shoals, as it is termed here, to Boston; that is they are to go between Martha's Vineyard and the Main, and so close round Cape Cod, into Cape Cod harbour, from whence an account is to be sent to Boston of their arrival. Pilots have been provided for the abovementioned pafsage, which is at all times a dangerous Navigation for ships of any great draught of water.

If they were to go round the Nantucket Shoals, they would be in danger, as light ships, of being blown off the Coaſt this boiſterous Season. All the transports go as Cartel ships, and the utmoſt care has been taken by Lord Howe to take out of them all Cannon, Arms, and Military Stores. Not even a Cutlaſs is allowed to be taken on board. All this is neceſsary to prevent the Rebels from having any pretence for detaining the troops or Moleſting the Ships.

There are 2000 barrels of Flour on board the transports, which is to be landed for the use of the Convention troops, in case the Rebels should under any pretence attempt to detain them, which is expećted they will endeavor to do. If the troops are permitted to embark immediately the flour is to be sent back here for the use of the troops on this Island, who have been served with Biscuit for five weeks paſt.

I am under great apprehensions, should the Rebels suffer the troops to embark, that accidents may happen to some of them before they reach England, as many of the transports now going for them are crippled ships, and were under orders to go to England from the Delaware at the time they received orders to come to this port to receive the Convention troops on board.

There are not more than 25 of them, and therefore the troops will be much crowded on board them; and as they may expećt to meet with Eaſterly winds about the time they get into Soundings, it is probable they will have a tedious paſsage.

12ᵗʰ Febʸ   Rain laſt night — Some Snow this morning. Clear weather and hard froſt in the afternoon. Wind W.

The Chatham, Tortoise, and Harcourt, got under way this Morning in order to proceed to Sea. The Harcourt got out, and went to Sea. The other ships after some unsucceſsful attempts, returned into the harbour.

About 30 Discharged Soldiers went home in the Harcourt, also some officers, and other paſsengers.

13ᵗʰ   Clear weather. Strong wind at S. W.

Came in the Brune Frigate, with several veſsels under her Convoy from New York. Part of her Convoy were forced on shore during the late Stormy weather on the Long Island side of the Sound, where two veſsels with Coals for this garrison were loſt.

Most of the vessels which sailed with the Sphynx on the 4th Instant were also forced ashore on Long Island by the late heavy gales of Wind.

The Brune has brought many letters which came by the December Mail to New York.

14th   Some Snow.   Cold weather.   Strong wind at W.

15th Feby   Cold weather and hard frost.   Wind W.   Light wind towards Evening.

At 8 this morning the signal was made for the Ships for England and Boston to get under way.   The Chatham, Buffaloe and Tortoise got out first, and proceeded on their voyage.   The Boston ships, under Convoy of the Juno and Cerberus, were all out by 2 o'Clock.

Previous to their going out, all the abovementioned ships got as close as they could under the Cononicut shore, near the ferry, as from thence, (with a Westerly wind) they go out with more safety, by turning close round the Dumplins, and keeping the Cononicut shore on board as much as possible; for the Ebb tide is thrown with such force on the shore of Brenton's neck, that ships going out with a Westerly wind are in danger of being driven upon it.

Came in a Brig with Coals from New York.

16th Feby — Wind N. E. all day, with some Snow.   Cold weather.   About 4 Inches of Snow has fallen within these three days.

The wind having come round last night to the Eastward, attended with Snow, the Boston fleet could not pursue their voyage; they were seen this morning plying between this Island & Block Island.

It appears by letters and Newspapers from England of the 11th Decr last, that the accounts of the latter operations and Surrender of Genl Burgoyne's Army, has caused a good deal of consternation, and given occasion to the Members of Opposition in both houses, to abuse the Ministry, and extol the Americans.

It Appears however that vigorous exertions are to be made, as an augmentation of 20 men pr Company to the Infantry, and 15,000 Seamen has been voted without a division.

17th Feby — Some Snow last night.   Cold weather, and hard frost.   Strong N. W. wind all last night and this day.

No appearance of the Boston fleet this morning.

A Rebel Ship escaped last night by way of the Naraganset passage. She was first discovered by The Lark's Tender, which lay about half a mile ahead of the Lark. As soon as the tender saw her she slipt her Cable, but before she could get under way the ship was near on board of her. The tender then followed her and kept firing small arms. The Lark having everything in readiness gave the ship a broadside as she passed, but without any apparent effect. The Somerset being also prepared in the Naraganset passage gave her a broadside from both Decks, notwithstanding which she got clear to Sea. The tender followed her as far as the Lighthouse. Neither the Lark or Somerset attempted to pursue her, nor did any Frigate go out of the harbour after her. It is probable she went into Bedford; as the wind would not admit of her going round Point Judith. She did not fire a Shot.

Came in this Evening a Privateer Brig of 8 Carriage guns, 6 Swivels and 51 men, taken by the Unicorn. She had been out but a few days from Portsmouth, New Hampshire, when taken, was bound to the West Indies, and had made no capture.

18th Fe^b Fine clear weather. Hard frost. Wind W.

Eleven men came in from the Naraganset side last night.

A party of an Officer and 36 British, went into the Country today, to be employed in cutting wood in a large Swamp on this side of Fogland ferry, for the use of the Garrison. It is computed that there are about 400 Cords in the Swamp, but it cannot be got at but during a hard frost.

We have had a party of a Captain, Subaltern and 50 men from the Garrison, cutting wood upon Cononicut, ever since the troops have been in quarters. They are relieved every fourteen days.

When Soldiers are employed in cutting wood for the public use, they are allowed 5s/. New York Currency, or 2s/11^d Sterling p^r Cord, which is paid them by The Barrack Master General.

In consequence of the difficulty of procuring fuel for the use of this Garrison, only two thirds of the regulated allowance has been issued since we came into quarters. The other third is paid for in Cash by the Barrack Master at the rate of four Dollars p^r Cord. — as the two thirds allowance is not sufficient for the Subaltern Officers, they are under the necessity of purchasing

what further quantity they want, at the rate of Nine Dollars p^r
Cord.

The Cord of wood measures 8 feet long, 4 feet wide, and 4 feet
high. The wood is generally cut in pieces of four feet in length,
but the actual quantity contained in a Cord depends much upon
the size of the pieces, their streightnefs, & the manner in which
they are piled up.

19th Fe^b   Fine clear weather.   Wind S. W.

The Centurion of 50 Guns, Captain Braithwaite, arrived laſt
night from New York in 36 hours. She came round Long Island
from Sandyhook. Letters of the 1st Inſtant from Philadelphia,
have been received by her.

Appendix 1778

Resolves of Congrefs, relative to the detention of Genl Burgoyne's army

In Congress — 8th January 1778

The Committee to whom the letters that pafsed between Genl
Heath and Genl Burgoyne and the letter from Genl Burgoyne
to Genl Gates, were committed, brought in a report, which was
taken into consideration, and agreed to as follows —

That they have considered with mature attention the Convention entered into at Saratoga between Major Genl Gates,
and Lieu^t Genl Burgoyne in October laſt, and find, that numbers
of the Cartouch boxes, and several other articles of Military
accoutrements annexed to the persons of the Non-Commis-
sioned Officers and Soldiers of Genl Burgoyne's army, have not
been delivered up, and that agreeable to the spirit of the Convention, and technical interpretation of the word, "arms," they
ought to have been delivered up — This opinion is warranted
not only by the Judgement of the moſt approved writers, but by
the interpretation and practice of British Officers in Similar
cases, in the course of the present war, particularly in the Capi-
tulation of St John's, on the 2^d Novr 1775 —

Your Committee farther report, that there are so many other
circumſtances attending the delivery of the arms and Military
ſtores, which excite ſtrong suspitions, that the Convention has
not been ſtrictly complied with on the part of Genl Burgoyne,
agreeable to its true spirit, and the intention of the contracting
parties; and so many instances of former fraud in our Enemies,

as to justify Congreſs, however cautious to avoid even the Suspition of want of good faith, in taking every measure for the
securing the performance of the Convention, which did not
impose any new condition, nor tend to delay its execution —

Of this nature your Committee consider the Resolution of
Congreſs of the 8ᵗʰ Novʳ laſt, directing Genˡ Heath "to cause to
"be taken down, the name and rank of every commiſsioned
"officer, and the name, former place of abode, occupation, size,
"age, and description of every Non-Commiſsioned Officer and
"private Soldier, and all other persons comprehended in the
"Convention of Saratoga." This cannot be considered as imposing any new condition, but as a measure, naturally resulting
from the Articles of Convention, which the conquering party
had a right to avail itself of — and which is ſtrictly juſtifiable,
had no suspicion of the want of good faith in the party surrendering, presented itself. Your Committee are of Opinion, that
the reasons which Genˡ Burgoyne adduces for refusing a Compliance, are inapplicable to the case; and they beg leave to
observe that he is totally miſtaken, in his appeal to the conduct
of Sir Guy Carleton and himself, with respect to the prisoners,
released from Canada, in Auguſt 1776. For notwithſtanding his
expreſs declarations to the contrary, in his letter of the 23ʳᵈ
Novʳ laſt, to General Heath, it appears from the Original liſt of
the Prisoners released from Canada, which is herewith presented, that the Provinces, Counties and towns, to which the
prisoners released belonged, were annexed to their respective
names, which for the security of the conquering party, were in
the hand writing of the respective prisoners.

Your Committee therefore cannot but consider Genˡ Burgoyne's refusal to give descriptive liſts of the Non-Commis-
sioned Officers, and Soldiers, belonging to his army, when connected with his former conduct, and ill-grounded aſsertion on
this occasion, in an alarming point of view; more especially
when they consider, that nine days previous to his refusal, he
had without juſt cause given, declared in a letter to Genˡ Gates,
that the publick faith, plighted in the Convention of Saratoga,
was broken on the part of these ſtates. This charge of a breach
of publick faith, is of a moſt serious nature, pregnant with
alarming consequences, and deserves greater attention, as it is
not dropped in a haſty expreſsion, dictated by sudden paſsion,
but is delivered as a deliberate act of Judgement, committed to

writing, and sent to the General with whom he made the Convention, and if credit is to be given to General Burgoyne's account of himself, in his letter to Gen¹ Heath of the 23ʳᵈ of Novʳ, he cannot be considered "of so light a Character, as to have "acted in a serious matter of State upon a sudden impression."

The reason upon which he grounds this charge is, That the Officers included in the Convention, have not since their arrival in Massachusetts-bay, been accomodated with quarters agreeably to their respective ranks; on which your committee beg leave to observe, that though from the sudden and unexpected arrival of so large a body of troops, the concourse of Strangers in and near Boston, the devastation and destruction, occasioned by the British army, not long since blockaded up in that town, and by the American army which besieged them: and considering that the Officers were not to be seperated from their men, and that the troops could not be quartered with equal convenience, in any other place, within the limits pointed out, and described in the Convention, as there are not a sufficient number of barracks, in any other part of that State: though from these, and many other unavoidable circumstances, the accomodations of Gen¹ Burgoyne and his Officers, might not be such as the public could wish or he expect, yet his charge of a breach of the public faith on this account is not warranted either by the letter of the preliminary articles, agreed on between himself and Gen¹ Gates, on the 14ᵗʰ Octʳ, or by the Spirit of the Convention, signed on the 16ᵗʰ of the same Month: since by an examination of these articles it will appear, that the stipulation, with respect to the quartering of Officers, was not to be construed in that rigorous sense, in which Gen¹ Burgoyne affects to consider it, but on the contrary, that it was "agreed to as far as circumstances would admit."

Your Committee forbear to lay any stress on the attempt of the Enemy to alter the place of embarkation from the Port of Boston to that of Rhode-Island, or the Sound, so contiguous to the port of New York, which as well as that of Rhode-Island, is at present in their possession: on the seemingly inadequate number of vessels, (being only 26 transports sent to Rhode-Island, as appears in a letter sent from Gen¹ Pigot to Gen¹ Burgoyne, Dated December 3ʳᵈ) for an army consisting of 5642, in a winters voyage to Europe; or on the probability of the Enemy's

being able on so short a notice, to victual such a fleet and army
for a voyage of such length; since the declaration of Lt Genl
Burgoyne, that the public faith is broke, is of itself sufficient to
justify Congrefs, in taking every measure for securing the performance of the Convention, which the law of Nations in consequence of this conduct will justify.

These facts and opinions, your Committee, in a matter of such
high moment to the honour and safety of these states, esteem it
their duty to report specially; and considering that Genl Burgoyne has not fully complied with the Convention of Saratoga,
particularly in not delivering up the Cartouch-boxes and Accoutrements: that he has exprefsly, and without just foundation,
charged these states with a breach of public faith: that in consequence of this declaration, whilst in our power, he may deem
himself and the army under him, absolved from their compact,
and may therefore have refused compliance with a measure
naturally resulting from the Convention, and which only tended
to render his Officers and Men insecure, in case the Convention
on their part was not complied with: considering farther, that
from the distance between America and Great Britain, there is
no opportunity of accomodating this dispute in any reasonable
period of time with the Sovereign of the State, in behalf of which
this Convention was made, and that the Operations of Genl
Burgoyne's army in America, would not only defeat the Main
object of the Convention, but prove highly prejudicial to the
interest of these states. Your Committee submit the whole to
the consideration of Congrefs, in order that such measures be
adopted, as are consistent with the safety and honour of the
United States.

Whereupon Congrefs came to the following Resolutions: —

Resolved, — That, as many of the Cartouch-boxes, and
several other articles of Military Accoutrements, annexed to the
persons of the Non-Commifsioned Officers and Soldiers, included in the Convention of Saratoga, have not been delivered
up; the Convention on the part of the British army, has not
been strictly complied with —

Resolved, That the refusal of Lieu^t Genl Burgoyne, to give
descriptive lists of the Non-Commifsioned Officers and privates,
belonging to his army, subsequent to his declaration, that the
publick faith was broke, is considered by Congrefs in an alarming point of view, since a Compliance with the resolution of Con-

grefs could only have been prejudicial to that army, in case of an infraction of the Convention on their part:

Resolved, That the charge made by Lieu^t Genl Burgoyne in his letters to Major General Gates, of the 14th Novr of a breach of public faith on the part of these States, is not warranted by the juft conftruction of any article of the Convention of Saratoga; that it is a Strong indication of his intention, and affords juft ground of fear, that he will avail himself of such pretended breach of the Convention, in order to disengage himself, and the army under him, of the Obligation they are under to these united States, and that the Security which these States have had in his personal honour, is hereby deftroyed:

Resolved, therefore, that the embarkation of Lieu^t Genl Burgoyne, and the troops under his Command, be suspended, 'till a diftinct and explicit ratification of the Convention of Saratoga shall be properly notified by the Court of Great-Britain to Congrefs.

By order of Congrefs
HENRY LAURENS, <i>Presid^t</i></div>

Atteft   CHA^s THOMPSON, <i>Secretary</i>

The Dispatch Sloop of War arrived this day from the Delaware. She brings letters of the 10th Inftant, at which time everything was quiet at Philadelphia.

Orders have been received by the Dispatch, to send as much forage as pofsible to Philadelphia, with the utmoft expedition.

20th Feb^y   S. W. wind and thaw 'till 3 oClock, when the wind came round to the Northward and it froze hard.

A party of Nine Rebels landed laft night near the lower Black point, from whence they proceeded to Elam's house, robbed the family of near 100 Dollars in Cash, and then got off undiscovered.

21st — Hard froft, and very cold N. W. wind.

22^d Feb^y   Froft. Wind N.

The Swift Sloop of War sailed for New York.

A small party of Rebels landed laft night about ten o'Clock under McCurrie's house, a mile N. of Fogland ferry, and, headed by one Hunt, whose Mother is maintained by Mc Currie, went up to it and Robbed it of five Blankets, some Woolen Cloth; wearing apparel, and other articles, and then made off. As soon as notice was sent to the Barracks at Fogland Ferry, a party was sent in pursuit of them, but they escaped.

A Flag of truce came down this morning from Providence — It appears by a Boston paper brought by her, that Congrefs have Resolved, for many trifling reasons, not to permit Genl Burgoyne's Army to embark until The Convention of Saratoga is fully ratified by The King and Parliament. A person who came in the Flag says, that part of the Troops have actually marched from Cambridge to Rutland, and some towards Worcester, where they are to remain for the present.

The reasons given for this very extraordinary step, evidently shews that Congrefs determined, at any rate, to prevent General Burgoyne's Army from going to England time enough to replace such troops as were likely to be sent from thence time enough for the opening the Campaign. It is to be hoped that this flagrant breech of faith will at laft convince the British Nation that the Rebel Chiefs are a set of unprincipled Scoundrels; and that it will rouse them to a spirited exertion of the Strength of the Country, which, if properly directed, will effectually crush the ungrateful and perfiduous wretches.

It is to be observed, that this resolve pafsed in Congrefs the 8th of January; and yet Sir William Howe's letters to Genl Pigot dated the 10th of February, make no mention of it. Nor has Genl Pigot at this moment any Official information of the transaction, either from The Commander in Chief, or Genl Burgoyne.

23rd Feb^y — Froft.   Wind N.

The Sentence of a General Court Martial lately held in this Island, by which three Soldiers of the 22^d Regiment were sentenced to receive Corporal punishment for the crime of Sheep stealing, having been laid before the Commander in Chief, he has directed the punishment ordered to be inflicted; but at the same [time] has signified in public orders, that he moft highly disapproves the Sentence pafsed upon them, and conceives those who adjudged the delinquents to receive Corporal punishment for a Crime deemed Capital by law, have not properly diftinguished the nature of their guilt. He has also ordered, that no Ensigns shall for the future be put on General Courts Martial, where a sufficient number of officers of superior rank is to be had for that duty.

24th Feb^y   Fine weather. Wind W.

Six men came in last night from Swansea. They say it was
The Warren, Rebel Frigate, which escaped down the Naraganset passage the night of the 16th Instant. This is confirmed by
some of the Rebel papers, but with this addition, that "she
almost destroyed one of The Ministerial Frigates which attempted to oppose her." The fact is that she was suffered to
escape, but did not fire a gun.

Came in The Venus Frigate last night, from a Cruize in Boston
bay, where she lately took a Privateer of 10 Guns, and destroyed
two or three other vessels. The Crew of the Venus is so very
sickly that she was obliged to come in to Port before the term
of her Cruize was expired. She has not above 30 men fit for
duty. The Sickness is imputed to the bad weather she experienced during her Cruize, which obliged her to keep the Ports
and Hatches down, & occasioned much foul air between Decks.

25th Feb^y —   Fine soft day. Clear and pleasant. Wind S.

I went and visited all the advanced posts this morning, where
every thing is perfectly quiet. The men who came over last
from Swansea say the Rebels have not above 300 men in the
Neighbourhood of Howland's ferry. Four of the men who came
from Swansea, having obtained permission to return, went back
last night. They have promised to bring over provisions occasionally, and said they had some hopes of being able to bring off
Col^o Campbell of the 71st, who is guarded in so careless a manner as to favor an attempt to escape.

26th Feb^b   Thick fog all day. Raw and cold. Wind S. S. W.

William Bennet, Private Soldier in the 54th Regiment, was
hanged this morning for Desertion, agreeable to the Sentence of
a General Court Martial, which has been approved of by The
Commander in Chief. A Captain, Subaltern, and 50 men from
each Regiment in Garrison, under the Command of the Field
Officer of the day, attended the Execution.

An example of this kind was much wanted on this Island in
order to deter the Soldiers from committing a crime, which,
altho it is in these times one of the greatest a Soldier can commit, has been too prevalent of late. The effect of the example
however, was a good deal weakened, by the punishment not
immediately following the apprehension, and condemnation of
the offender. Considerable delay has been unavoidably occa-

sioned by sending the proceedings of the Court Martial to The Commander in Chief for his approbation.

27th Fe^b   Thick weather. Some rain. Raw & unpleasant. Wind S. E.

28th —   About 2 Inches of Snow fell laſt night. Wind N. E. Froſt this morning, and clear weather.

The Detachments of the 43rd Reg^t for the relief of those of The Landgrave's Reg^t at the advanced poſts, marched from Newport at 7 oClock this Morning.

Seven transports with about 450 Tons of hay on board for the use of the troops at Philadelphia, went out this morning under Convoy of The Brune. One transport got ashore on Brenton's point, and another ran foul of the Dispatch Sloop, and carried away her Boltsprit; but the as wind was fair, and the forage is much wanted at Philadelphia, the other ships did not ſtay for them.

The Thames sailed for New York.

1st March 1778   Slight froſt laſt night. Raw weather. Wind S.

The 43rd Regiment marched this morning at 7 oClock to Windmill hill to relieve the Landgrave's Reg^t which marched into town at 4 in the afternoon. A Captain, Two Subalterns, and 76 men of the Flank Companies of the 54th marched at the same time to relieve the Heſsian Chaſseurs at Fogland ferry.

The roads are exceedingly bad at present.

Two officers of the 71st Regiment, and 8 Countrymen came in laſt night from Swansea. The officers made their escape lately out of Worceſter Jail.

Some people who came in lately from the Naraganset side say, that the Rebels having a few days before brought down an 18 p^r to fire at the Somerset ſtationed in the Naraganset paſsage, some friends of Government aſsembled in the night, spiked the Gun and knocked off the Trunnions, to the great mortification of the Rebels.

2^d March —   Strong gale of wind from the W. N. W. after 11 o'Clock laſt night, which continued moſt part of this day. Snow during the night, about 3 Inches deep. Very cold day.

Lord Howe has kept up the ſtricteſt discipline in the Navy since his arrival here, and busineſs is carried on with the utmoſt secrecy. The Ships of War receive sealed orders, and inſtructions to be ready to sail on the first Signal. Their signal is frequently made suddenly, and they go immediately out of the harbour without knowing their destination till they are fairly out of the Port. His Lordship applies himself with the utmost assiduity to the public business, and is very seldom seen on shore. A Conduct highly praiseworthy in a man who has the chief direction of affairs of such great consequence to the Nation. If he indulged himself after the fatigues of the Campaign, in even the most innocent recreations, it would give room for the malicious spirits at home to say he neglected the public concerns.

3rd March — Snow from about 1 oClock this morning, which continued all this day. Hard frost. Wind E. and very cold.

No account whatever has yet been received of the fleet which sailed on the 15th February for Boston, which causes some apprehensions for their safety.

4th Snow all last night, which drifted much with a strong N. W. wind. It lay upon an average 14 Inches deep this morning. Hard frost all day.

5th March. Hard frost. Wind N. E. in the morning, and S. in the afternoon.

A Soldier (a German) of the 43rd Regiment, deserted last night from the advanced post at Howland's bridge.

A Sloop came in from New York last night. She saw the Sphynx, with 10 Sail under her Convoy in Huntingdon bay, bound for this port.

The Amazon having got up a set of Jury masts, went out from the Inner harbour, and anchored near the Eagle.

6th Hard frost. Wind N.

The Centurion sailed. Her destination unknown.

Came in The Unicorn from a Cruize.

7th March. — Some Snow in the morning, which turned to rain in the afternoon. Wind E.

Came in The Maidstone Frigate from a Cruize.

A German Serjeant of the 43rd Regiment deserted last night from the advanced post at Common fence; he was pursued very soon by an Officer and 20 men, but they could not find him on any part of the neck.

Two men came in last night in a Small Sloop from Sandwich. They have fled from their homes to avoid taking a test which has lately been ordered to be subscribed by all the Inhabitants of Maſsachusetts bay. The Sloop is loaded with wood, which they have disposed of.

These men say that the ships for Boston sailed from Holmes's-hole in Martha's Vineyard, only two days ago, having waited there for many days for a fair wind to take them over a particular part of the Shoals.

8th March   Rain laſt night, which froze as it fell, and encruſted every thing with Ice. Rain this morning with a N. W. wind.

Five persons came in from Tiverton laſt night, among whom are a Colonel Holland of the Militia, and a Mr Eccleſton a Clergyman.

A fleet of 8 transports laden with Hay, sailed this morning for the Delaware, under Convoy of the Diamond.

Sailed the Amazon for New York, where she is to take in the Maſts of the Mercury, lately loſt in the N. River, and proceed thence to England.

9th March.   Cold raw weather.   Wind E.

Captain Griffiths of The Nonsuch having been appointed Commodore, and to Command on this Station when Lord Howe goes from hence, hoiſted his broad pendant yeſterday as soon as the Amazon went out of the harbour. He could not do it sooner, as Captain Jacobs of the Amazon is a Senior Captain.

10th   Froſt laſt night. Small rain moſt part of the day. Wind E.

Two men came in yeſterday in a small boat from Martha's Vineyard.

A German Soldier of the 43rd Regiment deserted laſt night from the advanced poſts.

11th March.   Rain and thick fog all day. Wind E. The froſt & Snow is going off faſt. The roads are now become extremely bad.

The diſtreſs of the lower claſſes of the Inhabitants of this town (Newport) is at present very great; particularly for provisions and fuel, which are scarce and dear. The Salt provisions which the Soldiers dispose of, supports many of them.

12th　　　Rain and fog most part of the day. Wind S. W. in the Morning, but afterwards E.

A large house on Brenton's neck, the property of Captain Brenton of the Navy, which has for some time past been uninhabited and going to ruin, is now taken for a Naval hospital, and is fitting up for that purpose. It is convenient and well situated, being about two miles from the town, & very accefsible to boats from the Ships. In consequence of its distance from Newport, many of the irregularities committed by the people in and about the hospital, will be prevented.

13th March — Fog and some rain. Wind S. The frost almost gone. The roads are at this time in very bad condition.

Some guns were heard in the offing this Morning, supposed to be from the Sphynx and her Convoy; but that they dare not venture to come in with the land on account of the Fog.

A Ship with Rebel prisoners went up to Bristol. They are released on parole. There has been a great Sicknefs among them of late; which is generally the case with the American prisoners; and they are so lowspirited and desponding, that when once taken ill, they seldom recover.

14th March.　　　Fog again this morning. Wind S. S. W. About 3 it cleared up and the day became very pleasant. Very little Snow remains except in those places where it had drifted to a great depth. But the Country is still very wet, and there is not the least appearance of Spring.

No birds have been seen yet, except such as remain here during the Winter, which are the Meadow-lark, or Swamp-Quail, the Snow bird, the Quails, and a few Snipes.

The Rebels having made a Signal from Papasquash point to speak with The Flora, a boat was sent to them, when they desired leave to bring down some officers to be exchanged: the leave was granted, but the Fog coming on very thick, they did not come off.

15th March　　　Warm pleasant day. Wind N. E. in the Morning, and S. in the afternoon.

Came in The Sphynx with a fleet from New York. They have been out three weeks, and have been detained most of the time in the Sound by contrary winds.

Came in also The Ariel from a Cruize, with several very valuable prizes.

Mr Mercereau, a Rebel Commissary came down from Bristol with five Officers and five Soldiers of General Burgoyne's Army, who were taken prisoners during the last Campaign, and are to be exchanged for Rebels of equal rank. The Officers are Capt Green, 31st Reg^t, Ensign Baron Salans, & Surgeon Sealy, 9th, Lieu^t York, Roy^l Artillery, and Lieu^t Durnford, of the Engineers.

Great flocks of Wild Geese were observed this day, going to the N. E. which, in most parts of America is looked upon as a sign there will be no more severe weather. Thier flight to the S. E. in the month of November is generally the forerunner of bad weather.

16th March.   Rain and thick weather all day.   Wind E.

The 43rd Regiment having undertaken to supply themselves with the necessary quantity of wood from Commonfence Neck, during the time they continued on duty at the advanced posts, & having employed several Carts yesterday in drawing away what had been cut near Hicks's Orchard, the Rebels fired 6 Cannon shot at them from the Fort above Howlands ferry, but without effect.

Four Rebel Sloops went through Bristol ferry this day into Bristol bay. Two of them were full of men. Our battery fired 12 Shot at them, but they passed through without any damage. Some of the Shot struck very near them.

17th Cloudy day, but soft and pleasant.   Wind S.

Many Blackbirds, Bluebirds, and Robins, seen this day.

A Colonel Johonnet came down from the Rebels to General Pigot on some business. He was permitted to come on shore and to walk about the town. An officer of the Garrison was ordered to attend him during the time he remained on Shore.

18th March.   Frost last night, and Strong wind at N. W. Wind W. during the day, and pleasant weather.

Three White-men and five Negroes came off in a small boat last night from South Kingston. They were taken up off Point Judith this Morning, and brought in here by the Royal George, a Letter of Marque from New York. Those men intended to come to Newport, having fled from their homes to avoid being obliged to serve in the Rebel Army.

The Royal George has brought 40 Chaldrons of Coals for the use of the troops. The Rose of 20 Guns may be hourly expected with ten sail of transports to take in Hay for Philadelphia.

The Maidstone Frigate sailed this day.

The Rebels have fired a good many shot these last two days at the parties of the 43rd Regiment employed in cutting wood on Commonfence neck. They also brought their Galley near, and fired at them, but without any effect.

19th March.   Fine weather. Slight frost. Wind S.

The Maidstone, which went out yesterday, Steered up the Sound. Another Frigate went the same course this morning.

There is no appearance of The Rose and her Convoy, and as they were left under way yesterday near Plumb-Island, and there has been a fair wind ever since, it is feared some accident has happened to them. The Warren, a Rebel Frigate of 30 Guns, was in New London harbour lately; and tis said a vessel of 40 Guns from France with Clothing & Military Stores, escaped our Cruizers a short time since, and got into the same port. If any of the Rose's Convoy should have got on shore, and the abovementioned vessels fall upon her and them, they will be an overmatch for them.

20th March.   Pleasant weather. Wind S. W.

Came in The Isis from New York. She has brought the letters which came by the January Packet from England.

The Rose and her Convoy were seen yesterday at anchor, near Gardiner's Island, in the Sound.

Came in also The Diamond from the Delaware; but has brought no letters, as she only gave up her Convoy to The Brune, and then returned. Two of The Brune's Convoy were taken by the Rebels in the Delaware, the lower part of which is infested with a number of small flat-bottomed Privateers, which run into shallow water out of reach of our frigates. But the Diamond having got intelligence of one of them, landed a party which marched 7 miles up a Creek, and cut her out, with a small loss. Lt Medell of the Marines, lost his arm in this affair.

The Haerlem Tender came in this morning from the fleet in Cape Cod bay.

21st March.   Strong gale of wind last night, & this day at N. W. Hard frost and very cold.

The Rose and her Convoy of 10 Ships from New York, attempted to get in this morning, but were driven out to Sea by the violence of the gale.

22ᵈ — Cold day.   Strong wind at N. W.

A Flag of truce came down from Bristol with Ensign Clerk of the 43ʳᵈ Regiment, who was taken prisoner in   last, on Commonfence neck. He was allowed to come in on his parole.

23ʳᵈ March.   Fine clear day. Slight frost in the morning, but a very mild afternoon.   Wind N.

Lord Howe, in The Eagle of 64 Guns, sailed out of the harbour at 12 this day for The Delaware. It is supposed he will call off Sandy hook, in order to have an interview with Commodore Hotham who commands at New York. There was no salute on his going out. His Lordship has been here since the 2ᵈ January last.

24ᵗʰ   Good weather.   Wind S.

Came in The Rose, and ten empty transports from New York, to load hay for Philadelphia.

The Hefsian Regiments stationed on this Island, put on their new Clothing this day for the first time. Altho it has been ready for three months past, they could not put it on until they received orders so to do from General Knyphausen, their Commander in Chief in America. These troops have received no clothing since they left Germany, in the beginning of the year 1776.

25ᵗʰ March.   Pleasant weather. Wind S. There is at present very little appearance of Spring.

A party of Colº Wightman's Provincial Corps having disguised themselves, and pretended to have just come over from the Eastern shore, went last night to the houses of some of the Inhabitants on the East side of this Island, by whom they were most favorably received, and where they fully discovered that nothing but the dread of The King's troops prevents the greatest part of the Inhabitants from joining the Rebels most heartily in any enterprize against them. One of the Inhabitants acknowledged that he was to have set fire to the Hay Magazine. In short they all discovered their eagernefs to inlist in the Rebel Army, or to give them every afsistance in their power. Three of them were apprehended this day by the General's order, and sent to The Provoſts.

About 90 men, drafted from the 22ᵈ & 43ʳᵈ Battalions, to complete their Flank Companies, embarked today on board the hay ships going to Philadelphia.

28ᵗʰ March.   Cold raw day. Wind E. Snow for about two hours in the Evening. About an Inch deep.

Many persons have come in lately from the Main. They in general agree in saying that a demand of 40,000 men, within 40 days, was lately made, in order to complete the Rebel Army; in consequence of which every means are used to raise them; but without much succeſs, the people in general being averse to entering into the service. Negroes, Indians, and persons of all descriptions are accepted. In the province of New Hampshire very few have been raised.

A man who calls himself Davis, and who appears by the papers found upon him to be a Serjeant in a Rebel Battalion, came over from the Seconnet side by himself the night before laſt in a Canoe. A considerable sum of money (above 600 Dollars) in Gold, Silver, Loan-office Certificates, & Continental bills, was found upon him. From many circumſtances it is ſtrongly suspeſted he is one of a gang of villians concerned in the Robbery & Murder of a Mʳ Spooner, at Brookfield in Massachusett's Bay; — which Robbery & Murder was lately committed, at the inſtigation of Mʳˢ Spooner, by some Rebel Soldiers. The fellow's story is, that he was employed to inliſt men for the Regiment, and having been entruſted with the money for that purpose, he deserted with it. He was sent to prison until something certain is known respeſting him.

27ᵗʰ March.   Fair pleasant weather. Wind N. E.

The fleet for Philadelphia sailed this morning under Convoy of The Apollo.

28ᵗʰ March — Pleasant weather. Wind N. E. all laſt night, but S. E. the latter part of this day.

The wood party consiſting of 100 men, under the Command of Major Martini of the Heſsian troops, embarked on board the fleet going to Shelter Island for wood for the Garrison.

About half after 10 oClock laſt night, the Lark Frigate Stationed off Greenwich, perceived a veſsel coming down, and made the Signal; on which The Commodore ordered The Maidſtone &

Sphynx, which were lying in the harbour, to slip their Cables and put to Sea; soon after which the Rebel vefsel came paft the Somerset lying in the Naraganset pafsage, who gave her many shot, and by the time she had got to the mouth of the pafsage, the two Frigates were ready for her, and gave her so warm a reception that she was obliged to run on shore within point Judith. As the wind died away towards morning they could not get near enough to deftroy her, which afforded the Rebels an opportunity of getting out part of her ftores, and bringing down some guns to protect her. As the Somerset sent no report to the Commodore, and nothing could be seen from the ships in the harbour this morning except our two frigates at anchor in the Offing, the Commodore knew nothing of the situation of the Rebel vefsel until Gen¹ Pigot sent him information of what was seen from the heights; upon which the Spitfire Galley was towed out of the harbour by the boats of the fleet, and every necefsary preparation made for deftroying her. As the wind came in from the S. E. in the afternoon the Frigates worked up and made a disposition for burning her, which was effected about 7 in the Evening, with great gallantry by the boats under the Command of Lieuᵗ Vashon of The Maidftone, notwithftanding a severe fire of Cannon & Musquetry from the Rebels. She proved to be the Columbus, a Continental Frigate, pierced for 36 Guns, Six of which were on a lower deck. She was on her way to New London where she was to have taken in moft of her Guns & men. The Rebels saved all the powder she had on board, part of her sails, and some other ftores; but the ship was entirely deftroyed. Seven Seamen were wounded in boarding her.

29ᵗʰ March. — Cold day. Some Snow this morning. Strong Wind at N. E.

The fleet from Cape Cod bay, under Convoy of The Juno and Cerberus, came in sight this morning from the Eaftward. Moft of them got in before night, but with great difficulty, as the wind was violent and contrary. Some of them got into the Naraganset pafsage, and four others, seeing it likely to blow hard and that they could not get in before dark, ftood out to Sea.

Two prizes taken by the Orpheus, and a ship retaken by her, came in with the fleet.

30ᵗʰ March. Strong gale of wind from the N. E. all laft night, & moft of this day, with heavy rain.

About 20 Non-Commiſsioned Officers & Privates of different Regiments, who had been prisoners with the Rebels, and were brought to Halifax to be exchanged as Seamen; were brought in with the fleet yeſterday. They came from Halifax in the Orpheus, and were put on board one of the Transports at Sea.

31ˢᵗ   Fine weather. Wind N.

Some of the transports which were obliged to run into the Naraganset paſsage on the 29ᵗʰ came into the harbour to-day.

General Burgoyne is expected here in a few days from Cambridge having obtained permiſsion from Congreſs to go to England.

1ˢᵗ Aᵖ 1778/   For Appendix

From the Maryland Journal. 10ᵗʰ Feᵇ 1778

I observed in the London Gazette a pompous liſt of the Killed, wounded and Prisoners of the Rebel army (so termed) in the Campaign of 1776. I therefore make no doubt, but the Publication of the following Authentic account of the killed, wounded and Prisoners of the British tyrants, since the Commencement of hoſtilities, will ballance the same, and be agreeable to many of your readers, who perhaps have not taken a summary view thereof.

In March 1776 the Parliament of Great Britain granted supplies for the support of 42,390 British and Foreign troops to serve in America, exclusive of 8000 Marines, for that Campaign, which Military force was shiped for, and actually did land on the Continent before the 1ˢᵗ of Septʳ following, amounting to 50,390 land and Sea forces, which was reduced by the armies of the united States as follows —

	Killed	Wounded	Prisoners
Commencement of hoſtilities, at Lexington & Concord	43	70	
At the Battle of Buncker's hill	746	1150	
Ticonderoga, at Sᵗ John's, & before Quebec	81	110	340
On the Lakes, by General Arnold	53	64	
At the attack on Fort Sullivan, S. Carolina	197	260	
At the Cedars, in Canada	40	70	
At Norfolk, and the great bridge	129	175	40
At different engagements on Long-Island	840	1600	65
At Haerlem and Hellgate	136	157	49
At New-York, on landing	57	100	
White plains	350	470	200
Carried forward	2672	4226	694

Brought over	2672	4226	694
At the attack on Fort Washington, & the lines before it	900	1500	
Fort Lee	20	35	
At Trenton — 26ᵗʰ Decʳ 1776	35	60	948
At Princeton	74	100	
In Boston road, by Commadore Harding	52	90	750
In sundry transports			390
At Danbury	260	350	
At Iron hill, Newcastle county	59	80	20
At Brandywine — 11ᵗʰ Sepᵗʳ 1777	800	1176	
On Reading road, by Genˡ Maxwell	40	60	
On Staten-Island, by General Sullivan...........	94	150	278
At Bennington, 4ᵗʰ October	900	1300	30
At Forts Montgomery, and Clinton	580	700	
At Forts Mifflin & Redbank	328	70	84
Of the army under General Burgoyne...........	2100	1126	5752
Prisoners and Deserters, before the Surrender.....			1100
British, and Foreign troops, killed, wounded and taken Prisoners, since the commencement of hostilities in America	8914	11023	10046

Total 29,983

1ˢᵗ April.   Fine weather.   Wind N.

Sailed The Diamond Frigate for Halifax, and The Apollo, with a fleet of hay ships for Philadelphia. 1010 Tons of hay has now been sent from hence to Philadelphia, which at 10 lbˢ pʳ Ration amounts to 226,240 Rations. Not lefs than 300 Tons of hay has been spoilt here during the laſt winter by bad management, and not securing the Stacks properly from the weather.

Eleven men came in laſt night from Freetown. They have all inliſted in the Provincial Corps here.

A man came in likewise from Bedford. As he has a considerable sum of money with him, in Gold, and appears to be of a suspitious Character, it is imagined he only came here with a view of getting a pafsage to France to purchace Merchandize and Military Stores for the Rebels.

A Sloop laden with Potatoes, Onions, Cyder, &c. &c., from Swansea, came ashore laſt night near the mouth of The Town pond at Briſtol ferry. The people who own her had been on the Island some time ago, and received afsurances from Lord Howe & Genˡ Pigot, that if they brought the vefsel, she and the Cargo, should be at their own disposal here. They were afraid to go through Briſtol ferry on account of the Rebel Battery there, therefore they run her ashore as above. As it was a high Spring tide at the time, it is feared they will not be able to get her off.

Huyne's Regiment marched this morning at 7 oClock to relieve the 43rd Regiment at Windmill hill and the 2^d Company of Hessian Chasseurs at Fogland ferry. The 43rd marched into town at 2 o'Clock.

During the time the 43rd have been on duty at the advanced posts, they have employed parties in cutting wood for their own consumption on Commonfence neck; besides which they have cut, and left piled at Commonfence Redoubt, 150 Cords, for the use of the Reg^t which succeeds them. They have been paid for all the wood they cut, at the rate of 4 Dollars p^r Cord. The Rebels Cannonaded their parties almost every day, but without effect.

2nd April.   Pleasant weather.   Wind S. E.

Lieu^t Col^o Anstruther of the 62^d Reg^t came down yesterday Evening in a flag of truce from Providence. He came here to endeavor to get exchanged for a Rebel officer of equal rank; but as there are no Rebel troops prisoners here, he will be obliged to go to New York to effect his purpose.

3rd Ap^l — Heavy rain from 7 last night till near daybreak, accompanied with Thunder, Lightning, & Strong wind at S. W. About 11 at night there was a very quick flash of lightning, and loud clap of thunder, which caused a good deal of consternation among the Inhabitants.

Clear pleasant day, but a heavy gale of wind at S. W. The Rebels with two armed boats, attempted last night to burn the Sloop which was on shore near The Townpond. They boarded her, but did not succeed.

4th   Fine day 'till 12 o'Clock, when the wind changed to the S. E., when it snowed hard 'till night, and then turned to rain. High wind in the Evening, and Cold. About 6 Inches of Snow fell, but it did not lie.

5th April. Heavy rain last night, Wind N. E. Some Snow this Morning. Clear and pleasant after 10 o'Clock this morning. Wind W. in the afternoon.

About 30 sail of vessels, went out this morning for Shelter Island for Wood, under Convoy of the Mermaid.

Sailed at same time The Maidstone, with a Convoy for New York.

6th   Very fine day.   Wind S. W.

Four men came in last night from Swansea. They say that a Mr Bradford, the Rebel Lieut Governor of this Province was put in Irons lately on suspition of carrying on a Correspondance with some of The King's Officers.

7th April.   Fine weather.   Wind S.

The Rebels burnt the Sloop at Bristol ferry last night, without lofs or opposition. Everything of value had been previously taken out of her.

Came in The Swan, with a Convoy from New York.

About 12 this day, General Burgoyne, attended by Colo Kingston his Adjutant General, Captain Stanley of the 20th, & Ensign Wilford of the 2d Regiment, his aides de Camp, Mr Wood, Surgeon of the Hospital, and Mr Geddes, Deputy Paymaster General, landed from Warwick point. They left Cambridge on the 5th Instant. The General has obtained permifsion to go to England on parole; and he intends embarking as soon as pofsible on board The Grampus, Storeship.

The General was received at the house allotted for him, by a Guard of a Captain, two Subalterns, & 50, British, & the Guards beat a March, &c.

Major Pollard, Aide de Camp to General Heath, and a Rebel Commifsary came with Genl Burgoyne. The latter is come to make an arrangement for supplying the troops of the Convention with provisions.

8th Apl   Cold day, but clear and pleasant.   Strong wind at N.

Orders were ifsued at Philadelphia the 3rd January, for the payment of 165 days forage money to the Army, "in consideration of the latenefs of the "Campaign, and the dearnefs of provisions." Only such Officers as have taken the field are to be included. The abovementioned order was received here yesterday.

9th   Fine weather.   Wind S.

A number of Transports are to go from hence to Europe under Convoy of The Grampus, and are to sail the first fair wind.

10th April — Very fine day. Wind S. W.

General Burgoyne, attended by Gen¹ Pigot, and most of the public Officers, made the tour of the Island, and visited all the posts. There was an assembly in the Evening, in compliment to the General, at which were present about 40 ladies and 100 Gentlemen.

11th   Cloudy, soft weather. Wind S. W.

Sailed The Swan, with 3 vessels under Convoy for New York. Arrived a vessel from Halifax, with Coals.

12th   Fine weather. Wind S. W.

The Somerset 64 Guns, came round the S. point of Cononicut, into the harbour, having been relieved in her station in the Narraganset passage by The Juno.

13th Ap¹   Pleasant weather. Wind S. W.

General Burgoyne is extremely uneasy at being detained here so long, being particularly anxious to arrive in England before the breaking up of Parliament.

14th   Thick weather. Wind S. S. W. Fog in the afternoon.

There is little or no appearance of Spring hitherto, and not a leaf or a blossom stirring.

15th Ap¹ — Rain last night, and this morning. Wind N. E.

General Burgoyne, and the other officers going to England, embarked this morning on board The Grampus, Storeship, which with the other vessels, immediately got under way; and about 11 o'Clock the whole fleet, consisting of about 30 Sail, were safe out of the harbour. No Salute was given, or other compliment paid to Gen¹ Burgoyne on his embarking. But he was accompanied to the waterside by The Generals, The Staff, and many other Officers. He expressed great satisfaction at the attention which had been shewn him during his stay here.

The flag of truce returned this day to Providence, with Maj^r Pollard, and the Rebel Commissary. Major Morrison, our Deputy Commissary General here, went with him to Boston, to settle finally everything relative to the supplying the Troops of the Convention with provisions. Major General Phillips succeeds to the Command of that Army.

At 4 this afternoon The Somerset sailed for New York. As the Crew of the Somerset are sickly, she is ordered round to New York for their recovery; fresh provisions and other refreshments being in greater plenty there than in this Island.

16th Ap^l   Fine weather. Wind S.

Mr Geddes, Deputy Paymaster General of The Convention Army returned in the Flag of Truce yesterday, and took with him a very considerable sum in Specie, for the use of our Troops at Cambridge.

17th   Rain all last night. Clear fine day. Wind N. W.

Sailed The Unicorn Frigate for Halifax, to repair some part of the Iron work about her Rudder, which cannot be done here. Sailed also The Haerlem Tender, with two Victuallers loaded with provisions for the troops at Cambridge.

Four hundred men from the troops in this town, have been employed for some days past, under the direction of the Commanding Engineer in damming up a small run of water which falls into Easton's pond, to the N. E. of Newport. The intention is, to overflow a Valley to the Eastward of the General Hospital, and by that means to reduce the extent of the front by which the Enemy can attack the town. I am of opinion it will not answer the end proposed, as there is not a drop of water runs there during three Months of the Summer, and the foundation of the present Dam is not so staunch as to retain the water which at this season may be collected.

18th Ap^l — Strong wind last night at N. W. Fine clear day. Wind N. W.

Two or three small vessels have arrived within a few days from Long-Island with Oysters, which are Sold at one Dollar p^r bushel.

Major of brigade Blomfield of The Royal Artillery, & Captain Montgomery of the 9th Reg^t arrived here last night from Providence.

Lt Col^o Campbell of the 71st Reg^t has at last obtained permission from the Rebels to go to Morristown in Jersey to endeavor to effect his exchange. His baggage under the care of an officer of the 71st came here a few days ago from Providence in his way to New York.

In consequence of a report at Boston that The King's Army had embarked at Philadelphia, The Rebels ordered the troops of the Convention at Cambridge, to be marched to Rutland 70 miles from thence; and the 1st Division, consisting of the Royal Artillery and the troops which composed the advanced Corps of that Army, have actually marched in consequence thereof. This is by many considered as an excuse for removing them from Cambridge, where we might supply them with greater ease with what they require, to a place where they will not meet with the like accomodation.

A Cartel sloop came in this day from New London, with five Prisoners, some of whom are Masters of vessels which went with the last Wood fleet from hence to Shelter Island, & were taken straggling about on Long Island. I think we should not suffer these fellows to enter the harbour when they please, under the pretence of exchanging a few prisoners, as by such means they gain exact intelligence of everything, and plainly observe the position of our Ships.

General Pigot has received certain intelligence that Mr Sullivan is daily expected at Providence to take the Command of the Rebel troops in this Neighbourhood; and as he is an enterprizing spirited fellow, it is likely he will succeed in his endeavors to collect a sufficient body of men to enable him to make some attempt on this Island before we receive any reinforcement, or have further time to strengthen our position. The Redoubts which it has been proposed to construct near The General Hospital, were begun upon this day by working parties consisting of 400 men. The Redoubts proposed are at Tomini Hill, Irishes, Bannisters, The General Hospital, and The Windmill; which will command all the Ground from Coaster's-harbour Island on the left, to the head of Easton's pond on the right: which is obviously the best position to be fortified for the defence of the town.

As we have at present no Camp Equipage, (except some old tents for about 500 men) I think we should immediately erect a respectable work on Windmill hill, capable of containing a Regiment, and not to be taken without breaking ground against it. The Enemy should by every means in our power be prevented from establishing themselves unmolested on Windmill hill; or any part of the Northern extremity of the Island, for if they should we shall find it extremely difficult to dispossess them; and a secure position there would enable them to land, without molestation, everything requisite for attacking us in force. If we possess a strong post on the N. end of the Island, and they determine on making an attack, they must make that [attack by] water, which, considering the disposition and extent of our naval force, will be attended with numerous and almost insurmountable difficulties.

Two Gallies and The Kingsfisher, are stationed in the Seconnet passage, and without a superior Naval force to cover the landing, the Rebels cannot expect to succeed in an attempt on that side; but should they by any accident make good their landing, it is very improbable they would leave such posts as Windmill-hill and the Artillery Redoubt behind them, unless they left a considerable force to observe them.

The three advanced Redoubts command the two Necks effectually. Windmill-hill commands part of the E. side, as the Artillery Redoubt does the West. The Enemy must therefore force most of those posts before they can advance into the Island. Should they make their attack in any other quarter, they must bring every thing by water.

A trifling temporary work should by no means be constructed on Windmill hill; for as it is the best spot on the Island for a work of consequence, and such a work will at one time or other be found necessary there, the erection of a trifling work would be throwing away so much time and money.

19th Ap^l   Fine weather.   Wind S. S. W.

An Oyster sloop arrived this morning from New York, which place she left the 16th Instant. She brought a letter which mentions that The Andromeda Frigate arrived the day before with dispatches from England, in consequence of which Lord Howe, then at Sandy-Hook, immediately got under way for The Delaware, altho the wind was contrary. Also, that Genl Howe is recalled, and Genl Clinton appointed Commander in Chief in his room. The Andromeda also brought drafts of two Bills which had been read in the House of Commons on the 19th February. The one for declaring the intentions of Parliament concerning the exercise of the right of imposing taxes in America: the other to Enable His Majesty to appoint Commissioners with powers to treat, consult, and agree upon the means of quieting the disorders now subsisting in America.

The Packet with the February mail from England was spoke with by The Apollo 14 days ago, going into the Delawar.

20th Ap^l Fine weather.   Wind N.

A Rebel Lieutenant came in the night of the 18th Instant. He had been in Jail for some time for attempting to desert to us, but as there was not sufficient proof against him, he was enlarged; and immediately took the first opportunity to come off.

21st — Good weather. Wind N. W.

Came in The Halifax Armed Schooner from New York, with two vessels under her Convoy. The letters brought by her confirm the accounts we received on the 19th.

General Pigot has received a Circular letter from Lord George Germaine, (with draughts of the acts before mentioned, dated the 19th February) declaring the wishes of The King & Parliament to restore peace to the Colonies, and desiring that the Bills may be dispersed immediately among the people at large, that they may be acquainted with the favorable disposition of Great Britain towards them.

Sailed two Brigs for Boston with provisions for the troops of the Convention at Cambridge.

22^d Ap^l   Cloudy, and some rain 'till 2 oClock, when it turned to a thick wet fog. Wind S.

A party of about 25 Rebels landed on Commonfence Neck yesterday and advanced as far as Hicks's Orchard. A Shot was fired at them from the 12 p^r in Bristol ferry redoubt, which falling very near them, they immediately retired.

Ten men came over to us last night.

23rd Ap^l   Fine weather. Fresh wind at N. W.

A Sloop came on shore on Sachawest beach yesterday Evening about 7 o'Clock, in the Fog. A Corporal and four men were sent there soon after, who by firing a few shot at her obliged one of the people to come on shore, which he did in a Canoe with great hazard. It appears she belongs to Nantucket, and went lately from thence to Bedford, where she took in a Cargo of Tar, Turpentine, Sails and Cordage, and cleared out for Nantucket; but the owners and people on board her being Loyalists, they determined to steer for Newport & dispose of the Cargo; but they mistook Sachawest bay for the entrance of the harbour and were driven on shore. The Cargo has been landed on the beach, but the vessel will be lost.

24th   Good weather, but rather Cold. Strong wind at N. W.

There has been no fish brought to market this season, except Perch. They are taken in Easton's pond and in the ponds near the Shore to the Southward of the town. They are from four to Nine Inches long, and sold for a shilling a Dozen.

25th Ap[l]   Pleasant Weather. Wind W.

Several copies of the Bills read in the House of Commons on the 19th February last, were sent this day by a Flag of truce to Providence, addressed to M[r] Sullivan who commands in the Military department there.

Captain Furneaux, late of the Syren, came down this day from Warwick, having been exchanged for M[r] Manley, late Captain of the Rebel Frigate Hancock. He brings information of the arrival of a French Frigate at Falmouth, Casco Bay, which sailed from Brest on the 8th March, and brought out M[r] Deane, and, as tis said, the Ratification of a Treaty of Alliance between France and the United States of America. This information relative to an Alliance is not credited, as at the time the Treaty must have been negotiating, France made declaration of her friendly disposition towards England; and it is by no means her interest to go to War with us at a time when we have so powerful a Fleet and Army assembled, with which we might immediately attack her most valuable Colonies in the West Indies. The giving assistance to our Colonies to throw off their dependence on the Mother Country, would also set a dangerous example to their own. It is by many imagined that this report is circulated in order to answer the temporary purpose of raising men to complete the Regiments for the ensuing Campaign.

26th Ap[l]   Fine weather. Wind N. W.

Sailed the Halifax, and a ship under Her convoy for New York.

27th   Fine pleasant day. Wind S. W. and fresh.

Came in two prizes taken by The Haerlem Sloop.

28th Ap[l]   Fair fine weather. Wind S. W.

Came in The Orpheus from a Cruize.

A flag of truce came down from Providence this morning. Col[o] Barton (the person who commanded the party that took Gen[l] Prescott) came in her, and having informed the Captain of the advanced ship that he had letters for Gen[l] Pigot which he was directed to deliver into his own hands, he was permitted to come to town. He brought a letter from M[r] Sullivan, who commands at Providence, on the subject of the Bills lately sent up. It is conceived in high and insulting terms, and informed the General, he had referred the Bills to the Governor & Council.

Mr Barton was allowed when he came on shore, to visit some of the Prisoners in the Provost; but he was so closely attended by an Officer, that it was not in his power to speak to, or have the least correspondence with any of the Rebel party here, which certainly was the secret motive for his visit to this place. The sending a fellow who they knew must be particularly disagreeable to us, merely to be the bearer of a letter, shews the insulting manner in which they act towards us. He was extremely prefsing to be allowed to remain on shore all night, but was obliged to go on board and return up the Bay at 2 o'Clock.

29th Apl   Cloudy weather.   Wind N. E.

General Pigot having received information that the Rebels intend shortly to carry off all the Stock from the Elisabeth Islands, has determined to send a detachment there immediately, and endeavor to be beforehand with them; and for this purpose the Flank Companies of the 54th Regiment, and a Company of The Hefsian Chafseurs have received orders to be in readinefs to embark on the shortest notice. Two transports are ordered for the reception of the Detachment which consists of about 200 men, and they are to be convoyed by a Frigate from hence, which, with the Unicorn frigate now there, is to cover them.

Major Morrison returned this day from Boston, having arranged every thing with the Rebel Commifsary there, relative to our supplying the troops of the Convention with provisions.

Major Morrison says, the Rebels burnt the drafts of The Bills lately sent up to Providence, under the Gallows there, by the hands of the common hangman; and that they have been treated with all pofsible insult and contempt in other places. But this proceeding is by no means to be considered as conveying the Sentiments of the bulk of the people, who are now so completely tyranized over, that they dare not exprefs their opinion upon any public matter, especially one of so great consequence. It is entirely the act of those who have afsumed all authority at present, and who must sink into their original insignificance in case of a reconciliation with Great Britain.

30th Apl   Rain all day.   Strong wind at N.

The three Companies embarked this morning at 6 o'Clock. They did not sail in consequence of the appearance of bad weather.

A party of about 20 Horsemen were seen within these few days on the S. point of Fogland. It is supposed Mr Sullivan was there reconnoitring.

It appears from an attentive examination of the ground near Windmill hill, that a Small redoubt on the right of the E. Road, and nearly in a line with Windmill hill, would be of great service should the Rebels make any attempt to land thereabouts, as the shore is advantageous for a landing and not seen from any of our posts. If the General has certain information that the Rebels intend to make an attack on this Island, an arrangement should be made for bringing all the Carriages, horses, and Cattle within our lines in due time, in order to render their advancing towards the town more difficult and tedious; — and I believe the best mode of proceeding in case they should effect a landing will be to attack them as soon as possible with all the force that can be collected.

1st May.   Rain all last night and this day. Wind N. E. Cold & raw.

The 54th Regiment marched this morning at 9 o'Clock to Windmill-hill to relieve the Regiment of Huyne; and the 2^d Company of Chafseurs at the same time to relieve the post at Fogland ferry.

The 54th are to construct a Redoubt round the Barrack at Windmill hill, for the present security of that post.

It is intended that the two Flank Companies of the 54th, and the two Companies of Hefsian Chafseurs, shall take a weeks duty each at Fogland ferry, during the time the 54th Regiment is stationed at Windmill hill.

The Providence Rebel Frigate of 30 Guns & 350 men escaped to Sea last night about 10 o'Clock. The night was very dark, with much rain, and the Wind at N. N. E. The Lark, stationed off Greenwich had sufficient notice of her coming down, and was under way when she came opposite to her, and they engaged till they came near the N. end of Connonicut, when the Lark, having received a good deal of damage, 3 men killed and 7 wounded, and finding the Providence had come under the fire of The Juno, came to an anchor. Many shot were exchanged between the Providence and the Juno, but as the latter did not get under way, the Providence pafsed her, and then fired several shot which raked her and shot away her Ensign Staff; after which she proceeded to Sea unmolested. The Commodore on observing the firing made a Signal for The Orpheus to slip, and go out of the harbour, which was not complied with, as neither the Pilot or Master would take charge of the ship under the circumstances of the weather. The night was so dark that it was above half an hour before the Commodore knew that the Orpheus had not gone out, he would then have gone out with his own Ship but it was too late. In short there appears to have been some misconduct on the part of our ships. The Lark should have endeavored by every possible means to have retarded the Providence, and even have run foul of her at any risque. If she had been lost and driven the Enemy on shore, the advantage would have been on our side. The Juno should certainly have engaged her, and followed her to Sea: her fire would have directed the ships from the harbour where to have gone to her assistance; and the Captain of the Orpheus, in such a case should have taken the charge of the ship upon himself: it was possible to get out, and if he had lost his ship, a Court Martial would have acquitted him. At any rate he was blameable for not giving immediate notice to The Commodore why he did not obey the Signal, as The Commodore might then have gone out with the Nonsuch, which lay in a more favorable situation.

By all accounts the Enemy's ship was worked & fought well, and in good order. She must have suffered considerably, as the Lark was very close, and fired a great deal at her.

2ᵈ May.   Thick weather and some rain. Wind N. E. Fair in the afternoon, and Wind N. W.

A Soldier of the 54ᵗʰ Regᵗ deserted last night from his post, and got clear off to the Rebels by way of Commonfence neck.

Three of the New Redoubts are now nearly finished, and the troops are employed in constructing a Redoubt on Tomini hill, which, from the nature of the situation, is capable of being made a place of great strength, and will cover the left of our position.

3ʳᵈ May.   Fine soft day. Wind N. W. early in the morning. After 10 o'Clock it came in from the S. W, so that the Orpheus and the ships with the Flank Companies and the Chasseurs lost the opportunity of going out.

Came in a Schooner laden with Sugar & Coffee, taken by The Maidstone.

We are in daily expectation of the arrival of a fleet of Victuallers from New York, with provisions for the Army, of which we have for some time been in want, and have been obliged to get a supply from the Navy on this Station.

By intelligence which the General has received from different quarters, the Rebels certainly intend, and are making preparations for an attack on this Island.

I think we should pay more attention to what they are doing on the Narraganset side, than we appear to do, lest they should make a descent on Connonicut and establish themselves there, previous to their attempt on this Island. The pofsesfion of Connonicut, would give them many advantages, and should they establish a Battery on the Dumplins, they would thereby command one side of the entrance to the harbour, and render a great part of the harbour itself very insecure. If the Rebels last October, had landed 2000 men on Connonicut, their grand Expedition would probably have ended more to their credit.

4th May. Fine weather. Wind S. S. W. Some rain in the afternoon.

The wood fleet came in this morning from Shelter Island, under convoy of The Sphynx, and Mermaid. They have brought about 300 Cords of wood for the use of the Army. About the same quantity has been brought by the vefsels belonging to the Inhabitants.

Seven men came in last night from the Narraganset side. Two of them are Soldiers of the Royal Artillery belonging to General Burgoyne's Army. They say the Rebels are collecting boats at Providence, Greenwich, and Warren, and that every movement in the adjacent Country indicates an attempt on this Island. Provisions, horses, Carriages, Ammunition, &c., are collecting in different places. They have for some time past been very cautious to prevent strangers from going into the town of Providence, where, 'tis said, they are building a number of boats and constructing floating batteries. An Expedition against this Island is the general talk of the Country, and they exprefs their hopes of being in pofsefsion of it before the middle of June.

They are raising a Regiment of Negroes in this Province to send to Washington's Army.

Great rejoicings have been made of late all over the Country, on account of their Alliance with France, which they say is now certain.

I am of opinion they really will attempt something soon, for as the spirits of the people are now high, on the supposition of an Alliance with France, numbers of them will be found willing to engage for a short time in an enterprize of that nature. It is certainly their interest to attempt it, and before we receive any reinforcements from Europe.

5th May.   Good weather. Wind N. in the morning, and about 6 o'Clock the Orpheus, and The Haerlem Sloop, with the two transports which have the Flank Companies and the Chasseurs on board; sailed for the Elisabeth Islands.

The wind changed to the Southward at about 9 o'Clock and brought in Six sail of Victuallers from New York, under Convoy of The Faulcon.

The 54th Regiment is employed at Windmill hill in throwing up a work round the large Barrack there.

Three of the Redoubts near the town are finished, and that on Tomini hill nearly so. When the works intended to be made from Green-end to the shore on the left of Tomini hill are finished, the town will be rendered very secure, as it is by much the best position for the purpose.

6th May.   Fine weather. Wind N.

The Rebels fired Six Shot this morning from their Battery at Bristol ferry at the boats of the Flora, which were fishing near Hog-Island; but without effect.

It appears by letters which were received yesterday from Philadelphia; that Sir William Howe has resigned the Command of The Army in America, and that Sir Henry Clinton is appointed General and Commander in Chief in his room. General Clinton is going from New York to Philadelphia; General Daniel Jones is to Command at New York, and General Robertson on this Island. Tis said that Genl Pigot is to go from hence on the arrival of Genl Robertson, but where, is not certain.

7th May.   Good weather. Wind N.

A Soldier of the 54th Regiment deserted from his post last night. As soon as he was missed he was pursued by a Serjeant's party, and at day break he was discovered at the extremity of Commonfence neck. He had just before fired his piece as a signal for a boat from the Rebels to take him off. The Serjeant, who discovered him first, endeavored to seize him, but when he got within Six yards of him, he fired and killed the Serjeant on the spot; then seeing the rest of the party coming up, he threw himself into the water intending to swim across, but several shot being fired at him, he sunk and was drowned. A boat was at this time coming over from the Rebel shore, but as soon as they heard the firing it returned. Col° Bruce having given orders that every deserter shall be immediately pursued, and if pofsible killed, it is probable no more of that Regiment will desert during the present month.

8th May.   Heavy rain from 5 this morning 'till 3 in the Afternoon.   Wind E.

In the disposition of the troops for the defence of this Island during the ensuing Summer, I think the placing of them in several small encampments at such places as appear moſt likely for the Enemy to land at, should be avoided as much as pofsible, leſt we expose them to be cut off, or insulted. The troops, in my opinion should be poſted in two separate encampments: one, on Windmill-hill for the defence of the North end of the Island; the other within the new Redoubts, for the defence of that position and the town, in which all our Stores are deposited. The Flank Companies and the Chaſseurs might be poſted at Fogland ferry, for the defence of the Battery there, and to furnish patroles & poſts of intelligence along the Eaſt Coaſt.

The Regiments of Landgrave and Ditfourth to be poſted at Windmill-hill; under the Command of Major General Losberg. They consiſt of near 1,000 men, their field pieces would be of great service there, they may be depended upon for the defence of the works, and Major General Losberg is the Second in Command on the Island.

The three British Battalions to be encamped as follows; 22d behind Green-end Redoubt; 54th behind Banniſter's; and 43rd behind Irishes; under the Command of Brigadier General Smith. These Battalions to furnish all the poſts along that front; and occasional patroles, to the Eaſtward towards Sacha-weſt beach and Taggart's, and Weſtward as far as Stoddard's.

The Regiment of Huyne to encamp near the Windmill, S. of the town, fronting Southward's; their field pieces commanding the roads to Brenton's neck and Churche's Cove. This Regiment to furnish poſts at the narroweſt part of Brenton's neck, and on the road to Churches Cove.

The Regiment of Bunau to encamp behind Eaſton's Redoubt, furnishing a Guard in it, and making patroles over Eaſton's beach, and round Eaſton's point. These two Regiments to furnish the town Guards, and to be under the Command of Major Gen[l] Huyne.

The three British and two Hefsian Regiments might alternately furnish 50 men, weekly, to Connonicut; or, if more adviseable, Wightman's Provincials might be posted there.

In the positions abovementioned, the Enemy would hardly attempt to make an attack of any consequence. A dispersed disposition would invite it. If they mean to attack us with a view to conquering the Island, they must either force our advanced posts, and the Redoubt at Windmill hill; or make a landing on one side, (probably the Eastern) of the Island; the former is extremely difficult, as they must carry the works at Windmill hill before they can advance forward, and secure the landing of their Artillery, Stores, and provisions. The latter is still more so, as immediately upon landing they would be liable to be attacked on both flanks, and to have their communication cut off by our Ships and Gallies. It is therefore to be supposed that if they are determined upon making an attack, they will endeavor to force our advanced posts, as by that means they would cover the landing of every necefsary article, place us in their front, and have both their flanks secure. Our attention therefore should be employed in strengthening the N. End of the Island. The Redoubt at Bristol ferry should be made more defensible; in its present state it might be taken by afsault with little lofs, and might be effectually defended against us. The pofsefsion of Bristol ferry would give them that of Commonfence, which is Commanded by it; and thus they would Command the pafsages from Bristol and Howland's ferries. The Security of Bristol Redoubt is therefore of the utmost consequence, and with a Redoubt which the General intends to have erected between Windmill hill, and Commonfence Redoubt, would effectually command the two Necks.

A Small Redoubt at Arnold's point would be of service in commanding the beach opposite Hog Island, which is a good landing place, and unseen from any of our works. It would also give that additional strength to the left of the position which is now wanting, the Artillery Redoubt being rather too distant for that purpose.

As it is difficult for the Enemy to collect any considerable number of boats in our Neighbourhood for the purpose of making a descent, without the General's having notice of it, (and he has at present very good intelligence) such a change in our disposition might, and should, be made, as the number and situation of the Enemy's boats, and their movements might point out as necefsary.

9th May.   Fine weather.   Wind N. W.

The transports from the Elisabeth Islands arrived laft night in the Seconnet pafsage. The troops have been very succefsful, and met with no opposition. The two transports have brought 884 Sheep and Lambs. — 150 of them were bought from such of the Inhabitants as were well affected, and willing to sell them. The reft, being the property of noted Rebels, were taken without payment. The party has also secured about 1,000 more sheep and lambs on a small Island under protection of the Unicorn, until the transports can return for them. The whole were taken from Nashawn Island, which is the largeft of the Elisabeth Islands; about 10 Miles long and 4 broad, and lies neareft to the Main. A Company of Rebels were pofted upon it, but they retired upon the appearance of our fleet. Our people burnt the Barracks they had occupied, and deftroyed two pieces of Cannon. Captain Coore of the 54th Grenadiers Commanded the party. The Sheep were landed this day at Sachaweft point, and the troops returned to town.

A party of an officer and 40 men embarked on board the Transports this day, and they are to return immediately for the remainder of the Sheep.

A Privateer sloop of 12 Guns lately taken by the Maidftone, arrived this Evening from New York, which place she left on the 7th.

The following is a lift of the Generals serving in the Rebel Army, with their Rank, and the Province, or Country they are Natives of. 9th May 1778.

Commander in Chief

George Washington .... Virginia

Major Generals

Charles Lee .... England
Philip Schuyler .... New York
Israel Putnam .... Connecticut
Horatio Gates .... Virginia
William Heath....................... Mafsachusetts
Joseph Spencer .... Connecticut

[*Major Generals* — continued]

John Sullivan	New Hampshire
Nathaniel Green	Rhode Island
William, Lord Stirling	New Jersey
Thomas Mifflin	Pensylvania
Arthur Sinclair	Pensylvania
Adam Stevens	Virginia
Benjamin Lincoln	Maſsachusetts
Benedict Arnold	Connecticut
Marquis de la Fayette	France
Robert Howe	North Carolina
Alexander McDougal	New York
Baron de Call	Germany
Thomas Conway	France

Brigadiers

William Thompson	Pensylvania
John Nixon	Maſsachusetts
Samuel Parsons	Connecticut
James Clinton	New York
Chriſtopher Gadsden	South Carolina
William Manyshell	South Carolina
Laughlin McIntosh	Georgia
William Maxwell	New Jersey
Mathew Alexis	France
De Roche Fermoy	France
P. Horne de Bou	France
Henry Knox	Maſsachusetts
Francis McNash	Maſsachusetts
Enoch Poor	New Hampshire
John Glover	Maſsachusetts
John Patterson	Maſsachusetts
Anthony Wayne	Pensylvania
James Vernon	Rhode Island
Peter Muhlenberg	Virginia
George Weedon	Virginia
William Woodford	Virginia
George Clinton	(Governor of New York)
Edward Hand	Pensylvania
Ebenezer Learned	Maſsachusetts
Jedidiah Huntington	Connecticut
Count Polaski	Poland
J. Stark	New Hampshire

Total	1 Commander in Chief
	19 Major General
	27 Brigadiers
	——
	47

10th May.   Good weather. Wind S. Some rain in the afternoon.

It appears by some of the letters received yesterday from New York, that Sir Henry Clinton is gone from thence to Philadelphia to take the Command of the Army, in the room of Sir William Howe who is going home. General Robertson it is said is coming to take the Command on this Island.

11th May.   Fine weather. Wind S. W.

It is still unknown here what became of the Providence, Rebel Frigate which escaped out of this port by the Narraganset passage the night of the 30th April. There was no account of her at New London the 8th nor at Boston the 6th Instant. The Officers of The Lark are of opinion she suffered a good deal from their fire.

12th May.   Very fine day. Wind N. in the Morning, and S. after 1 o'Clock.

Came into the Seconnet passage, the Sphynx, with the Transports and other vessels from the Elisabeth Islands, having about 900 Sheep and lambs on board, which were immediately landed at Sachawest point.

The Sheep and Lambs which were brought in on the 9th Instant were divided this day, and half of them were given to the Navy. The other half were reserved for the troops and the Military hospitals.

Three men came in last night by way of Bristol ferry. They say the Rebels find great difficulty in raising men in New England for Washington's Army; and that the men have a particular aversion to go to the Southward.

I shot a bird here this day, which is called here, The Quamquidle, or Bob-o'-Lincoln; but properly the Rice bird. The Inhabitants say it is never seen on the Island before this day of the Month, and never fails making its appearance on this day. As it is a bird of passage and comes from the Southward, it is probable *the Old May day*, is that on which they are usually first observed.

13th May.   Fine weather. Wind S.

The Haerlem tender came into the Seconnet passage to day from the Elisabeth Islands, having two sloops under her Convoy, with about 80 head of Cattle on board.

Sailed a flag of truce Vefsel for Boston, with provisions for the Convention troops, and a quantity of necefsary supplies and articles for the Officers at Cambridge.

14th   Heavy rain for about two hours this morning. The rest of the day fine. Wind N. E.

15th May.   Fine weather, and warm. Wind S. S.W.

16th — Fine day. Wind S. W.

The Sphynx went out of the Seconnet this morning, with several vefsels under Convoy for the Elisabeth Islands, to bring off Stock.

Came in a Sloop from Bermuda, lately taken by a Rebel Privateer, but retaken by the Maidstone Frigate.

A flag of truce vefsel came down from Providence, and brought several Officers of the Convention Army, who have made interest to get exchanged, or leave to go home on parole, vizt Major Agnew, 24th Regt; Maj^r Forbes, 9th; Captain Vigors, 29th; Lt Poe, Ensign Rotton, 47th; Lieu^t Waite, 20th, Lt Lord Napier, 31st; Ensign   , 53rd; Chaplain Mongan, 62^d; En^s Colquhoun, 71st; Volunteer McDougal 71st, & Commifsary Higgins.

17th May.   Very fine weather. Wind E.

The officers who came from Cambridge say there is great desertion from the British troops there; but as many of them are the best Soldiers, it is generally supposed they go off with a view of getting into some of the posts occupied by the King's Army.

18th   Fine day. Wind S. W.

A Schooner, late the Lady Parker tender, having been fitted out as a Galley, and named The Pigot, under the Command of Lieu^t Stanhope of The Navy, went out of the harbour this day for her Station in the Seconnet; where there are now Three Gallies; vizt The Alarm, L^t D'Auvergne; The Spitfire, Lieu^t Sauma, and The Pigot, Lt Stanhope.

When Lord Howe was here he saw how useful such vefsels would be for the defence of the Island, and ordered several of them to be fitted out. Another is now equipping at Goat Island.

19th May.   Good weather. Wind E.

Sailed The Mermaid and Lark on a Cruize.

Came in a prize vefsel taken by the Maidstone. She spoke

with a fleet of 27 sail from England bound to New York, a few days ago.

Accounts are received of the arrival of the Providence Rebel Frigate at Boston, with two prizes which she took on her passage, after her escape from this harbour. Her lofs in going out is not mentioned.

There is a large fleet of Privateers at Boston; many of them of force, and few lefs than 10 Guns. They have been very succefsful of late in bringing in prizes, some of which have been very valuable.

Five large French ships, armed, and which are called King's Frigates, are also at Boston. They muft have been very fortunate in escaping our Cruizers, or our Cruizers very remifs in observing Boston Bay.

The intelligence received from all quarters agree in ftating that an attack on this Island is intended, and will probably be soon attempted. It is not improbable that in case of an attack, the Rebel Fleet at Boston will make its appearance in the Seconnet, in order to cover a descent on that side.

Our new Redoubts are nearly completed, and everything else is in such readinefs as to put us in a respectable situation for the reception of the Enemy.

As there appears a great probability of the Rebels receiving afsiftance from the French, and affairs may have undergone a great change since the date of our laft accounts from England, I think it would be prudent to mount some heavy Cannon in the Battery at Brenton's point, and on Goat Island. The entrance of the harbour is at present totally undefended, and a few guns at those places may be of great service.

20th May. — Fine weather. Wind E. Fog at Sea moft of the day.

The Kingsfisher came round this day from the Seconnet, and brought with her the two transports and four Sloops which have been to the Elisabeth Islands for Stock. The Kingsfisher is come round to repair her Foremaft, and is replaced in that ftation by the Sphynx.

Many Cannon heard to the Eaftward between 10 this morning, and 6 in the Evening.

21st Fine weather. Wind S. Foggy at Sea.
The Pigot Galley came round from the Seconnet.

22^d May.   Fine weather.   Wind S. W.

The Rebels are certainly preparing for an attack on this Island; and the General having intelligence of the situation of their boats, is making arrangements for the destruction of them. An expedition against their principal collection of boats near Warren, will shortly be undertaken.

23rd   Good weather.   Wind S. W.

A Block Island fishing boat came in this day. The men say they were yesterday on board Admiral Gambier's Ship off Block Island, who had 24 Sail under Convoy bound to New York: 9 weeks out from England. But few troops on board the fleet.

24th May. — Good weather, but appearance of rain. Wind S. W.

The Spitfire Galley came out of the Seconnet this morning with an intent to come into the harbour, but the wind prevented her. She is intended to afsist in the Expedition against the Rebels boats, which is to take place this night.

25th May.   Fine weather clear.   Wind N. E.

The Spitfire Galley did not get into the harbour this day 'till one oClock, notwithstanding every effort. Some whaleboats from Point Judith, taking her for an unarmed vefsel, came off to attack her, but when within Gunshot they met with such an unexpected reception, that they with difficulty got off; and it was supposed with some lofs.

The 22^d Regiment, the flank Companies of the 54th, Captain Noltenius's Company of Hefsian Chafseurs, Some Artillery men and Guides, amounting in the whole to about 500 men, and under the Command of Lieu^t Colonel Campbell of the 22^d Regiment, marched from Newport at 8 o'Clock last night to Arnold's point, on the West side of the Island near Windmill hill, where they arrived at 11 o'Clock. It began to rain at the time the troops marched from town, and continued, with some intermissions till near 12. As the troops had no blankets, and waited near an hour on the beach for the boats, they were all thoroughly wetted. The boats arrived at the place of embarkation about 12 o'Clock, and consisted of 13 flat boats, and four or 5 barges and Whaleboats, under the direction of Captain Clayton of The Strombolo, afsisted by Lieu^t Knowles, Agent of Transports, and some other officers of the Navy. The whole of the troops were embarked and put off from the shore about ½ past 12. They immediately proceeded to The Flora, which lay opposite, and from thence up the Bay, and round Papasquash point to the mouth of Warren River, where they landed, undiscovered about half past 3 this Morning; one mile from Bristol and 3 miles from Warren. As soon as formed they proceeded to Warren (where the Company of Chasseurs were posted to observe The Neck, the road leading to Providence, and the Ferries over Warren River) and from thence to Kickemuit bridge, on the other side of which the Light Infantry of the 54th was posted to observe the roads that way. Here they found 125 boats, most of them large flat batteaux, capable of carrying 40 men each; a Galley mounting 2. 18; 4. 12; and 6. 4 pounders, besides Swivels; a Sloop loaded with Military Stores; a quantity of materials for building and repairing boats, a Store house, and a Corn mill; all of which, together with some houses, the Bridge, and some Gun Carriages, were burnt and totally destroyed. Many Cannon were found here, which were spiked, the trunnions knocked off, and otherwise destroyed. The troops then returned to Warren, where they set fire to a new Privateer Sloop of 16. 4 pounders complete: — A considerable Magazine of Powder and other Military Stores, was discovered in a house at Warren, which was set fire to; by which means the Church and many houses were burnt. A Park of Artillery, consisting of 2. 18; 2. 12; & 1. 9 pounder, on travelling Carriages, with side boxes for ammunition, Complete, was found at the entrance of Warren. The Guns were Spiked, the Trunnions knocked off, and the Carriages burnt.

After this service was completed, the troops returned by the way of Bristol, and, as the alarm had by this time become general and many of the Rebels had assembled, they were continually fired upon during their march, from behind Walls, trees, and houses by about 300 Rebels, with 2, 3 pounders; notwithstanding which they entered Bristol, where a small Magazine of Stores, the Church, and about 20 of the principal houses were burnt, and several Guns destroyed; after which the Detachment proceeded to the height above Bristol ferry, where they took post 'till the boats came round from Papasquash point.

On the landing of the troops in the morning above Bristol, Captain Seix with 30 of the 22d Regt was sent in a flat boat to take poſseſsion of the Enemy's Battery of 1. 18 pounder on that point, and which had fired on the Flora when she went round it to cover the Boats. This service they effected without any loſs, made a Captain and 9 men prisoners, and deſtroyed the Gun, Platform, Carriage, &c. &c. The flat boats, after the deſtruction of this gun, aſsembled at the point, and waited for a Signal from Briſtol ferry for their removal there to re-embark the Troops. The Signal being made about half after 10 o'Clock, they proceeded thence, with the Flora, up the Channel between Hog Island and Rhode-Island. The Flora anchored between the Islands, and the Boats proceeded to the Ferry, at which place the troops began to embark about ½ past 11. The Embarkation was completed about 12, under cover of The Flora, and the Pigot Galley. The Rebels continued an irregular fire upon the advanced parties of the Troops until they began to embark, but did not attempt making any attack during that time or when the laſt were embarking. When the laſt boats were putting off from the ferry, a few ſtraggling fellows fired from behind some Rocks, and soon after they brought forward one of their Field pieces and fired a few shots from it, but without any effect. From the time our troops quitted the hill above the Ferry until they were out of reach of Cannon shot, Our battery at Briſtol ferry Redoubt, and the Pigot Galley, kept a smart fire on the Rebels, which deterred them from appearing in numbers. The Flora also fired a few shot at them. 69 Prisoners were brought over from Briſtol point to Windmill hill, and were marched from thence to Newport. The troops returned in the boats to Newport, where they landed about 4 in the afternoon.

The whole of our loſs on this occasion was Lieut Hamilton and 4 privates of the 22d 1 Grenadier, & one Light Infantry of the 54th, and 4 Heſsian Chaſseurs, Wounded. Two Drummers of the 22d who after landing were sent back to the boats for some combuſtibles, were taken prisoners by the Inhabitants. The loſs of the Rebels could not be ascertained, nor could it have been considerable, as they never shewed themselves openly, or came very near.

During the Expedition about 40 pieces of Cannon, including those belonging to The Galley and the Privateer, were spiked or otherwise deſtroyed.

At the time The Flora and the boats were proceeding up the bay, the Pigot Galley and 6 armed boats, under the Command of Captain Reeves of the Nonsuch, paſsed undiscovered through Briſtol ferry into Mount Hope Bay; — The Pigot came to an anchor at the mouth of Taunton River, while the boats proceeded to Fall River, where a Rebel Galley called the Spitfire, lay at anchor. They surprized, boarded, & took her without the smalleſt opposition, and immediately towed her down to The Pigot. She mounted 2. 24 pounders in her bow, 2. 12 pounders in her Stern, and 6. 4 pounders in her waiſt, with 8 Swivels, and had when taken, the Captain and 15 men on board. Having secured the prisoners and got everything in order, and the wind about 9 oClock having sprung up from the N. E., the two Gallies and the 6 boats got under way to repaſs through the ferry. The Rebels had at that time 2. 18 pounders in their lower Battery, and as soon as they came within reach began to fire on them with both round and grape shot; but they paſsed without any other damage than one Seaman slightly wounded by a Grape shot. Captain Brady of The Royal artillery, who was in our Redoubt at Briſtol ferry, kept so brisk a fire on the Rebel Battery that they had not time to fire many shot. The Gallies anchored ahead of the Venus, off Arnold's point, (The Venus having replaced the Flora when she went above Papasquash point with the boats) where they remained till they were ordered up to cover the embarkation of the Troops. The Prize Galley however could not work up in time.

About 2 o'Clock this Morning the Guard house which the Rebels had on the N. point of Fogland, was burnt by some boats from the Armed veſsels in the Seconnet paſsage, without any loſs, although the Enemy had a Guard in it, and fired some Cannon shot from their Battery on the S. point.

These different attacks caused a general alarm throughout the Country: Signal guns were fired at Warwick point, at Providence, and other places; but it did not appear that the Rebels turned out or aſsembled with much alacrity, as the numbers opposed to our Detachment did not increase much towards the close of the Expedition, altho they were near Eight hours on shore, and the burning the boats at Kickemuit River, and the explosition of the Magazine at Warren sufficiently pointed out where our people were. The General knew, before the Expedition was undertaken, that Colonel Crary's Regiment, consiſting of about 250 men, was quartered at Briſtol.

The deſtruction of the Armed veſsels and so many boats, muſt undoubtedly prevent the Rebels from making any attempt on this Island for a considerable time.

Unfortunately for the Rebels, almoſt all the boats which they had at Howland's ferry, were sent over to Kickemuit the Morning of the 24th, to be repaired, and consequently were deſtroyed with the others.

The Expedition was well planned, and executed. The troops underwent much fatigue during the continuanace of it, but they supported it, and behaved with their usual spirit. The Flank Companies of the 54th acquired great credit for their addreſs and conduct in flanking, and covering the march of the Main body.

26th May.   Fine weather.   Wind S.

The Haerlem Sloop, coming into the harbour this morning from the Seconnet, was taken for an unarmed veſsel by some Rebel boats from point Judith, who put off to attack her; but a Signal being made by the Commodore for the Pigot and Spitfire Gallies to go out, and they being followed by some armed boats, the Rebels were afraid of being intercepted, and retreated precipitately.

27th   Fine weather.   Wind S. W.

The house of one Peleg Anthony, at the entrance of Brenton's neck, was burnt about 9 o'Clock laſt night, by accident.

28th May — Very fine weather.   Wind S. W.

The Sphynx came into the harbour from the Seconet paſsage.

The Ships of War in this Bay and harbour, are now ſtationed as follows, —

The Orpheus .... Off Warwick point.
The Juno .... In the Narraganset paſsage.
The Flora .... Off Papasquash point.
The Venus......................... Above Dyer's Island.
The Unicorn ⎫
The Alarm & ⎬ Gallies .... In the Seconnet paſsage.
The Spitfire ⎭
The Nonsuch
The Sphynx
The Kingsfisher
The Pigot, & ⎫ Gallies .... In the harbour.
The Prize ⎭

29th May.　　Good weather.　Wind S. W.

The four Hefsian Battalions in this Garrison, with their Eight Field pieces, were out this day together, and went through several Manoeuvres. They made a fine appearance.

30th May.　　Fine weather.　Wind S.

Captain Ford of The Unicorn having been up as far as Gold Island near Howland's ferry this Morning at day break, to reconnoitre; on his return fell in with a Rebel boat with five Soldiers in her, which he took without opposition. They belong to a Col° Topham's Regiment ſtationed at Howland's ferry; and say, that the Rebels had several men killed and wounded on the 25th Inſtant, and among the latter Colonel Barton (who took General Prescott) mortally. They also say the people of the Country are much alarmed and discontented; and that great blame is thrown on Genl Sullivan for neglecting to place proper Guards on their boats, &c.

The 22^d and 43rd Regiments have received orders to hold themselves in readiness to encamp.

The General's reason for encamping these Regiments, although they have only some old Camp Equipage, is to have some troops out upon the Island, in readineſs to repel any attempts of the Enemy to retaliate for their loſses in the late Expedition.

31st May.　　Cloudy day.　Cold wind at S. S. E.　Some rain in the Evening.

The General and the Commodore having determined to attempt deſtroying some Saw Mills, and a quantity of Plank for building boats, which they had upon Fall River; the Pigot Galley, A Gunboat, some Flat boats, and the boats of the Flora, Juno, Venus, Orpheus, & Kingsfisher, under the direction of Captain Christian of The Kingsfisher; with 100 men of the 54th Regiment under the Command of Major Eyre of that Regiment; were ordered for this service. At 12 oClock laſt night they paſsed through Briſtol ferry, unperceived by the Rebels, and proceeded up Mount Hope Bay, except the Pigot, which unfortunately run aground in the upper part of the Paſsage, which gave an alarm to The Rebels, who immediately communicated it by firing Signal Guns which were repeated on both sides of the Bay. The boats waited some time in hopes of being joined by The Pigot, but finding the Alarm was given, they moved on to their deſtination without her, and on approaching the shore near Fall River, they were fired on by a Guard of about 40 men; but pushing directly in, the Troops landed and dispersed the Enemy. They then proceeded to the Firſt Mills, where one Saw-Mill, a Corn Mill, 9 large boats, and about 15,000 feet of Plank was burnt. On advancing a small diſtance towards the other Mills, they found a considerable Number of the Enemy poſted at, and above them, from whom they received a heavy fire by which 2 men were killed, and an Officer & 4 men wounded. It being then judged imprudent to attempt forcing the poſt, or to continue longer on shore, the troops returned to the boats, and re-embarked without moleſtation. No other loſs than that abovementioned was suſtained. The boats then returned down the bay, and landed the troops on the North point of Commonfence Neck, and went to the afsiſtance of The Pigot, which had continued all the time aground, and under the fire of the Rebel Battery at Briſtol-ferry, by which she had suffered considerably; but by the afsiſtance of the Boats, and more particularly the well directed fire of our two Guns in Briſtol ferry Redoubt under the Command of Capᵗ Brady of the Royal Artillery, who twice dismounted one of the Enemy's Guns, and by a continual fire almoſt deſtroyed their work and prevented them from firing so quick and so well as they would otherwise have done, she was at laſt got off. Lieuᵗ Congleton of The Flora loſt an arm, and 3 Seamen were killed by this unfortunate accident. The Galley received several shot in her hull; and had her boom cut in two and some of her Rigging much damaged by the Enemy's shot. 160 Shot were fired from the two guns in our Redoubt.

Came in one of the ships which had been sent to Boſton with provisions for the troops of the Convention Army.

1ˢᵗ June.   Thick weather.   Wind S. E.

The Regiment of Bunau marched at 6 o'Clock this morning to Windmill hill, to relieve the 54ᵗʰ Regiment, which came into town about 1 o'Clock.

A Detachment of a Captain & 80 men from the three Heſsian Regiments in Newport, marched at the same hour, and Relieved the firſt Company of Chaſseurs at Fogland-ferry.

The Lark and Mermaid came in this Morning from a Cruize, and brought with them two small prizes. Came in also The Ship Fanny, a letter of Marque in 53 days from Liverpoole, with a Cargo of Beef, Flour, Wines, beer, Groceries, &c. This is the first veſsel which has come directly from Europe to this port, since we have been in poſseſsion of the Island; except the Ariel, and she was bound for New York, but on being informed at Sea that Lord Howe was in this port, she altered her deſtination and came in here.

It appears by some Papers brought by The Fanny, that a War with France is inevitable, The French having declared the Independance of America, and concluded a Treaty of Amity and Commerce with the Rebels. The reſpective Ambaſsadors had returned home; but war was not declared the 8th of April.

Orders were given this day for the 22d and 43rd Regiments to encamp toMorrow, the former on Quaker-hill, and the latter on Turkey hill.

2d June — Heavy rain all laſt night and all this day. Wind S. E.

The General laſt night countermanded the march of the 22d, and 43rd Regiments, on account of the heavy rain; the neceſsity for encamping not being so great as to endanger the health of many men. The encamping for the firſt time in bad weather, or on wet ground, should always be avoided as much as the nature of the Service will admit. If the firſt two or three days of the Campaign are wet, the Soldiers generally contract disorders which deſtroy many and render them unfit for Service during the remainder of the Campaign. Too much attention cannot be given at all times to preserve the health of the Soldiers.

3rd June — Rain and thick weather moſt part of the day. Wind N. E.

The fleet deſtined for New York, got under way this Morning at 8 o'Clock, under Convoy of The Sphynx, Strombolo Fire ship, and Haerlem Sloop. The laſt is to proceed to The Delaware with the General's dispatches.

Captain Welsh, aide-de Camp to Genl Prescott, who has remained with Genl Pigot, since Genl Prescott was taken, went in The Strombolo. Several officers of the Convention Army, and some Heſsian Officers, went in different veſsels.

The new Chain of Redoubts lately conſtructed for the defence of Newport, are now completed. The ground is in all parts extremely advantageous; but I think some of the Redoubts are not well placed, and that in general they are too confined. They are called, Green-end, Dudley's, Banniſter's, Irishes, and Tomini;

and on the left of Tomini, in the bottom, is a small open work, intended to ſtrengthen the line to the left, and defend the passage round the head of a small Creek. The Redoubt at Green-end is very small, tho intended for three large Guns. The Parapet is formed En Crainioulle. The reason given for this is, that the Enemy by erecting Batteries at 600 yards diſtance, might plunge into the work. But as this kind of Parapet is only intended to preserve the defendants from a plunging fire of Small arms, and as the front and flanks of this Redoubt cannot be exposed to such a fire, it confines the defence so much, as to render it almost useleſs. The top of the Parapet is at leaſt 9 feet above the upper Banquet. The man poſted at each of these diminutive Embrazures, can only fire directly forward; and should a Cannon shot ſtrike one of these little Merlons, it would immediately fill up two of them. In short it appears as if The Engineer wanted to exhibit unusual kinds of Parapets, to shew his fancy.

Dudley's Redoubt is certainly placed too far back. If it had been about 60 yards forwarder, it would have answered every purpose much better.

Banniſter's and Irishes have a very good command of the adjacent ground. The right flank of Irishes might have been conſtructed so as to have defended Banniſter's better.

Little Tomini should certainly have been formed as an outwork to the great hill. A Single gun, En Barbette, in a small work, open behind, would have been of service, as it would command a good deal of ground unseen from Great Tomini. Little Tomini is now a cover for the Enemy, within 150 yards of the principal work; and as the surface of the ground within Great Tomini Redoubt, is a Rock, and there is not a Traverse in the Redoubt, should the Enemy during a Siege lodge themselves in front of Little Tomini, and place one or two small Mortars there, the Redoubt could not long be defended.

I am of opinion it will be found necesſary to conſtruct another Redoubt to the right of that at Green-end, in order the better to command the head of Eaſton's pond. The Dams which have been made to ſtop the little Rivulet, & thereby overflow the ground above Eaſton's-pond, I am certain will not answer the General's expectation of rendering that ground impaſsable to an Enemy. They were improperly made at firſt; and when the hot weather comes on, there will be little or no water remaining there.

4th June 1778 — Rain and thick weather moſt part of the day. Wind N. E. Cold and disagreeable.

This being the King's Birthday, The Ships of War in the harbour, and the different parts of the Bay, fired 21 Guns each, at 1 o'Clock. 21 Guns were fired by our Artillery at Windmill-hill; and the Reg[t] of Bunau fired three Vollies, at 12 oClock.

5th Thick weather 'till 3 o'Clock, when it cleared up, and proved a fine afternoon. Wind N. W.

The Kingsfisher went round into The Seconnet. The 54th Reg[t] received orders to hold itself in readineſs to encamp.

6th June. Very hazy at Sea. Wind S.

Came in The Maidſtone with a Brig, one of Admiral Gambier's Convoy, laden with 200 Ton of provisions, which she retook yeſterday off Block-Island. She was taken a few days before by a Rebel Privateer out of Bedford. The Rebels on board took to their boat when chaced, and got on shore at Block-Island.

7th June. Rain greateſt part of the day. Thick weather. Wind S. E.

Came in a Schooner, prize to the Maidſtone.

The Unicorn sailed for Halifax, to repair some part of the Iron work about her Rudder.

There was a great alarm among the Rebels at Howland's ferry laſt night, without any cause that we know of. About half paſt 11 they fired two Cannon shot from their upper work, and soon after some Small arms, and some more Cannon. The firing continued about 20 Minutes.

The late expeditions have made them extremely alert, and apprehensive of an attack on that poſt, which is their principal one in our Neighbourhood.

8th. Heavy rain some part of laſt night, and until 10 this day. Wind S. Hazy during the day, and a thick fog in the Evening.

9th June. Fine clear weather. Wind W.

A Flag of truce came down the Bay this Morning from Providence. She has brought a long letter from M[r] Sullivan to Gen[l] Pigot, complaining of the exceſses and inhumanity of the troops on the late Expedition, the cruelty of carrying off inoffensive Inhabitants, and the burning of houses. He threatens

retaliation, and says the patience of the Americans is nearly ex-
hausted. It is the usual ſtile of all their public correspondence,
calculated to inflame the minds of the people, and to impose on
those unacquainted with the real ſtate of the case. In one part
of his letter he desired to know upon what terms the prisoners
will be released.

A person who knew nothing of the late Expedition but from
the abovementioned letter, would conclude that every poſsible
exceſs and inhumanity had been wantonly committed. The
fact is, Mr Sullivan is extremely mortified that we should have
so completely deſtroyed the preparations he had been making
at a great expence for the invasion of this Island.

Some persons who came down in the veſsel, say, that The
Royal Army was preparing to embark from Philadelphia, and
they are expected to visit Connecticut, or The Maſsachusetts'
Bay.

(24th June, 1778)   (From the Providence Gazette)

Letter from Genl Sullivan, to Genl Pigot

Providence, 4th June 1778

Sir —

The repeated applications of the diſtreſsed families of those
persons who were captured by your troops, on the 25th Ultº induce me to write you upon the subject. As those men were not
in actual service, or found in arms, I cannot conceive what were
the motives for taking them, or gueſs the terms upon which
their release may be obtained. Had the war on the part of Britain, been founded in Juſtice: and had your troops in their
Excursion, compleated the deſtruction of the boats, and our
Military preparations in that quarter, without wantonly deſtroying defenceleſs towns, burning houses consecrated to the
deity, plundering and abusing innocent Inhabitants, and drag-
ging from their peaceful habitations unarmed and inoffending
Men; such an Expedition might have shone with Splendour.
It is now darkned with savage cruelty, and ſtained with in-
delible disgrace.

In your laſt letter to me, you gave it as your opinion, that the
Inhabitants of America at large, would entertain more favour-
able Sentiments of the views and intentions of Great Britain,
than I seemed inclined to have. If, Sir, the unprecedented

cruelty of your troops, displayed upon every petty advantage, since the commencement of this contest; the inhuman and un-exampled treatment of Prisoners, who, by the fortune of War, have fallen into your power, had not sufficiently convinced the Inhabitants of the united States, that they had nothing to expect from that Nation, but a continuance of those tyrannical and cruel measures which drove them to a seperation; the conduct of your party, in their Excursion, must have stamped it with infallible certainty.

The law of Retaliation has not as yet been exercised by the Americans. Humanity has marked the line of their conduct thus far, even tho' they knew that their tenderness was attrib-uted to base timidity: but if a departure from the laws of hu-manity, can in any instance be justified, it must be, when such relentlefs destroyers are entrapped by the vigilance of the party invaded. Perhaps at some such period, the Americans, fired with resentment of accumulated Injuries: wearied with the long exercise of a humane conduct, which has only been rewarded with barbarity and insult: and despairing to mitigate the hor-rors of war, by persisting in the practice of a virtue, which their Enemies seem to have banished from their minds; may, by sud-denly executing the law of Retaliation, convince Britons, that they have mistaken the motives of American clemency, and trifled too long with undeserved lenity. Should such an event take place, the unhappy sufferers may charge their misfortunes to the Commanding Officers of the British army in this Coun-try, whose mistaken conduct has weaned the affections of Americans from your Nation, driven them to disavow alle-giance to your Sovereign, and at length roused them to acts of Retaliation.

I should not have wrote you so particularly upon this sub-ject, had I not observed in the Newport Gazette, that the Con-duct of your troops, employed on the late expedition, had received your approbation, and warmest thanks.

Your favouring me with a line, informing upon what terms a release of those unfortunate persons may be obtained, will much oblige, Sir —

Y^r Most Obed^t & very humble Servt

M. Genl Pigot   JOHN SULLIVAN

S^r. — Newport 10th June 1778

I received your very Extraordinary letter, and as you request nothing more than the favour of a line, to inform you upon what terms the Prisoners taken the 25th of last Month, can be obtained, it is unnecefsary to trouble you with a reply to any other part of your letter.

You are pleased to say, you cannot conjecture upon what terms their release may be obtained. You certainly must know, that by the laws of this country, every man above 16, and under 60, is obliged to serve as a Soldier under very severe penalties, and have General and Field Officers appointed to lead them, whenever called forth: and I have no doubt but many of those very persons, whom you call peaceable Inhabitants, have been marched, on the late intended Invasion of this Island, by Genl Spencer. This being the case, I do not see there can be any objection made to their being exchanged for Soldiers or Seamen. Any one who does not come under the above description of being between 16 and 60, shall upon your pointing him out, be immediately set at liberty without exchange. Should this proposal be agreeable to you, I am ready to make the exchange as soon as you please: but in case it does not meet with your approbation, I am sorry to acquaint you, that not having it in my power to accomodate the Prisoners so conveniently and well as I could wish to do, must be under the necefsity, when an opportunity offers, of sending them to New York, where they will be better attended to, and more at large, & I wish I could say their Exchange more easily effected.

I am Sir, Y^r Most Obed^t Humble Servt

M. Genl Sullivan ROBERT PIGOT

S_{IR} — Providence, 20th June 1778

As it was not in my power to Comply with the terms proposed by you, in your letter of the 10th Ins^t respecting the exchange of the persons taken by your troops on the 25th of last Month; I could not give you an answer without consulting the Council of war, who request me to send a flag, in which Governor Bradford goes, with some proposals, which he will communicate.

We have some Seamen here taken by our vefsels of War, others we expect will in a few days be brought on from Boston.

The Council wishes to know whether you will exchange the Prisoners whose names are contained in the lift sent by Governor Bradford, for an equal number of the troops of this ftate now in your hands, and send out the residue on parole. Should this proposal be agreed to, the persons mentioned in the lift shall be sent you immediately after the return of the flag, and those sent out on parole, shall be exchanged as foon as prisoners can be collected for the purpose.

You may depend on as speedy a performance as pofsible on the part of the State, and that I shall do every thing in my power to forward to Rhode Island persons in exchange for such as you may send out.

> I have the honour to be Sir
> Y^r Moft Obed^t Humble Servant

Maj^r Genl Pigot   JOHN SULLIVAN

                                        Newport 22^d June 1778
SIR —

I had the favour of your letter laft night by Govr Bradford, but before his arrival every thing relative to the release of the Soldiers and Inhabitants taken the 25th May, was settled with Mr Mercereau, the Commifsary of Prisoners. Finding by Govr Bradford, it would be agreeable to you to give Sailors in Exchange for the Inhabitants, I have given my consent thereto. Mr Mercereau, the Commifsary, will wait upon you with the agreement, which I doubt not will be complied with as soon as pofsible.

> I have the honour to be, &c.

P. S. Some of the Inhabitants   ROBT. PIGOT
being old and infirm, I have discharged
them, without looking for others in
Exchange.

It is reported that an Expedition went up the Delaware about the beginning of May, and that all the Rebel Frigates, Gallies, Boats, & c.; in short the whole of their Water force on that River was deftroyed.

It appears probable that this ftep is preparatory to the Evacuation of Philadelphia, and that the Army will march through Jersey to New York. If the Campaign is to be opened in New England, and our operations confined to the Provinces Eaft of

Hudson's River, it certainly is proper to destroy all kinds of vessels in the DeLaware; Philadelphia should be burnt, and the Jersies laid waste as much as possible: — By proper disposition of the ships of War in The Hudson, the Rebel Army would find it very difficult to get into any part of New England time enough to prevent General Clinton from acting as he thought proper in it; and a considerable part of it might be laid waste before any considerable force could be collected to oppose him.

If The Congress refuse to treat with the Commissioners, (as it is almost certain they will) the most effectual means of reducing the Country to subjection, is to burn and destroy every thing the Army can get at. The great body of the people are desirous of a reconciliation and long for a return of that state of ease and happiness which they enjoyed a few years ago. Very few parts of America know, as yet, what the horrors of War are, and if their houses, farms, and other property was destroyed and laid waste, their resentment would turn upon Congress, and their numerous other rulers, who, in order to retain their usurped power and authority, have refused those very terms which they formerly claimed, and for which the War was professedly undertaken. The bulk of the people are so heartily tired of the distresses they already labour under, and the exorbitant taxes they pay, that if one Province was firmly to declare their readiness to accept the terms offered by Great Britain, the power of Congress would be shaken. But they are so completely tyrannized over by their new masters that it is highly dangerous for any man to speak of reconciliation or treaty.

As lenient measures, and great concessions have had no other effect on the Americans, than to encrease their obstinacy, Great Britain would certainly be justified in the opinion of the World, (especially if they should enter into an Alliance with France) in using the severest means of reducing them to obedience and subjection.

It is expected that Gen¹ Clinton will burn Philadelphia; — If he does not, we have possesed it, at the expence of a whole Campaign, to very little purpose. As this Country must, sooner or later, be under subjection to Great Britain, it would be good policy to prevent the Americans from having any great City in a situation inaccessible to our Ships of War. Citadels, with respectable Garrisons, at Boston, Rhode-Island, New York, and other proper places to the Southward, would keep this Continent in a state of subjection for many years.

It is probable Gen¹ Clinton will open the Campaign in New England, as the War cannot be carried on in any other part of the Continent with so much prospect of advantage. Nothing can be done to the Southward of Pensylvania; and in that Province Washington will never give an opportunity of bringing him to a general action. Should our Army march through Pensylvania & Jersey, it would be attended with no solid advantage, unlefs they were to burn & destroy as they went. The people would rise up as Enemies as soon as the Army had pafsed, and the Country would remain unsubdued. As the principal Strength of the Rebellion lies in the New England Provinces, our whole force should be collected there, and all our efforts made against them: — The pofsefsion of The Hudson, (which renders the Communication with the Southern Provinces extremely difficult) the ports and harbours in The Sound, this Island and Bay, and the Entrance of Boston Bay, would surround them in such a manner as to prevent them from receiving afsistance or Supplies, and they Would at the same time be under apprehensions of attacks from Canada. It is therefore highly probable that New England will be attacked; — and while the main body advances against their principal force, one or two small Squadrons should act on the Coast, and on every occasion land some troops, & burn the towns & settlements. Such operations would divide and harrafs the Enemy, and prevent the whole force of the Country from afsembling at one point. Such a mode of Warfare might appear cruel, but it would be the most effectual towards a conclusion of the War, and in the end the most Economical. We have dispersed our force too much; and in search of lukewarm friends, have in every place met with inveterate Enemies, who never could have been brought together to any one point from whence we had chosen to carry on our operations.

10ᵗʰ June — Fine weather. Wind S.

The 22ᵈ, and 43ʳᵈ Regiments, marched this morning at 6 o'Clock, and encamped: — The former on Quaker hill, and the latter on Turkey hill.

11ᵗʰ — Good weather. Wind S.

About 10 o'Clock last night a fleet arrived from New York, under Convoy of The Cerberus; having on board Brigadier General Brown's 1st Battalion of the Provincial Regiment Called

The Prince of Wales's American Volunteers, consisting of about 400 men.

12ᵗʰ June — Very fine weather. Wind S.

The 54ᵗʰ Regᵗ marched this morning from Newport, and En-camped at The Blacksmith's on the East road, about 4 miles from Newport.

The Prince of Wales's Volunteers disembarked this day, and Encamped; 6 Companies behind Green-end Redoubt; two be-hind Irishes; and 2 in the work on Tomini hill. They appear to be a very good body of men, and are well Clothed and Armed. They are provided with new Camp Equipage.

The Rebels moved one of their guns from their battery at Bristol ferry last night.

The Pigot Galley gave chace out of the Seconnet this Morn-ing to a Snow which appeared to be coming in there, and about 7 o'Clock she struck without resistance. She was brought round into the harbour this Evening, and proves to be a French vessel from Bourdeaux to Bedford, laden with dry goods and Salt. She mistook the Seconet passage for Bedford.

Brigadier General Smith came out with the troops that en-camped on the 10ᵗʰ Instant, and has the Command of all the troops at the North part of the Island.

13ᵗʰ June.　　Very fine weather. Wind S.

Commodore Griffith is going from hence immediately in The Nonsuch. It is said all the line of Battle ships are to assemble in the Delaware, as a French Squadron, convoy to a fleet of American store ships, is expected there.

The following are the present stations of the troops on this Island. — *Bunau's Regᵗ* — At Windmill hill: This Regᵗ fur-nishes all the posts at the North End, in front of a line drawn from their right & left to the Shore.

22ᵈ Regᵗ　At Quaker hill on the East road, their right to the Seconnet. They furnish the posts on the East shore, from Ewing's, as far as McCurrie's.

43ʳᵈ Regᵗ　On the left of the West road, near Turkey hill: four Companies with their right to the W. Road; and four Com-panies, 200 yards to their left. They furnish the posts on the West shore, from the left of Bunau's Regᵗ as far as the Creek of Layton's Mills.

A Detachment of 80 Hessians from the three Battalions in Newport, at Fogland Ferry. This detachment furnishes the post at Fogland, and Patroles as far as little Sandy-point, on their right.

54ᵗʰ Regᵗ At the Blacksmith's on the E. road. Their right to the road, and to that which leads up from Lopez's house; furnishing the posts from Sandy point to Black point.

All the abovementioned Troops report to General Smith, and furnish a chain of posts and patroles from Black point on the E. side, round to Layton's Creek on the West.

The Regiments of { Landgrave, Ditfourth, & Huyne, and The Royal Artillery } are in Newport.

The Prince of Wales's Volunteers are Encamped behind the New Redoubts near the town.

A Detachment of a Captain & 50 men (relieved weekly) from Newport, is posted in the Redoubt at Connonnicut.

14ᵗʰ June. Fine weather. Wind S.

This Island abounds at present with a great variety of Birds, some of which are very beautiful.

We have been greatly neglected of late with respect to the supplies of Provisions for the troops, and have been furnished for some time by The Ships of War. If it had not been for the Cargo of the retaken Victualler brought in lately by The Maidstone, we should now have been in distress for a Supply. The Flora was under orders to proceed to New York to solicit an immediate supply, when that vessel was brought in, but was then Countermanded.

15ᵗʰ June. Very fine weather. Wind E.

The Flank Companies of the 54ᵗʰ Regᵗ encamped this day at Fogland ferry, and relieved the Detachment of Hessians posted there.

The Rebels pitched about 40 Tents this Morning between the upper and lower Forts at Howland's ferry. They appear to have about 200 men at that post.

Having observed several times last winter when shooting on Brenton's Neck, a place where there was the appearance of very good Turf, and conceived that the troops might be supplied with a part of their fuel from hence, if made at a proper Season; I mentioned it to The General, about a Month ago, and by this desire a trial was made of it, which promised well. It has since been more accurately examined, and found very good; in consequence of which he this day ordered 48 men from the British Regiments to be employed, under the direction of Lt Cooke the Barrack Master, in cutting it; and it is expected that a considerable part of the Winter's firing for the Garrison, may be procured there this Season. It is within a mile and half of the town, easily freed from Water, and of considerable depth.

The supplying this Garrison with Wood from Long Island, is attended with many difficulties and great expence. The parties usually sent from hence to cut wood on Shelter Island, have consisted of about 100 men. They generally were out about four or five weeks, and seldom returned with more than 400 Cords.

Five or six transports, with a Frigate for their Convoy, and protection while there, were employed on this Service with each Detachment. The consumption of Wood for the Garrison last Winter, was about 300 Cords p^r week. It would be lefs expensive to send Coals from England.

16th June.   Fine weather.   Wind S.

A party of Wightman's Provincials went last night to the Narraganset shore, to bring off some Recruits; but having mistaken the landing place, they were discovered by the Rebels on shore, who fired into the boat, and killed one man; on which they returned.

17th June.   A very warm day.   Wind S. after 11 o'Clock. Some thunder, lightning and Rain about 8 in the Evening.

A Detachment of 2 Captains, 4 Subalterns, and 200 men of The Prince of Wales's Volunteers, under the Command of Lieu^t Colonel Pattinson of that Corps, embarked this Morning. They are going to Lloyd's Neck on Long-Island to cut wood for the use of this Garrison. When they have cut a quantity, Ships are to be sent for it.

A Soldier of the 22^d Regiment was hanged this Morning in front of that Reg^t on Quaker-hill, for quitting his Post, Robbery, and Desertion. The 22^d Reg^t, the Picquets of the three British Regiments, and the Regiment of Bunau, attended the Execution.

18th June.   Fine weather. Wind N. E. in the Morning, which the Nonsuch, and some vessels under her Convoy for New York took advantage of, and went out of the harbour.

The wind came round to the S. E. after 1 o'Clock, and brought in a Fleet from New York, under Convoy of The Brune, with Provisions, and some Recruits.

A Soldier of the 54th Regt deserted yesterday afternoon. Having procured brown Clothes, he passed over the Creek at the mouth of The Town-pond below Bristol ferry Redoubt, at which place the Hessians have neglected to keep a Sentry during the day.

A Flag of truce came down from Providence. Four Officers of the Convention Army who have obtained leave to go to New York on parole, came down in her.

19th June.   Very fine day. Wind S. W.

Came in a ship from Boston, which sailed from hence some time ago with provisions for the Convention Army. Several Officers of that Army came in her, on parole.

20th   Good weather. Wind S. W.

The ships which arrived last from New York, brought about 60 Recruits, the Camp Equipage, and about 14 days provisions.

21st June.   Some rain last night. Close sultry day. Wind N.

A flag of truce came down from Providence this Evening, with Mr Bradford, the Deputy Governor. He is come to conclude the arrangements for the exchange of the Prisoners taken on the 25th May. Some people imagine he is come about affairs of much greater consequence.

22d.   Thick raw weather. Some rain. Wind N. E.

Mr Bradford returned to Providence.

See Appendix No   for letters[1] which passed lately between Genl Pigot, & Mr Sullivan relative to the late Expedition and the Exchange of Prisoners.

23rd June.   Thick weather. Wind N. E.

Sailed The Brune, with some vessels under her Convoy for New York.

Two 6 pounders, with a proper Detachment of Artillery men, were sent from town this day to the 43rd Regt; and the same to the 54th. They are to remain attached to them 'till further orders.

There are 2, 6 pounders with the 22d Regiment.

---

[1] The letters are printed on pages 294–297.

24th June.   Thick weather 'till 11 oClock, when it cleared up, and proved a very fine afternoon.   Wind S.

An Eclipse of the Sun this Morning; almost total.   It began about half paſt 8.   Greateſt darkneſs, 15 Minutes paſt 10. — at which time there was a fine opportunity of viewing it through some thin Clouds.

Appearance of the Eclipse, 24th June 1778, 15 Minutes paſt 10, in the Morning.   6 Miles N. of Newport, Rhode-Island.

25th June.   Very warm day.   Very little wind till 1 o'Clock & then S.

The Brune and her Convoy were in sight yeſterday, to the Eaſtward of Block-Island.

The Ships of war now on this Station are placed as follows: Flora, in the harbour.   (Captain Brisbane being the Senior Captain acts as Commodore) Orpheus, off Warwick; Juno, in the Narraganset paſsage; Lark, off Pappasquash point; Cerberus, below Dyer's Island, and opposite the Channel between Prudence and Connonicut; Kingsfisher, with The Alarm, Pigot, & Spitfire, Gallies, in the Seconnet paſsage.

The quantities of fish of various kinds, that are now in the different Rivers, and Creeks in this Bay, are aſtonishing.   The Inhabitants might take as many as they pleased with Seines; but they have neither boats nor Nets.   Indeed they are not to be truſted with the former, on account of their inclination to carry off deserters, and to supply the Rebels with whatever can be had from this Island.

26th June.   Warm weather.   Wind S. W.

Thirteen Cannon were fired yeſterday afternoon at Providence, and this Evening above 70 were fired there.   It is expected the Rebels have received some favorable accounts from the Southward.   Probably of the Evacuation of Philadelphia.

27th June 1778.   Very warm day.   Wind S.

Two of the 24 pounders in the Battery at Fogland ferry, were removed this day to Newport.

A report was sent this Morning to Genl Pigot from The Lark, that between 4 & 8 yeſterday Evening, four Sloops, each containing from 60 to 70 men, had paſsed from Warwick to Briſtol.

The Rebels hoiſted the 13 Stripes this day at the upper Fort at Howland's ferry.   They have certainly received some favorable news from France, or from the Southward.

The Regiment of Bunau has conſtructed a Redoubt between that at Howland's bridge and the one at Commonfence. It is now completed, and has a very good command of moſt part of the ground on both the Necks.

There are ſurprizing quantities of Moſkitoes at present in all the low grounds on the Island. The late warm weather has produced them in ſuch numbers.

28ᵗʰ June.   Very warm day.   Little wind at S.

Eighty men are now employed daily in making turf at Brenton's Neck.

29ᵗʰ June.   Very warm. Wind S. W. A great Thunder Storm towards Providence; but no rain fell on this Island.

The Regiment of Ditfourth marched out of Newport this morning, and encamped behind Irishes Redoubt. Huyne's Regiment marched out also, and encamped to the Southward of the town, facing Brenton's Neck.

The two Companies of Heſsian Chaſseurs under Capt Malsburg, encamped near Elam's house, between Fogland & Blackpoint.

30ᵗʰ June.   Very warm. Wind S.

The Sphynx arrived laſt night from the Delaware. It appears by the accounts received by her, that part of the Army had left Philadelphia, and were to march through Jersey to New York.

The Thames arrived off the harbour this day with some Victuallers from New York, and after having seen them ſafe in, ſtood off to Sea. The accounts received by these veſſels are, that the King's Army evacuated Philadelphia the 18ᵗʰ June, and were marching through Jersey to N. York. At their departure, a large fleet was seen off Sandy hook, ſupposed to be that under Lord Howe from the Delaware.

A flag of truce came down this day from Providence, with some prisoners in exchange for those taken the 25ᵗʰ of May laſt.

It now appears that the firing at Providence a few days ago, was on account of the Evacuation of Philadelphia.

1ˢᵗ July.   Very hot weather. Wind S. W. The Inhabitants say they never remember such hot weather on this Island, as we have had for ſome days paſt.

A change was made to day in the disposition of ſome of the troops. The 22ᵈ Regt marched at day break from Quaker hill, and encamped behind the Redoubts on Windmill hill, in place of Bunau's Regiment, which marched at 6 oClock, and encamped to the Southward of Newport, on the left of Huyne's Regiment. The Landgrave's Regiment marched at 5 in the morning from Newport, and replaced the 43rd at Turkey-hill; which Regiment replaced the 22^d at Quaker-hill.

The duty of the advanced posts is done entirely by the 22^d Regiment.

2^d July.   Warm day. Fresh wind at S. W. Some thunder Lightning and Rain from the Westward about 7 this Evening.

The Prince of Wales's Volunteers passed over to Connonicut this day, and encamped there. They are to be employed in making Hay, and in other public services on that Island.

3rd July.   Thick weather. Wind S. W.

Came in two vessels from Boston which had been sent there with provisions for the Convention Army.

A Boston paper brought by one of these vessels mentions that a Lieu^t Brown of the 21st Regiment had been shot by a Rebel Sentry for refusing to stop when ordered; and that Genl Phillips was confined to his room by order of the Rebel Genl Heath for demanding permission to send to acquaint Genl Clinton of the event.

4th July. Rain this morning 'till near 10 o'Clock. Thick and Cloudy 'till 2 in the afternoon, when it cleared up, and proved a remarkable fine Evening. Wind S. W.

A working party was employed this day in repairing our Redoubt at Bristol ferry. The Rebels fired three Cannon shot at them; one of which went through the Guard room and lodged in the inside of the opposite parapet. No damage was done.

This being the 2^d Anniversary of the Declaration of the Independance of America by The Congress, many Cannon were fired at 12, and 1 o'Clock, at Providence, Warwick, Warren, Bedford, &c. About 6 in the Evening there was a great discharge of Cannon and Musquetry at Providence, which continued without any intermission, for near an hour: during which time near 300 Cannon were fired. As the Evening was then very still, the Eccho down the Bay had a remarkably fine effect.

5th July.   Very fine weather. Wind S. W.

The Inhabitants are now in the midst of their Hay harvest, and the crops are very plenty and good.

6th   Very pleasant weather. Wind S. W.

Two of the 18 pounders were removed this day from the Battery at Windmill hill, to Bunau's Redoubt, near Commonfence.

7th July.   Warm day. Wind S. W.

The Faulcon arrived laſt night with dispatches from New York. She brings an account of an Action on the 28th June at Freehold, near Monmouth in Jersey, in which the Rebels attacked the rear Guard of our army, were repulsed by it, and suffered considerably. The loſs of The King's troops on this occasion amounts to about 330, in Killed, wounded, & Miſsing. Preparations were making near Sandy-hook, for the embarkation of the Army.

8th July.   Very warm. Wind S. W. A heavy thunder shower in the afternoon.

It appears by a Providence paper brought down this day by a flag of truce, that The Commiſsioners appointed by The King, have, in a letter to the President and Members of Congreſs, acquainted them with the heads of the terms on which they are authorized to treat with them for the purpose of accommodation. The Rebels seem to have treated this overture with great contempt; and have answered, that they will not treat with the Commiſsioners, unleſs the British Fleet and Army is withdrawn, or America, declared, in the moſt explicit terms, Independent.

The Commiſsioners are arrived at New York.

9th July.   Warm weather. Wind W.

The Rebels fired three shot yeſterday at our working party at Briſtol ferry; but without any effect.

Some men of ours employed in cutting trees on Common fence Neck for an Abbatis round Bunau's Redoubt, were fired upon from the hill above Howland's ferry: but the shot fell short.

The Rebels have erected a Beacon lately on the hill a little to the Northward of the upper Fort at Howland's ferry. They have hung a pitch kettle out at the top, in order to give a Speedy alarm to the Country, in case of neceſsity. They are now busily employed in making a Redoubt round it.

Two brace of Woodcocks were shot this day on this Island. They breed here. The bird is much smaller than those in Europe, and there is some difference in the plumage; particularly in the feathers of the breast and under the wings, which are of a buff Colour.

10th July.   Very warm. Wind S. E. Thick fog, with a S. Wind after 7 o'Clock this Evening.

Sailed The Faulcon, with a fleet for New York, and a number of Wood Vessels for Long Island, under her Convoy. A Privateer Schooner, fitted out by some of the Inhabitants of Newport, sailed at the same time on her first Cruize.

Twenty Seamen, lately taken by the Rebels, were brought over this morning by way of Howland's ferry. They are exchanged for the like Number of Rebels taken the 25th May at Warren and Bristol.

As the appearance of a Squadron of French ships of War on the Coast of America, may be daily expected, it has been thought proper to make some additions to our means of defence in case they should attempt this harbour; some heavy guns are therefore placing in a battery which the Rebels made on Brenton's point, and which is well situated for the defence of the harbour.

Lord Howe has assembled as many of the large ships as he could at Sandy hook, where he is now waiting the arrival of some others from the Northward; and to learn, with some certainty the motions of the French Fleet. Admiral Byron, with a respectable fleet from England, is supposed to be on his passage to Halifax.

11th July.   Close, warm weather. Rain last night for several hours. Wind S. W.

The Faulcon and her Convoy came back into the harbour last night, the wind not permitting them to go up the Sound.

12th July.   Warm weather. Wind S. E.

The Fleet sailed again this morning.

It appears by a Rebel paper brought this morning by a flag of truce from Providence, that the Despenser Packet, which sailed from England the 10th of May, was taken lately by a Rebel privateer and carried into New London. The Mail was sunk.

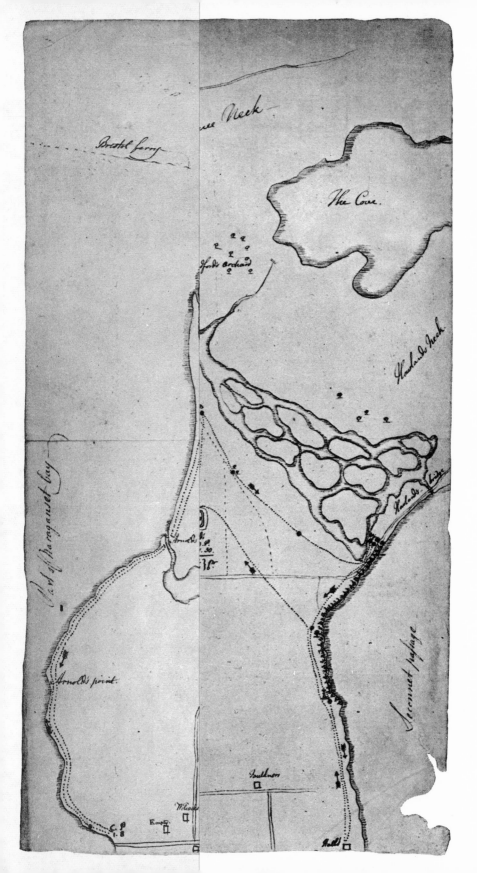

13th July.   Pleasant cool day.   Wind S.

A Garrison Court Martial sat this day in Newport, before which, Mr Goldthwait, a Merchant of the town, was accused by Lieut Kersteman of the Engineers, "of insolence & public abuse to him." The Court, upon the examination of the Evidence was of opinion, "that Mr Goldthwait was guilty of using expressions "unwarrantable and insolent, when addressed by him to Lieut "Kersteman, and which could not be justified by any part of "Lieut Kersteman's conduct towards him, and therefore ad- "judged him to pay a fine of five pounds Sterling for the use of "the Poor."

An Inhabitant of Newport was last winter sentenced by a Garrison Court Martial, to pay five pounds for buying a Sol- dier's necessaries.

As no Civil Government exists in any of the places occupied by The King's Troops in the Rebel Colonies, offences of a tri- fling nature, wherein Inhabitants have been concerned, have generally been tried by a Garrison Court Martial. When In- habitants have been accused of Capital crimes, they have been tried by a General Court Martial.

14th July.   Some rain in the Morning.   Fine weather.   Wind S.

15th July.   Fine weather.   Wind S. W.

About 12 o'Clock the Rebels fired 13 Cannon at Howland's fort, and the like Number at Bristol ferry. At 3 o'Clock they fired a number of Cannon at the abovementioned places, and at the town of Bristol. The Regiment encamped at Howland's ferry was also under arms, and fired vollies. We could at the same time distinguish some person of consequence there, who appeared to be reviewing the Regiment, as it marched past him and performed some Manoeuvres. There appeared to be about 500 men under arms, besides about 50 who were drawing three field pieces with the Regiment.

About the same time, a Regiment of nearly the same num- bers, was seen under arms, and firing, near Bristol. It is sup- posed that Mr Sullivan was at Howland's ferry, and that this is a day of Muster for the troops in this Neighbourhood.

A fleet of 18 Sail came in this Evening under Convoy of The Fowey from New York, having on board The 38th Regiment, The two Battalions of Anspach, and Colonel Fanning's Regiment of Provincials, with about 50 of The Royal Artillery; amounting in the whole to about 2000 men, under the Command of Major General Prescott. There are five Provision ships in the fleet.

16th July.   Warm day. Wind S.

The troops which arrived last night, disembarked this day and encamped. The 38th in the field behind Gen¹ Pigot's quarters; The Anspachers near Green-End Redoubt, and Fanning's behind Bannister's Redoubt.

The Army under the Command of Sir Henry Clinton, has entirely quitted the Jersies, and is now encamped on Long, New-York, and Staten, Islands. The troops embarked at and near Sandy hook, and proceeded from thence to their respective destinations; where it is probable they will remain until it is known what is the destination of the French Squadron; which The Maidstone Frigate lately fell in with near the mouth of The Delaware; and was supposed to be going in there, or into the Chesapeak.

Lord Howe is anchored within the bar at Sandy-hook, where he has with him 6 sail of the line, 5 ships of 50 Guns, and about 12 frigates; with two fire ships and two Bombs; the whole exceedingly well manned; having received 1300 Volunteer Seamen from the Transports and Merchant ships at New York. Many Masters and Mates of vessels have entered voluntarily to serve on board the fleet on the present occasion.

We must now remain upon the defensive, as no operation of an offensive nature can be undertaken until the strength and intentions of The French Fleet is ascertained. 'Tis said they consist of 12 Sail of the Line and four Frigates; under the Command of Count D'Estaing.

17th July.   Pleasant weather. Wind S. E.

'Tis said that General Pigot is to resign the Command here and go home; and to be succeeded by General Prescott. But it is not probable he will relinquish the Command of this important station at the present juncture.

It appears extremely fortunate that the Evacuation of Philadelphia, and the withdrawing the Shipping and Stores from the Delawar, was effected with so much expedition, and before the appearance of the French fleet before the Mouth of that River.

If any of our ships had remained in the Delaware until the arrival of the Enemy's Fleet, they must have inevitably fallen into their hands, or been deſtroyed; and a dimunition [diminution?] of the force of our fleet must have rendered the paſsage of the Army from Sandy hook to the Islands, very hazardous.

18ᵗʰ July.   Fog laſt night.   Fine clear day.   Wind S.
    Came in a Prize sloop taken by The Sphynx.